WHO CONTROLS TEACHERS' WORK?

WHO CONTROLS
TEACHERS' WORK?

Power and Accountability
in America's Schools

RICHARD M. INGERSOLL

HARVARD UNIVERSITY PRESS
Cambridge, Massachusetts, and London, England

First Harvard University Press paperback edition, 2006

Library of Congress Cataloging-in-Publication Data

Ingersoll, Richard M.
Who controls teachers' work? : accountability, power, and the
structure of educational organizations / Richard M. Ingersoll.
p. cm.
Includes bibliographical references and index.
ISBN 0-674-00922-3 (cloth: alk. paper)
ISBN 0-674-01990-3 (pbk.)
1. Teachers—Professional relationships—United States.
2. Educational accountability—United States.
3. School government—United States.   I. Title.

LB1775.2 .I55 2003
371.1—dc21   2002027274

ACKNOWLEDGMENTS

CONDUCTING RESEARCH and then turning it into a book is a large undertaking, far more than I had anticipated when I began this work. It is also inherently collaborative; without the help of many others I would never have completed this project. I originally began the line of research that culminated in this book as a graduate student. My largest debt is to my professors in the Department of Sociology at the University of Pennsylvania, who guided me during my years as a graduate student and have continued to do so—Fred Block, Jerry Jacobs, Charles Bosk, and Marshall Meyer. Far more than they probably realize, each imparted a great deal to my intellectual growth and to this project. I would be remiss if I did not mention several others who, in one way or another, provided me with invaluable help, feedback, and advice during the years I was doing this research. They are Harold Bershady, John Kimberly, Frederick Frey, Michael Useem, and Charles Bidwell.

I am also grateful to the agencies that provided the information on teachers and schools on which this study is based. I thank the National Center for Education Statistics (NCES), the statistical arm of the U.S. Department of Education, for the use of their Schools and Staffing Survey, and the American Educational Research Association for a research fellowship, which allowed me to spend a couple of years in Washington, D.C., analyzing this wonderful source of information on teachers. In particular, I am very fortunate to have had the opportunity to work with Sharon Bobbitt and Dan Kasprzyk, then members of NCES's Special Surveys and Analysis branch, both of whom gave me invaluable assistance throughout my fellowship and beyond. Many others helped me during my fellowship, but among those to whom I owe a special thanks are Jeanne Griffith and Paul Planchon, then associate commissioners at NCES.

I am also indebted to Bruce Wilson, formerly a researcher at the Research for Better Schools laboratory in Philadelphia, for extending me the use of the lab's School Assessment Survey and for providing me with aid, friendship, and even employment.

In addition, I thank those who made it possible for me to talk firsthand with educators who actually work in schools. Foremost among these are the two dozen teachers and principals who graciously consented to be interviewed, and who, for reasons of privacy, I will leave unidentified. In addition, I thank the respective central school administrators of the four schools in which I conducted my interviews, for granting me access to their school faculties and staffs.

Thanks also are due to Elizabeth Knoll, Kirsten Giebutowski, and Julie Hagen of Harvard University Press, and to a number of anonymous reviewers of the manuscript, all of whom provided me with many helpful comments. Henry May provided invaluable help with the advanced statistical analyses.

Finally I want to thank my wife, Constance Marino Ingersoll, for her help, encouragement, and patience.

CONTENTS

LIST OF TABLES AND FIGURES

Tables

Figures

WHO CONTROLS TEACHERS' WORK?

1

INTRODUCTION

THIS BOOK IS ABOUT the work of teachers in American schools. Unlike most research on schooling, it is not, however, primarily concerned with education itself, nor even with the teacher's role in the learning process. My concern is with the character of teaching as a job, teachers as workers, and schools as workplaces. I begin with the simple but often overlooked fact that teachers, in addition to being mentors, instructors, and surrogate parents, are also employees in organizations. My objective is to reexamine the character of these organizations and the implications for those working within. The route by which I came to writing this book was circuitous, and my own biography bears brief mention here because it plays an important role in the genesis of this research and in the viewpoint that I adopt.

Early in my career I taught secondary school, first in western Canada and subsequently in the eastern United States, in both public and private schools. At the time I was especially struck by how different my Canadian and American teaching experiences were. There were numerous reasons for this, but most simply put, I found teaching in

Canada to be far superior as a job. Two contrasts, in particular, stood out for me.

The first concerned the degree of conflict in the schools. The American schools in which I taught, both private and public, were extraordinarily adversarial places in which to work. The schools often felt like battlegrounds, and indeed, we teachers described our work as "life in the trenches." Student misbehavior and verbal abuse directed at teachers was an everyday fact of life. And I was surprised by the degree of distrust, disrespect, and dislike directed toward teachers not simply by students but also by parents and administrators. I quickly became aware that these conditions reflected the widespread public image of school teaching in the United States. The level of respect accorded teachers in Canada and the United States seemed markedly different. In the United States, even among teachers themselves, I found a pervasive sense of disparagement for teachers and the teaching occupation. I would often hear that teachers did not work very hard, were not very smart, were overpaid, and had easy jobs because of their long summer vacations. On a regular basis I read news reports and commentaries blaming teachers or their unions for a host of societal ills—teenage delinquency, the breakdown of morals, the poor achievement of American students compared with those in other countries, the decline in American economic competitiveness, the persistence of sexism and racism, and so on. We teachers called it "teacher bashing," and it seemed to be an acceptable national pastime.

A second contrast that stood out for me was how differently schools in the United States and Canada were run and, more specifically, who ran them. I found that teachers in the American schools had far less input into how their schools operated and what their jobs were to be. This was true for a range of issues. For instance, even though my background was in sociology and history, I found myself required each year to teach any number of subjects—algebra, economics, civics, special education—many of which I had little knowledge of or interest in. I quickly found that teachers had little control over what they were assigned to teach. School principals reserved such decisions for themselves, often to the great frustration of the faculty, who had to live with, and often were blamed for, the consequences.

Certainly, many of us who enter teaching do so knowing that it has, in most cases, never been a highly paid or highly prestigious occupation. But I was taken aback by the lack of understanding or regard for the teaching job. It seemed completely counterproductive to me that many intrinsic rewards, such as the satisfaction of making an impact, of imparting one's knowledge, of working in a supportive and positive environment, and of having input into the way things operate, were lacking.

I began to wonder if my experiences were typical. The small number of schools in which I had taught were not stereotypically "tough." All were in small-town, rural, or suburban settings. I wondered what teachers' jobs might be like in other schools and elsewhere in the United States. Were they also characterized by low levels of teacher input into the operation of the school, and if so, why? How much control and influence do American teachers as a whole have over their work, and in what areas of their jobs are they most constrained? In what types of schools do teachers have the greatest say? In turn, I wondered if there was any connection between the degree of teacher input into how schools function and how well they function. In particular, I wondered if there were significant differences in the degree of conflict and strife in schools, and if these might be connected to the way schools are organized and run. It was these questions that eventually led to this book.

As I began to explore what has been written about the organization and operation of schools and the character of the teaching occupation, I became aware that my personal questions have also long been of great public interest. Indeed, I found them to be a source of heated controversy and debate in several distinct realms: educational research, educational policy and reform, and popular opinion. These topics were also, I came to believe, the source of a great deal of confusion and misunderstanding.

I wish to illuminate the extent to which teachers' individual troubles in the workplace are neither unique nor isolated, but are really public issues, invisibly but indelibly shaped by the larger societal and organizational contexts in which they lie. By closely examining these contexts, I hope to further our understanding of the problems and issues involved—a way of looking that the famous sociologist C. Wright Mills called using the "sociological imagination."

The Debate over the Control of Teachers' Work

Concern over the issue of who controls the work of teachers and who runs schools is neither new nor surprising. Elementary and secondary schooling are mandatory, and it is into the custody of teachers that children are legally placed for a significant portion of their lives. The quality of teachers and teaching are undoubtedly among the most important factors shaping the learning of students. Teachers are also expensive; the largest single component of the cost of education is teacher compensation.

Schooling is, moreover, important not simply because it instructs children in the "three R's" and passes on essential academic skills and knowledge. Schools are one of the major institutions for the socialization of the young. Teachers do not just teach subjects, they teach values and behavior, and they teach them to children—*our* children. The job of teachers is to help make socialized adults of unsocialized

4

youngsters; schools and teachers quite literally help pass on our society's way of life and culture to the next generation. Schools' role as surrogate parent—in loco parentis—is not new. Aristotle was among the first to point out that the purpose of schooling is to develop not simply the intellect but also the morals, behavior, and character of the young.[1] Poll after poll has shown that the public overwhelmingly believes one of the most important goals of schools is and should be to shape conduct, instill motivation, develop character, and impart values. It is this expectation, and the apparent failure of teachers and schools to adequately fulfill it, that lies behind so much of the "teacher bashing" mentioned earlier. To the public, well-behaved children and youth are among the most important outcomes of schooling.[2] Indeed in recent years, with numerous highly publicized episodes of violence in schools, issues such as student discipline, lack of respect for teachers, and improper behavior in classrooms have become even more pressing concerns. The task of deciding which behavior and values are proper and best for the young is neither trivial, neutral, nor value free. Hence, it is no surprise that those who actually do this work—teachers—and how they go about it are matters of intense concern. And it is precisely because schooling is so crucial that there has always been much controversy over who controls what teachers do.

Two opposing views dominate thought and policy on this subject. The first view, popular among a large number of education reformers, policymakers, researchers, and members of the public, holds that schools are far too loose, too disorganized, and lack appropriate control, especially in regard to their primary activity—the work of teachers with children and youth. These critics argue that school systems are marked by low standards, a lack of coherence and control, poor management, and little effort to ensure accountability. The predictable result, they hold, is poor performance on the part of teachers and students. In short, this viewpoint—which I call the school disorganization perspective—finds schools to be the epitome of inefficient and ineffective bureaucracy.[3]

For many of those who subscribe to this view, the obvious antidote to the ills of the education system is to increase the centralized control of schools and to hold teachers more accountable. Their objective has been to "tighten the ship" in one manner or another, through increased teacher training and retraining requirements; standardized curricula and instructional programs; teacher licensing examinations; performance standards; more school and teacher evaluations; merit pay programs; and, more recently, state and national education goals, standards, and testing.[4]

Over the past several decades this viewpoint has drawn a great deal of theoretical and empirical support from the interdisciplinary field of organization theory and from social scientists who study organizations, occupations, and work in general. To analysts in these fields of research, schools are an interesting anomaly—an odd case. From this viewpoint schools are unusual because, while they appear to look like other large, complex organizations, such as banks, agencies, corporations, and plants, they do not act like them. In particular, they do not seem to have the degree of control and coordination that such organizations are supposed to have. Schools have all the outward characteristics of other complex organizations, such as a formal hierarchy, a specialized division of labor, and a formal structure of rules and regulations, but in actuality, according to these organizational analysts, schools exert very little control over their employees and work processes. Because of this seemingly contradictory behavior, organization theorists have adopted a colorful vocabulary to identify such settings. Educational organizations, they hold, are extreme examples of "loosely coupled systems" and "organized anarchies." In this view, schools are oddly debureaucratized bureaucracies and, paradoxically, disorganized organizations—a situation, they conclude, that is often satisfying and of benefit to the staff involved, but also a source of inefficient and ineffective organizational performance.[5]

There is, however, a second and antithetical view of the educational system that is also popular, but among a different group of education reformers, policymakers, researchers, and members of the public. Schools are not too decentralized, this view holds, but exactly the opposite. These critics argue that school systems are marked by too much centralized control and too much bureaucracy. The predictable result, they hold, is poor performance on the part of staff and students. In short, this alternative viewpoint finds the school system to be the epitome of top-down, undemocratic bureaucracy.

There are multiple versions of this antibureaucracy, anticentralization viewpoint that differ according to which groups are deemed to be most disempowered. One version focuses on communities, families, and parents and makes the argument that local constituencies do not have adequate input into their children's and community's schools.[6] A second version of the antibureaucracy viewpoint focuses on teachers and their working conditions. The central problem in this view is that factorylike schools unduly deprofessionalize, disempower, and "demotivate" teachers—a situation that is dissatisfying to teachers and a source of school inefficiency and ineffectiveness. In short, to these critics teachers have very little control over their own work in schools. Not surprisingly, in this version of the antibureaucracy view, the obvious antidote to the ills of the educational system is to decentralize schools by increasing the power, autonomy, and professionalization of teachers. Of the many variants of antibureaucracy, anticentralization thinking, it is with this latter version that I am primarily concerned. I will refer to it as the teacher disempowerment perspective.[7]

Like the disorganization perspective, the teacher disempowerment perspective also draws extensive theoretical and empirical support from the interdisciplinary field of organization theory and from those who study organizations, occupations, and work. A long tradition of applied research in this field has illuminated the ways in which overly centralized organizational structures have a negative impact on employees and has advocated enhanced employee participation in workplace decision making.[8]

Neither this debate nor these two contrary viewpoints are new to educational theory or educational policy. Educational philosophies and reforms, it is often noted, run in cycles.[9] Since the advent of the American public school system, important and fundamental issues, such as who controls the work of teachers, have periodically surfaced as subjects of intense concern—and intense disagreement. However, in recent years this tension seems to have become the center of both increasing debate and decreasing consensus. Indeed, in the decade since I began this research, conflict over control and accountability in schools has become, if anything, even more prominent. These issues are the crux of many of the most significant education reforms of our day—school choice, education vouchers, charter schools, school restructuring, the standards movement, teacher and student testing, teacher professionalization, and so on.

At the heart of these reforms are questions concerning the degree to which schools in general—and teachers in particular—are and should be controlled and held accountable. At issue is how much say teachers have over what they do with youngsters and how much they should have. The school disorganization view holds that teachers are not adequately controlled. The teacher disempowerment view finds teachers to be overly controlled. Both perspectives appear to make a great deal of sense. Both have lead to extensive research. Both have fostered a wide range of reform and policy initiatives. Both are widely known and embraced by the public. But both cannot, it would seem, be correct.

The Research

It is the tension between these two views that provides the backdrop for my research. This book undertakes a close reexamination of the organizational structure of schools and the character and conditions of the teaching job. I have made use of theory and methods drawn from the field of organization theory and from the larger study of organizations, occupations, and work, and my objective is to address the school-control debate, to reconcile these two antithetical views, and to provide an alternative explanation for the anomalous and contradictory character of educational organizations.

In this book I address three sets of questions:

1. *Are schools centralized or decentralized?* Are schools top-down, highly centralized organizations or are they more participatory and decentralized workplaces? Are teachers' levels of input and autonomy equivalent to that of autonomous professionals or more akin to that of low-level employees? Does the control exercised by teachers over their work vary across key tasks within schools? Moreover, does the control exercised by teachers over their work vary from school to school ? Are some schools more centralized or decentralized than others?

2. *Do schools have the means to control the work of teachers and hold teachers accountable?* Are schools places where, behind the closed doors of their classrooms, teachers largely do what they want, with few rules, little supervision, and even less accountability? Or are schools highly rule-bound,

factorylike workplaces with much oversight and supervision of the work of teachers and compelling means of enforcement? What are the methods, if any, by which schools coordinate and control the work of teachers?

3. *Does school centralization or decentralization matter?* What difference does the amount of centralization or decentralization in schools make for how well schools function? Does increasing the amount of influence exercised by teachers in schools have a positive or a negative impact on life inside schools? Do highly centralized schools perform better or worse than highly decentralized schools? Is the "good" school decentralized, centralized, or does it not matter?

At the inception of this research I found myself, given my own experience as a teacher, to be sympathetic to the teacher disempowerment viewpoint—that schools are overly centralized and teachers lack sufficient autonomy. And indeed I still am personally sympathetic to the arguments and reforms promoted by that perspective. Nevertheless, as a taxpayer and a parent of school-age children, I have also found myself sympathetic to the view that schools and teachers need coordination, control, oversight, and accountability.

As I will argue, a close examination of schools reveals important limitations to each view's portrait of the organizational character and conditions of schools. This is not surprising. Teaching children and youth is an unusual occupation, and schooling is an unusual "industry." They comprise an unusual combination of "clients," "technologies," and "products," and they are—understandably enough—not well understood. My objective, however, is not to suggest that we discard either of the above viewpoints; instead, we must build on their insights and strengths. Both of the views of control in schools are partly true, but neither goes far enough. The disorganization perspective is correct: accountability and control are very important, and many schools are, indeed, disorganized and inefficient. But this is true in a different and more consequential manner than many have so far conceived. Likewise, the disempowerment view is also correct: allowing teachers autonomy and a substantial voice in how schools are run is very important, and in fact many schools are highly centralized organizations. But again, this is true in a different and more consequential manner than many have so far conceived.

In brief, my analysis shows that assessments of organizational power and control are highly dependent on where one looks, the criteria one uses for evaluating them, and how one examines them. First, how one defines the job of teaching is important. When it comes to assessing how centralized or decentralized schools are and examining how much input and autonomy teachers do or do not have, most researchers assume, reasonably enough, that classroom academic instruction is the primary goal and activity of schools and teachers and the most important place to look for evidence. Analysts typically focus on who chooses textbooks, who decides classroom instructional techniques, and how much say teachers have over the determination of the curriculum. Moreover, when it comes to evaluating the organization of schooling, most analysts look at the effects of school characteristics on student test scores. This approach makes sense, but it also misses a very important point.

Schools are not simply formal organizational entities engineered to deliver academic instruction, and schools do not simply teach children reading, writing, and arithmetic. Schools are also social institutions; they are akin to small societies whose purposes are in important ways like those of another social institution—the family. As noted earlier, schools are one of the major mechanisms for the socialization of children and youth. This is so fundamental and so obvious that it is easily taken for granted. One of the central contributions of sociology, in particular, to the study of schooling has been to uncover and stress the importance and necessity of this fundamental social role. Sociologists hold that this social role involves two highly charged tasks, both of which profoundly shape the lives of children. The first involves the rearing and "parenting" of the young—in short, teaching children how to behave. The second involves the sorting of the young according to their capacities and abilities, perhaps the most crucial part of which has become the determination of whether students are "college material" or not.

An empirical emphasis on the academic and instructional aspects of the job of teachers has meant a deemphasis of the social dimensions of teaching in research on control in schools. To fully understand control in schools, it is necessary to examine the control of these *social* aspects of the work of teachers in schools. In fact, when we look closely, it becomes clear that among the most crucial, most highly controlled, most highly consequential, and most overlooked aspects of schooling is the socializing and sorting work of teachers.

Second, assessments of organizational power and control are highly dependent on the criteria one uses for evaluating them. Typically, researchers have decided that schools are loose or tight, centralized or decentralized, in comparison to traditional ideals and models drawn from the study of occupations and organizations. This makes sense, but confusion arises because different analysts tend to use different yardsticks to evaluate schools. The disorganization view of schools favors the traditional bureaucratic model, sometimes called the "machine model," of organization, of which perhaps the most extreme example is the modern industrial factory.[10] It finds schools loose in comparison. The disempowerment view favors the ideal of traditional professions, the highest example of which is the medical profession. It finds teachers highly disempowered in comparison. I will try to show that by clarifying the distinctions underlying these competing models of occupations and organizations, it is possible to arrive at a consistent criterion on which to anchor one's evaluation of the amount of control and centralization in schools.

Third, assessments of organizational power and control are highly dependent on how one examines them. In school research, as in much organizational research, analysts often focus on the more direct, visible, and obvious mechanisms of control, accountability, and influence—such as rules and regulations, "sticks and carrots." It is important to recognize, however, that control and accountability can be exerted in different ways in schools, as in other workplaces. Among the most effective mechanisms by which employees are controlled are those embedded in the day-to-day organization of the work itself and, hence, invisible to insiders and outsiders alike. A closer look reveals that school administrators, like managers in other organizations, have access to a host of alternative means by which to supervise and sanction the behavior of teachers. The data reveal that teachers in most schools are subject to a great deal of constraint through a variety of both formal and informal modes of workplace control. Indeed, contrary to some critics, a close look at the job of teaching reveals that teachers are pushed to accept a remarkable degree of personal accountability, in the face of a remarkable lack of accountability on the part of the schools that employ them.

Accurately assessing the distribution of decision-making influence and the breadth and depth of organizational control and accountability in schools is important because, as I will show, the distribution of control and influence in schools profoundly affects how well schools function. The public's concern over the social aspects of life in schools is well founded. Many studies document the problems of student discipline; lack of respect for teachers; improper behavior in classrooms; and conflict, distrust, and turmoil between teachers and administrators. But the data also show that schools vary widely in the degree to which they suffer from these problems. What we learn from this analysis is how these problems are directly connected to the distribution of power and control in a wide range of schools.

My findings have important implications for an array of policy initiatives and educational reforms. I will show that reforms concerned with either increasing organizational control and accountability or, alternatively, increasing teacher autonomy are often based on a limited or inaccurate view of how schools are organized and of the character of the teaching job. As a result, while some are worthwhile, many reforms not only fail to solve the very problems they are designed to solve but also make things worse.

Reconciling the debate about the control of teachers' work is the primary objective of this book, and its intended audience is those concerned with the problems of education and teachers. But it is also my hope that this research may be of use and interest to an additional audience. Along with showing how an organizational analysis has something to contribute to our understanding of schools, a second operating assumption of this book is the reverse—that research on schools has something to contribute to the substance and method of organization theory and the larger study of organizations, occupations, and work.

Organizational control, centralization, and employee autonomy are among the most important topics in these fields. The tension between the two polar views of organizational control is, of course, not prevalent simply in research on schools. With minor variations, these views are also leading perspectives across the wider study of occupations, management, and work. One would be hard-pressed to find any type of organization, private or public, service or production oriented, to which they have not been applied. Researchers and reformers concerned with manufacturing plants, municipal bureaucracies, and hospitals have all made the same kinds of contradictory claims. Are these types of organizations overly centralized or unduly decentralized? Are their employees granted adequate autonomy or highly constrained, and with what consequences? In a range of industries and occupations, there is widespread debate over the degree to which employees and their work are and should be controlled.

This tension has political undertones. The two perspectives on control in both school and organizational research are in important ways motivated by two competing ideologies and sets of values concerned with how best to organize our workplaces. On the one side is a rationalistic viewpoint that stresses the importance of workplace coordination, predictability, and accountability for the success of collective enterprises. On the other side is a humanistic viewpoint that stresses the need for workplace democracy, worker autonomy, and employee well-being for organizational success. These counterarguments are central to a larger discussion among social scientists of the character of middle-class employment as a whole—is it proletarianized or professionalized? Are essential white-collar occupations like teaching more akin to professional vocations, based on expertise, training, and skill, or are they closer to factorylike jobs, which underutilize human resources and alienate employees? And what should they be?

Schools are, however, not simply another case. They are an important site of this debate and of these conflicting perspectives. In the first place, education is a big "business" in modern America, and teaching is a large occupation—it represents 4 percent of the entire civilian workforce in the United States. There are, for example, more than twice as many elementary and secondary teachers as there are registered nurses and five times as many teachers as either lawyers or professors.[11]

But it is primarily because of the place that educational organizations assume in the larger study of organizations, occupations, and work that a reexamination of the organization of schools is useful. As I noted earlier, schools are an odd case to analysts of workplaces and bureaucratic organizations. They have been a puzzle and have held a theoretical fascination for many researchers in the field of organization theory over the past several decades. For this reason, a study of schools can make a valuable contribution to our understanding of how to examine and assess organizational power and control.

Thomas Kuhn persuasively argued in his seminal study of the progress of science that it is by focusing on the anomaly and the exceptional that a particular theoretical perspective, or paradigm, is best able to advance.[12] Schools are such an anomaly in the field of organization theory. Despite numerous studies, educational organizations continue to be the target of the two highly contradictory theories, both of which enjoy widespread popular and empirical support.

Kuhn argues that the anomalies in any given paradigm are resistant to solution because they are a product of the paradigm itself. They are the perennial, self-induced blind spots. Hence, it is only through a close examination of the previously unexamined assumptions of a theoretical perspective that investigations can advance. This is what I propose to do in this book. It is my contention that schools provide a stark illustration of the limitations of the two conflicting perspectives—both important paradigms underlying scholarly studies of organizations. I wish to show that the anomaly of educational organizations and the confusion of contradictory explanations of school structure are to a large extent by-products of the theoretical frameworks by which these organizations have been studied.

My own approach to resolving this debate and to understanding the control of teachers' work draws from what has been referred to as the power/conflict perspective of organizations and work. This approach is often associated with the work of William Foote Whyte,

Reinhard Bendix, Rosabeth Kanter, and Charles Perrow, among organization theorists, and Harry Braverman, Richard Edwards, and Michael Burawoy, among work and labor theorists. By undertaking close empirical research, using a range of data, on power and control in a controversial kind of setting, I hope to make a contribution to this line of thought.

Definitions and Focus

A great deal of confusion in the debate over who controls the work of teachers arises because different observers and analysts use different definitions for the same phenomena, or use similar definitions for different phenomena. Therefore I will begin by clarifying my use of key concepts and terms.

Among the most confusing of concepts is bureaucracy. In common parlance, "bureaucracy" is a pejorative label for government agencies and is associated with red tape, inefficiency, and inflexibility. To organization theorists, however, bureaucracy is among the more efficient modes of organization, common to both the private and public sectors. Following organization theory, I will use bureaucracy to refer to one particular mode of organizational administration and one particular means of managing large numbers of individuals organized to undertake large-scale, complex tasks.[13] Bureaucracy's distinguishing characteristic is rationality, which is also a confusing term. Again following organization theory, here I am referring to formal or technical rationality—the use of standardized, specialized, and formalized rules and roles to accomplish organizational ends in as efficient a manner as possible. That is, bureaucracy is a kind of organizational administration in which large numbers of individuals are coordinated and controlled through impersonal formal systems of selection, training, assignment to delimited tasks, standardized operating procedures and routines, written records and rules, and specified salaries. Organization theorists have also shown that bureaucracy is a variable: organizations vary in their degree of bureaucratization and in the degree to which they exhibit the characteristics of formal rationalization and formal routinization.

One of the most fundamental characteristics of organization is hierarchy. Hierarchy, by definition, refers to the vertical ranking of persons and roles, accompanied by a corresponding unequal distribution of valued goods and resources. Among these goods are rewards, privileges, tasks, benefits, status, and, especially, power. In bureaucratic organizations, hierarchy usually takes a rationalized form. Power, for example, is hierarchically distributed in a standardized, routinized, specialized, and formalized fashion. That is, in bureaucracies there is usually a standard chain of command formalized by rules, routines, and written descriptions that legally define the power and responsibility associated with different positions.

The hierarchical distribution of power lies at the heart of the debates concerning school organization and is the subject of this book. Power and related concepts—control, autonomy, influence, authority—are also defined in a variety of ways. Following organizational analysts, "power," as I use it here, is synonymous with control; it is a relationship wherein an individual or group influences or controls particular issues, decisions, behavior, or other individuals.[14] By "authority," I will refer to the case in which power or control is considered legitimate by those controlled. By "autonomy," I will refer to the case in which individuals hold a high degree of control over issues that are directly connected to their daily activities.

When examining the hierarchical distribution of power in a system, it is also important to be clear about which groups or actors one is referring to. The debate about control in schools suffers from confusion over precisely this issue. In my analysis I will look at the control over teachers' work held by different groups, both governmental and nongovernmental. But the primary focus of this book will be the control held by teachers themselves, both individually and collectively, within classrooms and schoolwide, over the terms and content of their work and over different kinds of issues, both academic and nonacademic. Teachers are, of course, not a monolithic group. Within schools, teachers are divided into departments that may vary in their power, and the latter are often run by chairpersons who may hold an unusual degree of power. I will pay some attention to these differences, but my primary focus will be the interface between teachers and administrators within schools and the control held by teachers compared with that of administrators. As I will show, the differences in power among teachers within schools are far less pronounced than those between teachers and administrators.

In this book, school centralization and decentralization refer to the relative levels of power and influence of these two groups—teachers and administrators—*within* schools. When I refer to a decentralized school I mean one in which there is a great deal of teacher control—where teachers hold substantial control over their work, relative to school administrators. A centralized school is one in which there is a great deal of organizational control—where school administrators hold a lot of control over teachers' work, relative to teachers themselves.

I have chosen to focus on secondary schools. They are a natural site for examination because they are the subject of much disagreement and are thought to be the site of the most problems concerning both control and conflict.[15] My objective is to learn what role the degree of centralization and decentralization in secondary schools plays in their problems.

Along with describing what this book is about, it is perhaps also useful at the outset to note what it is not about. First, unlike the vast majority of school studies, this book does not focus on the effects of school characteristics on student test scores. I do look at important outcomes in schools. As mentioned, the third overall question and topic of this book asks whether control, centralization, and decentralization matter. In that portion of my investigation, again following my emphasis on schools as socialization institutions, I focus on the implications of the amount of control exercised by teachers for the character of the relationships among students, teachers, and administrators in schools and how well schools function as communities.

Second, unlike most research on teachers, this book does not focus on the process of teaching children, the creation of curricula, or the nature of instruction. I am interested in teachers as employees and schools as workplaces. Third, unlike much current organizational research, this book does not focus on the relations between organizations and their environments—the field of interorganizational relations. Similarly, unlike much research on the politics of education, my primary focus is not the relationship between school districts and state or federal governments. My focus is primarily on intra-organizational relations within schools. I am well aware of these other bodies of research, and indeed my research has elements in common with all of them. But this book does not fit neatly into any one of these important literatures or fields.

Data and Methods

In this volume I bring together the findings from a series of related studies I undertook over a ten-year period. These investigations ranged from a field study involving in-depth interviews with teachers and administrators in a small number of secondary schools, to advanced statistical analyses of several large-scale surveys. Research combining statistical analysis of quantitative survey data with interpretive analysis of qualitative interview data is unusual, but advantageous. The former approach allows one to discern with confidence the levels, distribution, and effects of control across a wide range of schools. The latter allows one to look more closely at the processes by which school administrators do or do not coordinate and control the work of teachers in particular settings. This combination of data and methods has allowed me to look simultaneously at general patterns and detailed processes.

As I discuss my findings in the chapters that follow, I provide further information about my data and methods in the text and endnotes. My objective throughout the text is to present the data in a clear, accessible, and nontechnical manner. Detailed and technical information on the data, the methods used, and the analyses undertaken, can be found in the Appendix.

My quantitative data are primarily from the nationally representative Schools and Staffing Survey (SASS) conducted by the National Center for Education Statistics (NCES), the statistical arm of the U.S. Department of Education. Four cycles of SASS have been done: 1987–88, 1990–91, 1993–94, and 1999–2000. I used data primarily from the first three cycles; the last cycle was not officially released until June 2002. SASS is the largest and most comprehensive data source available on teachers and schools. Each cycle obtained information from about 5,000 school districts, 11,000 schools, and 55,000 teachers, and included an unusually wide range of types of schools in both the private and public sectors. From this sample, NCES gathered information on the characteristics, work, and attitudes of teachers and administrators, and on the characteristics and conditions of schools and school districts across the country. The survey's depth of data on the staffing, occupational, and organizational aspects of elementary and secondary schools and its large and diverse teacher and school samples set it apart from prior NCES databases used in research on school organization, such as the National Educational Longitudinal Study of 1988 and High School and Beyond, and made SASS especially useful for this project.

In numerous places throughout this book I supplement the SASS data with analyses and presentation of quantitative data from other sources. One of these additional sources is the School Assessment Survey, a large-scale survey of teachers that was conducted in the 1980s by Research for Better Schools, a federally funded regional educational research laboratory located in Philadelphia. This survey gathered information on the characteristics of administrators and faculty and the climate and organizational conditions of public schools in the mid-Atlantic region. Although smaller and less comprehensive than the nationally representative SASS, this data source proved valuable because of its unusually large number of questionnaire items on school organizational characteristics.[16]

Another supplementary quantitative data source I used was the International Survey of the Locus of Decision-Making in Educational Systems, conducted by the Center for Educational Research and Innovation, a part of the Organization for Economic Co-operation and Cultural Development (OECD). OECD is a leading international research and development organization based in Paris and one of the best sources of international data on education; this particular survey collected information on the control of schooling across a range of nations in the 1990s.[17] This source proved valuable because it allowed me to compare the system of school governance and control in the US to that in other nations.

Finally, I also undertook a field study of four schools in the Philadelphia area, chosen to be as varied as possible. My fieldwork included observing life in school cafeterias, halls, meetings, and classrooms; conducting in-depth interviews with administrators and teachers, and examining school documents, faculty manuals and policy handbooks.

Of the four schools, the first, which I will call Catholic High, was a large, urban, less-affluent, parochial high school, grades nine through twelve. It was one of many schools operated by the Catholic archdiocese, which enrolled almost a quarter of all students in the city. Catholic High reflected the qualities that have come to be associated with Catholic education—safety, discipline, decorum, and community. The students wore uniforms, the halls were clean, the classrooms were orderly.

In the 1980s a number of problems beset the city's Catholic school system. The diocese was forced to close several of its schools due to declining enrollments and the accompanying fiscal difficulties. Even though tuition at Catholic High was low relative to other private schools, a large proportion of the students served by the diocese school were from lower-middle-class and working-class families who had difficulty affording the cost of private education. As a result, a growing proportion of the student body was non-Catholic—25 percent of the 1,480 students at Catholic High. Forty percent of the student body was minority. Sixty-five percent went on to college.

The archdiocese's fiscal uncertainties created tensions for the faculty at Catholic High. Changes in enrollments meant a more heterogeneous student body and, according to some teachers, more discipline problems. School closings meant faculty layoffs and fiscal restraint and resulted in an atmosphere of distrust between faculty and the administration. In the 1980s the faculty of Catholic High joined a teacher union—the Association of Catholic Teachers. However, the ability of the union to provide protection for staff in the face of a bleak fiscal outlook was mixed. For instance, salary increases led to tuition increases, which in turn exacerbated enrollment difficulties. As a result, teachers' salaries remained relatively low. The starting salary for teachers was lower than in the public school district, and the gap widened progressively with teachers' experience.

The second school, which I label Urban High, was a large, urban, public high school, grades nine through twelve, that served predominantly low-income students. It was one of many schools operated by the city's public school district. Like the Catholic archdiocese, in the 1980s the public school district was forced to close some schools due to declining enrollments and accompanying fiscal difficulties. Declining enrollments resulted in little new faculty hiring, and the majority of the faculty at Urban had been teaching for more than twenty years. As in other urban environments, the proportion of white students had significantly declined. Ninety-eight percent of Urban High's 2,600 students were from minority groups. Thirty-six percent were college bound.

Urban High, however, did not fit the negative stereotype of the troubled inner-city school. It had a good reputation among the city's schools. It boasted a successful athletic program and included among its alumni several well-known professional athletes. Moreover, it had had several dynamic principals and had been a key site of school reform and innovation. Its halls were clean and well kept. Graffiti was quickly removed, and a sense of order prevailed. This is not to say Urban High was free of problems. It faced the same intractable conditions that all inner-city schools confront—absenteeism, dropping out, drug use, teenage pregnancy, and racial tension. The faculty spoke forcefully of continual discipline problems—a situation most saw getting worse.

Urban's faculty were all members of the local affiliate of the American Federation of Teachers (AFT)—one of the two large national teacher unions. Traditionally, the union had primarily focused on "bread and butter" issues. Salaries, while lower than those in some suburban school districts, were relatively good for the occupation. In addition, the union had successfully bargained for a number of contractual agreements designed to protect teachers from such things as arbitrary dismissal, overly large class sizes, course overloads, nonteaching duties, and involuntary transfers.

The third school, which I label Suburban High, was a smaller, more affluent, suburban public high school, grades nine through twelve, with a 12 percent minority-student population and 1,000 students overall. It was one of several schools in a public school district located just outside of the Philadelphia city limits. Suburban was a well-known school in a well-known district. Average income levels of the residents in the district were among the highest in the state. This was reflected in the school in a number of ways. The school, a large well-maintained complex, offered an array of educational resources and a wide range of curricular programs. Students inevitably achieved at high levels, and 90 percent of the students were college bound. Teachers' salaries were among the highest in the state. Not unexpectedly, few teachers left and, hence, few were hired. Eighty percent were veterans with more than twenty years of teaching experience, and there was a sense among them that they were better off than teachers in most other schools.

Despite this relatively positive environment, or perhaps because of it, there had been some tensions in recent years between the faculty and the administration at Suburban. The faculty, long accustomed to having a large hand in the creation of school curriculum and the content of their courses, had resisted efforts on the part of the central administration to standardize course offerings and course content across the district. To teachers, initiatives to standardize courses were assaults on their hard-won professional autonomy. To administrators, initiatives to standardize courses were necessary efforts to achieve accountability and ensure that all students received equal and uniform instruction. This tension seemed to epitomize the opposition between the two polar perspectives of school organization.

Teachers at Suburban were all members of the local affiliate of the National Education Association (NEA)—the second of the two large national teacher unions. Like the AFT, traditionally, the NEA had primarily focused on "bread and butter" issues. There was a sense that this was changing and it had become far more common for local association representatives to try to add issues of professional autonomy, school decision making, budget policy and curricular planning to contract negotiation sessions. At Suburban this had become the case.

The fourth school, which I call Friends School, was a smaller, more affluent, private, combined (elementary and secondary) preparatory school situated at the edge of the city limits. Sixteen percent of its 480 students in grades seven through twelve were minorities.

Friends was one of the many Quaker schools for which Philadelphia is well known. An early radical Protestant sect, Quakerism evolved from a deep dislike for the hierarchy, conformity, and intolerance its founders associated with European Catholicism. The history of this now-declining religious group includes leadership in numerous liberal causes since the founding of Pennsylvania as a Quaker colony: religious tolerance, abolitionism, female suffrage, universal education, and pacifism.

Friends School reflected the qualities that have been associated with Quaker education—rigorous academics, liberal politics, consensus-based decision making. Student individuality was respected, but there was also great pressure for academic achievement. Teachers enjoyed great autonomy but were also expected to pay close attention to student needs. School decision making strove to be inclusive and democratic, and thus numerous meetings and committees required teachers' time and energy. Halls and classrooms were clean but not sterile, nor even well kept. An intensity reigned at Friends.

Education at Friends was relatively expensive—tuition was more than four times that at Catholic High. Nevertheless, Friends was highly selective and there was a waiting list for student applicants. Classes were rigorous; at the senior-high level students were often assigned college-level material. Virtually all of the students went on to college, most to highly selective schools. Teachers were relatively well paid compared with those at other private schools, but most received less than they would in commensurate positions in public schools. At the same time, their working conditions were significantly different than in the other three schools. Teachers at Friends had smaller classes, taught fewer courses each day, had fewer discipline problems, and could count on a greater degree of parental support.

The Plan of the Book

The next chapter, Chapter 2, reviews how the organization of schools has become an important problem and an unresolved puzzle among those who study organizations and occupations. It describes in more detail the two prominent theoretical and research perspectives of control in schools and the wide array of policy initiatives and educational reform they have fostered and supported. I then explain what I believe are the limits of each perspective's portrait of the distribution of power, the degree of centralization or decentralization, and the organizational hierarchy within schools.

Chapter 3 presents a range of data to establish the distribution of decision-making influence within schools. I first briefly describe the larger context and the educational system within which schools must operate. I then turn to my primary focus—an examination of the levels and variations in the decision-making influence and control held by teachers in schools. I distinguish how the influence of teachers varies across different types of decisions and tasks within schools and the extent to which it varies among different kinds of teachers. I compare the control held by teachers with that of both school and district administrators, and, finally, I investigate the extent to which the decision-making influence of teachers and the hierarchy of control varies among different kinds of schools.

Chapters 4 and 5 examine the mechanisms and processes by which schools hold teachers accountable and control the work of teachers. These two chapters move beyond the earlier statistical portrait of the distribution of control in schools by closely examining both the formal and informal organization of schools and of the work of teachers. I examine the direct and indirect mechanisms by which school administrators supervise, account for, and regulate the activities of their teaching employees. My objective is to show what kinds of boundaries exist for teachers' work within schools, as well as how and to what extent these are enforced.

Chapter 6 turns to the question of what effect organizational centralization and decentralization have on how well schools function. To answer this question I present the results of a series of statistical analyses examining the impact of teacher decision-making influence on the degree of conflict, cooperation, and cohesion among teachers, students, and administrators in schools.

Finally, in my concluding chapter, I summarize the findings of this book. I return to the two opposing views of control in schools and recapitulate the implications of this research for theory and research on schools, for theory and research on other organizations, and for educational policy and reform.

2

THE DEBATE OVER CONTROL

WHY IS CONTROL and accountability such an important issue for organizations like schools? What is our existing state of knowledge about the organization of schools, their degree of centralization or decentralization, and the control of teachers' work? What have education researchers, reformers, and policymakers concluded about the control of schooling in America? What are the strengths and weaknesses of existing theory and research on school centralization and decentralization? These questions are the subject of this chapter.

The Study of Organizational Control

Every workplace, whether in a private company, public bureaucracy, nonprofit agency, or member-owned enterprise, in one way or another must confront the same basic challenges inherent in organizing numbers of individuals to accomplish collective tasks. How does one define, supervise, and reward the activities of employees so that they act in the interests of the employer? How are the cooperation and consent of members best garnered in order to meet the goals of the organization? Among those who study organization this is often referred to as the problem of control and consent.[1]

If they are to succeed, organizations must, obviously, coordinate and control their individual members. But organizations, perhaps less obviously, are also dependent on the cooperation, expertise, and goodwill of those same individuals. On the one hand, too much control may demotivate, underutilize, and, ultimately, antagonize employees. On the other hand, too little control may undermine the performance and viability of the organization as a whole. Thus, a basic tension confronts all organizations—how to harness employee expertise and still meet the simultaneous need for both control and consent, for both accountability and commitment, for both organizational predictability and employee autonomy.

Hence, it is not surprising that those who study organizations and workplaces have long deemed organizational control and coordination to be "primordial" issues and prime "points of convergence" among the social sciences that investigate complex organizations, and a voluminous body of research is concerned with decision making, centralization, organizational control, employee compliance, types of authority structures, employee commitment and participation, worker autonomy, and power within organizations.[2]

In the interdisciplinary field of organization theory, analysts usually frame these issues of organizational coordination and control in the vocabulary of rationalization. Since the translation of Max Weber's famous studies of bureaucracy, this concept has been central to the study of organizations.[3]

To Weber, bureaucracy is the modern embodiment of formal rationality—the methodical creation of systems of impersonal rules, routines, regulations, and procedures as the means to accomplish predetermined ends with maximum efficiency. The bureaucratic model of organizational administration is characterized by a hierarchical chain of command, a specialized division of labor, standardized operating procedures and routines and, of foremost importance, control. Its guiding image is that of the smooth-functioning machine. Following Weber, the basic assumption of the rational perspective in the study and design of organizations is that bureaucracy, compared with other modes of organizational administration, is the most efficient and functional method for those concerned with the problem of coordinating and controlling large numbers of individuals organized to accomplish complex, large-scale tasks.[4]

But, while he celebrated the efficiency of bureaucracy, Weber also lamented the "iron cage"—the rigidity, inflexibility, and inhumaneness—wrought by rationalization. Similarly, the study of complex organizations has, since its inception, been characterized by debate over both the theoretical and practical usefulness of the classic Weberian bureaucratic model of organizational administration. Numerous studies have sought to determine which aspects of which types of organizations are accurately represented by Weber's model. Much of the research in this field has been part of an extended argument over the consequences of organizing different kinds of workplaces more or less bureaucratically. At the heart of the debate are two questions: To what extent are modern complex organizations the controlled and coordinated entities described by the bureaucratic model? And to what extent should they be?[5]

From the viewpoint of understanding research on the organization of schooling, the most significant event in this long tradition was the ascendancy of a group of organization theories, beginning in the 1970s, that offered a new and colorful vocabulary to describe work and organizations that are difficult to bureaucratize: "loosely coupled systems," "organized anarchies," and "decoupled organizations." This group has focused on understanding complex organizations that, on the one hand, provide products and services requiring the kinds of coordination and control afforded by bureaucracy but, on the other hand, involve work that is not easily or effectively bureaucratized.[6] The result is organizations that appear to be rational—that is, the coordinated, coherent entities described by the bureaucratic model—but do not act like bureaucracies. Loosely coupled organizations are oddly disorganized organizations and, paradoxically, de-bureaucratized bureaucracies. Predictably, a great deal of ambiguity holds in this research when it comes to the questions of whether organizational looseness is necessary or unnecessary, functional or dysfunctional, efficient or inefficient, effective or ineffective. Moreover, among analysts the concept is used in a variety of ways, but there is agreement on one thing: at the root of organizational looseness is control; loosely coupled organizations have little hierarchical control by a central authority.[7]

These parallel tensions—between control and consent and between bureaucratic and nonbureaucratic modes of organizing collective behavior—are more acute in some kinds of work and occupations and less acute in others. Most agree they are especially exacerbated in human-service and people-intensive jobs, particularly in the white-collar occupations employed within complex organizations. These kinds of occupations involve tasks, knowledge, and skills that are less tangible and more indeterminate than those of traditional production-oriented occupations. In such settings, the production process itself involves employees working on or with people, not raw materials. In such settings, cooperative relations are not only conducive to productivity but, in many cases, *are* productivity. Work, in such settings, often requires increasing amounts of both employee autonomy and employee cooperation, and is less amenable to rigid bureaucratic control. In short, these kinds of jobs seem to intensify the fundamental tension between control and consent and, as a result, are primary sites of loose coupling.[8]

Elementary and secondary schools hold a central place in this perspective. Schools, these researchers have concluded, are the archetypal loosely coupled systems.[9] Over the past few decades the conventional wisdom among those who study organizations is that schools are an example of an extreme case of decoupling and debureaucratization.[10] As John Meyer and Richard Scott, two prominent figures in this line of research, put it: "the standard social science portrait of schools depicts weak and ineffective organizations with little internal rationalization of work, and little capacity to produce useful effects as measured by student performance."[11]

The Anomaly of Educational Organizations

The notion that educational organizations, and especially elementary and secondary schools, are unusual bureaucracies is not new. Since early in the twentieth century, educational theorists, such as John Dewey, have stressed the inherent incompatibility between bureaucratization and the work of schools' primary employees, teachers. Perhaps the most insightful accounts of the tensions in educational organizations come from Charles Bidwell, Dan Lortie, and other educational sociologists, based primarily at the University of Chicago.[12] The contribution of this group of scholars has been to translate issues of school organization into the framework of organizational theory. The insights embedded in their theoretical framework have shaped thinking on school organization for the past four decades.

The objective of the public school system is, as this group has pointed out, to provide a mandatory, publicly funded service for a mass clientele. Hence, the job of those charged with administering this system lies in seeing that large numbers of students are similarly educated as efficiently as possible. From a management viewpoint, one obvious mechanism by which to undertake this kind of task was and is rationalized bureaucracy.

Although the mass character of education suggests the use of the bureaucratic mode of organization, other aspects of education do not. While the bureaucratic model is preferable from an administrative viewpoint, it is not, they argue, from a teaching viewpoint. Like other human-services occupations, teaching is inherently nontangible, fluid work; it requires flexibility, give and take, and making exceptions. This is all the more true, they argue, because the clients of schools are children and adolescents—they are neither mature adults nor voluntary participants.

From their viewpoint, this unusual combination of "clientele," "technology," and "products" places limits on the bureaucratization and rationalization of teachers' work. The task of teaching, requiring a personal orientation and professional autonomy, clashes with bureaucratic rationalization, which requires an impersonal and hierarchical orientation. In short, while the large-scale and mass character of schooling dictate bureaucracy, the character of the work itself—teaching—dictates the opposite. The result, Bidwell, Lortie, and others in this tradition conclude, is that the work of teachers, compared with other occupations, is necessarily subject to few rules and regulations, receives little administrative surveillance, and has lots of room for the exercise of personal discretion and decision making by teachers, especially within the confines of the classroom. As Lortie concludes, behind the "closed door," "classrooms are small universes of control with the teacher in command."[13]

These characteristics, the members of this tradition have persuasively argued, make schools a theoretically significant case of modern bureaucratic organization. Due to their apparent "structural looseness," schools offer one of the clearest illustrations of the limits to rationalizing human-service and client-serving work.[14] Hence, schools, while necessarily bureaucratized are, also necessarily, debureaucratized. The tension between these contrary tendencies, in this view, is both inevitable and a source of never ending problems. It is also the source of never ending debate.

The Debate

Notably, members of the research community have not been the only group to adhere to this traditional view of teachers and schools as loosely structured and relatively undercoordinated and undercontrolled. Since the turn of the twentieth century, this has been a recurrent and popular theme in the realm of school reform and educational policy. However, although organizational researchers generally have come to mixed conclusions concerning the positive and negative consequences of loose structuring and whether change is necessary, beneficial, or even possible, this is less true for those involved with educational reform.[15] Indeed, if schools lack control and coordination, then one obvious conclusion has been to "tighten the ship." This desire to increase control over what goes on in schools and what teachers do in their classrooms resurfaces on a regular basis as a central tenet of education reform. Educational critics and reformers have traced the causes of a bewildering variety of larger societal problems to loosely controlled and poorly performing schools, in general, and to loosely controlled and poorly performing teachers, in particular.

On a recurring basis, critics have, for instance, blamed these aspects of schools for society's economic problems. Such critics have argued that diminishing educational performance is one of the main factors behind diminishing U.S. economic performance and competitiveness, especially in the international arena. Behind this perspective is the idea that lax standards in schools have lead to poor student academic achievement, which, in turn, has lead to lower workplace productivity. Proponents of this view typically use terms like *competition, world-class, excellence, accountability, standards* and *raising the bar* to describe their ideas for school reform. A good example of this line of thought is the influential and widely cited National Commission on Excellence in Education's 1983 report *A Nation at Risk,* which warned of a "rising tide of mediocrity" engulfing our schools. In its view, one of the most important reasons for low standards in schools is low-quality teachers and teaching. Not enough academically able students are being attracted to teaching, these critics declared, and too many teachers lack adequate training, use ineffective teaching methods, and lack sufficient commitment to their work. Successful reform, this view holds, must guide schools "back to basics," promote educational excellence, emphasize a standardized core curriculum, upgrade requirements for students, and focus on raising the performance and accountability of teachers.[16]

Along with economic decline in our society, on a recurring basis school critics have also blamed lax standards in schools and among teachers for moral decline in our society. Proponents of this view argue that a host of social ills and youth problems, such as teenage delinquency, pregnancy, crime, and the decline of the nuclear family, can to a significant extent be traced to a decline in behavioral standards in schools.[17] In particular, such critics hold, teachers no longer teach—or are not allowed to teach—basic values, virtues, and especially self-discipline. Instead, a moral relativism pervades the schools, wherein children are handed the rights of adulthood but not held to its responsibilities. The solution, they conclude, is for schools to make traditional cultural values, character traits, and moral virtues, such as respect, hard work, honesty, and punctuality, more central features of the curriculum in schools. Proponents of this view typically seek to have schools require courses in "character education" or "moral literacy" and to impose behavioral codes for students and also for teachers. Such efforts are often associated with political conservatism, but this is not always the case. In recent years, liberal critics under a "communitarian" banner have also criticized schools for failing to promote sufficient character and values development.[18]

Those of a liberal-left orientation, however, often resist increasing either academic or behavioral standards for children and youth. In their view, if equality of educational opportunity and resources do not first exist, then increases in the requirements, accountability, and standards for students are unfair. In the absence of the former, these critics argue, disadvantaged youths end up being punished for shortcomings that are not their own fault. Many such activists, for instance, oppose raising high school graduation requirements or increasing the use of high-stakes student testing if inequities in the resources provided to children are not first addressed.[19] One of the most important of these resources is, of course, the quality of teachers and teaching. Among those concerned with issues of educational equity, it is widely believed that students from disadvantaged backgrounds do not have equal access to quality teachers. For these reasons, some civil rights activists have opposed increasing standards for students until there are increased standards for teachers.

Civil rights activists have long argued that the persistence of racial discrimination, minority stereotypes, and a minority gap in educational performance are directly attributable to the curriculum and culture of schools, in general, and the attitudes and behavior of teachers, in particular. Proponents of this view hold that schools, even where they serve predominantly black student populations, are dominated by white administrators and white teachers who are all too often insensitive to the needs and values of students from other racial and ethnic groups. White educators, they argue, are overly prone to mislabeling minority and black students as troublemakers or slow learners.[20] Groups such as the National Association for the Advancement of Colored People (NAACP) and the U.S. Commission on Civil Rights have argued that black and other minority students are disproportionately singled out for punishment in schools and that overly harsh zero-tolerance programs in schools, for instance, "may accelerate students' likelihood of falling into a life of poverty and crime."[21] These groups have pushed, often successfully, for greater supervision of teachers' disciplinary practices, multicultural sensitivity training for new teachers, Afro-centric curriculum requirements, legislation assuring due process for minority students, an end to student tracking and ability grouping, greater scrutiny of new teacher hires, and the recruitment of more black and minority teachers to schools with predominantly black student populations.

Along with economic, moral, and racial problems, it has also been popular in recent decades to hold teachers partly responsible for still another societal problem—gender discrimination and sexism. Proponents of this view argue that the persistence of unequal gender roles and the male/female gap in educational performance are directly attributable to the curriculum and culture of schools and, in particular, to the attitudes and behavior of teachers. Teachers, both male and female, in this view, tend to treat boys and girls differently in a number of ways, including paying more attention to and having higher expectations for boys; not encouraging girls to take science, math, and computer courses; ignoring sexual harassment in classrooms; and not challenging students' ideas about traditional, gender-typed careers. Typical of this genre of criticism is the American Association of University Women's influential and widely cited 1992 report *How Schools Shortchange Girls* and their followup 1998 report, *Gender Gaps*. One reform prompted by this movement was the Women's Educational Equity Act, originally passed by Congress in 1974 and since amended. In addition to a host of initiatives aimed at higher education and athletics, this legislation promoted the retraining of elementary and secondary teachers to make them more sensitive to issues of gender equity and pushed for greater scrutiny of the behavior of teachers in classrooms to curb discriminatory practices.[22]

The above four policy and reform streams represent only a small subset of the variety of groups and movements that are critical of teachers and schools. Moreover, my brief review here does not do justice to the long and varied intellectual and political history of educational reform concerned specifically with academic and moral standards or racial and gender equity. I focused on this subset to illustrate two points about education reformers concerned with the quality of teachers—their diversity and their commonality. Some among these four groups, for instance, are on the liberal left, while others are conservative in their political orientation. Some view teachers sympathetically, as victims of a poorly functioning or unjust education system. Others see teachers less sympathetically, as the root of the problem. Some hold that schools and teachers have shirked their responsibility to teach basic values and morals; others hold that schools and teachers err in the opposite direction—that they indoctrinate students with too many of the "wrong" values and morals. Some of these reformers have been successful in garnering support; others less so.

Although they appear to have little in common, there is, however, common ground among these very different reform groups when it comes to their diagnoses and prescriptions for schools. All these reform movements believe teachers and teaching matter—that is, all hold, implicitly or explicitly, that teachers have an crucial impact on our children and youth and, hence, our society's future. All argue that in one way or another schools currently are not doing a very good job, resulting in serious societal problems. All assume that education is far too important to be left to the control of educators, and all assume that it is altogether fitting and right that concerned citizens and groups, such as themselves, intervene to fix the problems of schools. All believe that teachers—their training, capabilities, performance—are a key source of problems in schools. As a result, all seek to improve the performance of teachers, through a variety of requirements and regulations. In other words, all seek to solve educational problems through the exertion of more external control, of one sort or another, over the work of teachers.[23]

These and other reformers have often been successful in this endeavor. Numerous school districts and state governments have, in recent decades, enacted legislation or regulations mandating a variety of (at times contradictory) reforms designed to provide more accountability, control, and oversight for teachers. These include higher entry standards for teachers, teacher licensing examinations, career ladders, behavior and dress codes, merit and incentive pay plans, more stringent teacher evaluations and supervision, and standardized curricula.[24] There have, moreover, been parallel efforts at the federal level. Particularly notable is the movement for national standards, national education goals, a national curriculum, and national testing that gained impetus beginning in the late 1980s, with the first of a series of unprecedented education summits between state governors and the president.[25]

The view that schools and teachers suffer from a lack of control, coordination, and standards—the school disorganization perspective—is prominent and pervasive. But it is not the only prominent viewpoint concerning the control of teachers' work. There also exists a very different perspective of school organization and control that has also been a popular theme in American education and also resurfaces on a regular basis in both the research and policy realms.

Like the school disorganization view, proponents of this second perspective also believe that schooling is crucial and that teachers have
an important and profound impact on our youngsters and, hence,
our society's future. They also believe that poorly managed and
poorly performing schools and teachers are a leading cause of many
larger societal problems. However, contrary to the disorganization
viewpoint, proponents of this second view argue the cause of many
education problems lies not in lax standards or a lack of top-down,
external, centralized control and coordination, but in precisely the
opposite. Schools are not too decentralized, this contrary view holds;
rather, they are far too centralized. The road to improvement, these
critics hold, lies not in more layers of rules, more oversight, and
more accountability, but in more delegation, deregulation, and decentralization. Imposing standards from the top down does not work
well, they say; instead of looking for ways to impose more control, it
is necessary to explore options for empowering those directly involved in schools. (Figure 2.1 outlines both perspectives.)

There are actually several competing versions of this second
viewpoint. They differ according to the school group or groups—
students, parents, principals, or teachers—held to be most disempowered and, hence, most in need of empowerment. Often this perspective is couched in terms of public-private comparisons—and
typically private schools are deemed to be far more decentralized
than public schools.[26]

One of the most prominent versions focuses on community control and makes the argument that local constituencies and parents
do not have adequate input into their children's and community's
schools.[27] This became a popular education reform theme in the late
1960s and early 1970s, when numerous groups sought to reform
schools by implementing community control,[28] by creating parent-
run alternative schools, and by instituting increased student input

	Control	→	Performance
Disorganization perspective	Decentralized decision making Autonomous teachers Too little accountability Few standards	→	Inefficiency and ineffectiveness
Teacher disempowermen t perspective	Centralized decision making Disempowered teachers Too much accountability Top-down standards	→	Inefficiency and ineffectiveness

Figure 2.1 Two perspectives on control and performance in schools

into school affairs.[29] More recently, some advocates of school choice and charter schools have adopted the same arguments and rhetoric—that powerful, central school bureaucracies deny families any voice in their children's education.[30]

Another version holds that school principals are unduly disempowered. In this view, principals, especially in public schools, are overly constrained by school-district governing boards and centralized district bureaucracies and, as a result, do not have the power to manage schools effectively.[31]

These two versions of disempowerment in the school system are often confused with yet another version of this perspective—teacher disempowerment—that has also been an important theme in educational research and reform throughout the last century. Reformers and researchers often assume that these different versions of the disempowerment perspective are synonymous. They do share common ground, but there are also important differences among them that are often overlooked. Each agrees that schools suffer from too much top-down bureaucratic control, but each has its own idea as to the solution. For example, the community and parental control version of school reform, ironically, often advocates reform measures similar to those offered by the school disorganization viewpoint. The objective of community control, charter schools, and school choice reforms is to *increase* the accountability of both schools and teachers by shifting substantial power from the education bureaucracy and from school staffs to parents and communities. These kinds of reforms inevitably illustrate a basic conflict, often forgotten, between the interests of parents and teachers. These two groups are frequently at odds; indeed, they have been termed "natural enemies."[32] Similarly, some proponents of the principal-empowerment version hold that teachers, and especially teacher unions, already hold too much power, and they advocate reform measures designed to *increase* the accountability of teachers.

In contrast, the teacher disempowerment view holds that efforts to exert more top-down control and accountability are part of the problem, not the solution. Research in this tradition does not find teachers to be highly autonomous and undercontrolled, but rather finds they have very little influence over important school decisions and issues that affect their work. Factorylike schools, this perspective holds, deny teachers the autonomy and authority and flexibility necessary for caring, engaged, efficacious, committed teaching. The inevitable result, in this view, is that such schools deprofessionalize and demotivate teachers; foster alienation and apathy—or, alternatively, misbehavior and disruption—on the part of students; generate frustration on the part of administrators; and ultimately resulting in school inefficiency and ineffectiveness.[33] The assumption underlying this view is that precisely because the education of children is so important, it should be left to those closest to the process and, thus, the most expert—teachers.

Efforts to upgrade the authority and professional standing of teachers have long been a part of educational reform, but they resurfaced with much fanfare and gained new momentum beginning in the mid-1980s. A new genre of major education policy reports began to appear that shifted the focus from criticizing the inadequacies of teachers, to making recommendations for improvements in teachers' working conditions and emphasizing school decentralization. Examples of this wave of reform included the Carnegie Forum on Education and the Economy's 1986 report *A Nation Prepared,* the Holmes Group's 1986 report *Tomorrow's Teachers,* the National Governors Association's 1987 report *Results in Education,* and later the reports issued in the 1990s by the National Commission on Teaching and America's Future. Typically, proponents have advocated teacher empowerment, teacher professionalization, and related initiatives designed to increase the authority and autonomy of teachers. In this view, rather than having to implement decisions made by external groups, teachers—like professors—should have far more control over the teaching goals, programs, and requirements of schools and far more autonomy over what they do in their classrooms—analogous to what is called academic freedom in higher education. Numerous school districts have experimented with forms of school decentralization and restructuring, with such names as school-based management, site-based management, and shared decision making.[34] Prominent among those supporting these kinds of reforms have been the two national teacher unions, the American Federation of Teachers and the National Education Association.[35]

Like school disorganization research, teacher disempowerment research draws extensive theoretical and empirical support from the interdisciplinary field of organization theory and from among those who study organizations, occupations, and work. The thesis that overly centralized organizational structures have a negative impact on employee behavior and attitudes has long had a place in organizational research. Analysts in this tradition typically advocate the efficacy of job redesign, employee empowerment, and participative management for improving the quality of work life and productivity in a range of workplaces and employment settings. The distinguishing feature of this line of research is its humanistic orientation and its focus on the role of the structure of organizations, rather than the attributes of individual members, in the genesis of problems in organizations.[36]

As a result of these conflicting perspectives in educational policy and research, there is a large-scale, ongoing public debate over the degree to which schools and teachers are and should be controlled. This tension is neither new nor surprising. It is precisely because the schooling of the next generation is so crucial that there has always been controversy over the issue of school control. Educational philosophies and reforms are often cyclic. One set of ideas dominates for a period, only to lose momentum in the face of increasing domination by an opposing set of ideas. A decade or two later, the first set of ideas often will reassert itself, perhaps in a different form and under a new banner. This has long been true for the issue of control over the work of teachers. But the debate over control seems to have come to a head in an especially prominent way in recent decades and brought to widespread attention long-standing and basic disagreements over what schools are and should be. Calls for school decentralization, teacher empowerment, and school-based management have been a dominant theme in the realm of reform, side by side with calls for more centralized control and accountability. Underlying this tension are starkly contradictory images of what schools presently are—overly decentralized or overly centralized—and what they should be—more centralized or more decentralized. This inconsistency cries out for explanation.

The contradictory views of control in schools also reassert the fundamental organizational problem of control and consent introduced at the beginning of this chapter. One view claims schools lean too far in the direction of employee autonomy; the other claims schools lean too far in the direction of organizational control. In either case, if the way schools are organized is counterproductive, it is necessary to account for how schools continue to function. On the one hand, if schools are loosely coupled systems, how is organizational control achieved, if at all? On the other hand, if schools are overcontrolled, how is teacher cooperation and commitment achieved, if at all? How do we reconcile these antithetical views of control in schools and explain the anomalous character of educational organizations? Answering these questions requires a close look at the different approaches each perspective takes to the work of teachers and the way they examine power and control in schools.

The Limits of Research on Control in Schools

What determines who is powerful in an organization? Power, organizational analysts have long held, accrues to those individuals or groups that control important resources, issues, and decisions in an organization. For employees, the key questions are, how much control do they have over their own work, and to what extent do they influence the decisions that directly and indirectly affect the character, content, processes, and evaluation of what they do in the organization?[37] To answer these questions, one must address three critical issues. First it is necessary to define what are the most important decisions and issues on which to focus in assessing the power of a particular group or groups and the character of an organization's hierarchical structure. Second, once the issues are defined, one must determine the standards and criteria by which to evaluate the distribution of control among members of an organization. Finally, once the issues and evaluative criteria are defined, one must decide how to adequately and confidently measure who has control in regard to the issues and decisions in question. In other words, assessments of organizational power and control are highly dependent on where one looks, the criteria one uses for evaluating them, and how one examines them. Each of these questions presents particular difficulties.

DEFINING THE WORK OF TEACHERS

Organizational analysts have long stressed that it is important to distinguish which issues and activities are central to the roles and work of particular groups and which are not. The power held by particular groups or individuals in an organization is a function of the extent to which they influence the decisions that are most central to their work. Control of these issues is most consequential. Responsibility for and control over less important or less central issues and decisions is not real power; indeed, the delegation of control over marginal and nonessential issues is often used as a form of co-optation and a subtle means of centralizing power. In such cases, employees can be led to believe they have a voice in the management of their jobs and their organization, when in fact they do not.[38]

What are the key decisions, issues, and activities involved in the work of teachers in schools? Most theory and research on the organization of schools subscribes to what has been labeled the "zone view" of school structure and processes. In this view, school activities are divided into two separate zones: a schoolwide zone and a classroom zone. The schoolwide zone consists of administrative activities: school coordination, management, planning, and resource allocation. The classroom zone consists of teaching and educational activities (see Figure 2.2).[39]

This classroom/school dichotomy has its roots in organization theory; it is an adaptation of a traditional framework that divides organizations into technical and managerial systems.[40] This model of

	Activity	Group controlling
Classroom zone	Academic instruction	Teachers
Schoolwide zone	Allocation and coordination	Administrators

Figure 2.2 Conventional zone view of the distribution of control within schools

organizational life assumes a functional separation between productive activities in the "technical core" and administrative activities in the "managerial structure" of organizations. In the realm of education, almost all researchers, whether representing the disorganization perspective or the disempowerment perspective, have adopted this conventional zone view. Where the two perspectives differ most distinctly is in deciding which is the most important zone and which set of activities to emphasize. The disorganization viewpoint tends to focus on the control of the classroom zone. When these researchers analyze how centralized or decentralized schools are, they commonly ask how much control and autonomy teachers have over educational matters within classrooms. They find teachers to have high levels of discretion over many issues of classroom instruction and thus conclude that schools are decentralized.[41]

Proponents of the disempowerment perspective typically do not deny that teachers have substantial influence over some issues of classroom instruction. Their contribution is to broaden the focus, to draw attention to a wider range of decision-making dimensions and, especially, to the importance of the schoolwide zone. Typically, they hold that teachers ought to have input into a school's allocation, planning, and strategic policies. When analyzing how centralized or decentralized schools are, they commonly ask how much say school faculties have over schoolwide policy matters outside of classrooms. They find very little faculty influence in overall school policy, planning, programs, and budgets, and conclude that schools are overly centralized.[42]

The different conclusions of the two perspectives are, to an important extent, a result of their different emphases. Each draws attention to different types of activities and different levels of analysis. One view emphasizes the lack of organizational control of teachers and their work. The second view emphasizes the lack of professional influence exercised by faculties over the way the schools are run. But, notably, both agree on the existing distribution of control within schools: "Schools are marked by a 'traditional influence pattern' in which decisions are differentiated by locale and position . . . administrators make strategic decisions outside of classrooms and teachers make operational decisions inside of classrooms."[43]

Moreover, and this is my central point here, despite their large differences in emphasis, focus, and findings, both views adopt a similar definition of the of the work of teachers and of the educational and productive core of schools. Most research on the organization of schools assumes, reasonably enough, that the core of what teachers do is academic instruction in classrooms. This is, of course, true. But it is also not the entire story.

The substance of teachers' work and the goal of schooling, as I noted in the previous chapter, is not simply to instruct youngsters in the "three R's" and pass on academic skills and knowledge. Schools and teachers are also responsible for passing on society's way of life and culture. This social dimension of schooling has been a central theme of educational theory since the beginning of the twentieth century. Beginning with the classic education studies by John Dewey and Emile Durkheim, continuing through midcentury mainstream educational theory, and up to the revisionist and critical educational analyses that dominated the last quarter of the twentieth century, social science has held that a major purpose of educational organizations lies in their social function.[44] Both Dewey and Durkheim, for example, argued that schools have, in essence, the same purpose as religion—to pass on moral order. Moreover, more recent researchers, such as James Coleman and Thomas Hoffer, have argued that this social role is expanding as schools are being increasingly called on to accept responsibility for tasks once reserved for parents, churches, and communities.[45] In short, educational theory has long held that among the central goals of schooling is helping to rear the next generation.

This line of education theory draws attention to the fact that what students learn in schools has as much to do with social relations as with the content of the academic curriculum. Much of this social activity is implicit, informal, and unstated, prompting observers to use the term "hidden curriculum" to refer to the norms, behaviors, and roles transmitted to students. Although often integrated with the "official curriculum," this social learning is distinct from academic learning.

Perhaps one of the clearest attempts to capture this academic/social distinction is in the contrast between the concepts of "human capital" and "social capital" popularized by Coleman and Hoffer in their research on schools. In the context of education, human capital refers to the skills and knowledge passed on to students by schools, and social capital refers to the social relations that establish and communicate norms and sanctions. Just as financial capital and human capital are valuable assets to be acquired, social capital, while less tangible, is no less valuable a resource.

Sociologists, in particular, have distinguished two overlapping types of activities within the social dimension of schooling—socialization and stratification. The first involves the inculcation of societal norms and rules, in short, the "parenting" of children. The second involves the assessment, sorting, and channeling of students into ranks, roles, and statuses according to their abilities and behavior, often referred to as the tracking of students.

Despite widespread recognition of the theoretical importance of the broader social goals and dimensions of schooling, these are often deemphasized in empirical research on education. Many analysts begin with the assumption that what teachers do in the educational and productive core of schools is primarily classroom academic instruction. In turn, researchers often assume that the ultimate and most important outcome of schooling is student academic performance. Finally, many end up assuming that student scores on mass-produced, standardized tests are "the bottom line" and the "be all and end all" of education.

Underlying this view is an economic, production-oriented model of schools that, like the zone view, is drawn from organization theory and research in industrial settings. In this framework, the objective of schools, like industrial and business organizations, is to produce outputs from inputs. The inputs usually include teacher, school, and student characteristics and resources; the output is student academic learning. Even those who stress the importance of the social aspects of schooling and look at things such as "community," "climate," and "ethos" in schools often end up treating these as subsidiary preconditions, as inputs, necessary for academic learning to take place.

Again Coleman's research provides a prime example of this tendency. In much of his later work he insightfully illustrates the importance of "functional community" and social capital in schooling, especially in illuminating the differences between public and private schools. But in his analyses these concepts are largely treated as inputs into the process of schooling, and he ultimately justifies their importance because of their positive effects on the "real" output of schooling—student test scores.[46] Others have gone even further in blurring the distinction between academic and social learning by assuming that student scores on academic achievement tests are *themselves* accurate measures of behavioral maturity, character, moral growth, and other key aspects of social learning.[47]

My point is not that academic instruction and achievement and student scores are not important—they are clearly important. Nor am I arguing that they are not integrally related to the socialization and sorting processes in schools—they are clearly related. Indeed, instructional and social objectives and processes are often inextricably mixed and merged within classrooms. My point is that the academic goals and activities of schools and the social goals and activities of schools are not the same. The behavioral growth and learning of students, the transmission of norms and roles, the character of the social relations themselves are all equally important aspects of the job of teachers and equally important outputs of schooling. Schools are formal organizations—in the sense that they are tools engineered to do a job—and hence they are in some ways similar to production-oriented industrial operations. But schools are also social institutions—in the sense of small societies infused with normative values and purposes. In this latter sense the purposes of schools overlap with those of another socialization institution, the family.[48]

The emphasis on the academic and instructional aspects of the job of teachers has meant a deemphasis of the social dimension of teaching in empirical research on control in schools. When it comes to examining the organization and control of the core educational activities in schools, researchers usually focus on the control of decisions commonly associated with formal academic instruction, such as the selection of instructional texts and the choice of teaching methods. In contrast, researchers less often examine who controls decisions surrounding behavioral, social, and normative activities in schools.

For instance, tracking is one of the most important topics in sociological research on education, and it is the subject of voluminous research, much of it focused on the extent to which the sorting of students in schools is based on background factors, such as their socioeconomic status, or on students' actual ability and achievement. In essence, tracking is concerned with how students are to be stratified into low, middle, and high ranks—one of the most crucial teaching and educational activities that transpires within classrooms and schools.[49] But in research on school centralization and decentralization, there has been little examination of who controls tracking. There has been, for example, almost no investigation of the extent to which teachers control or influence decisions surrounding these "gatekeeping" processes and what the implications are for schools.

Likewise, student discipline is one of the most important aspects of the social side of schooling. In the first place, classroom order is fundamental—without the maintenance of some degree of classroom order and student discipline, education cannot proceed at all. Student discipline is, however, not simply a necessary prerequisite for the successful transmission of instruction. Teaching discipline— the ability to behave according to social norms—is at the heart of school socialization and, ultimately, societal survival.[50] Moreover, the issue of discipline concerns which and whose set of values are to dominate school life—one of the most crucial educational decisions.[51]

However, researchers often do not place great importance on student discipline in schools. For example, a national poll of professors of education, who represent a large portion of those doing research on schools and also those who teach future teachers, found that most place student discipline, along with the importance of neatness, punctuality, and manners, at the bottom of their list of priorities for teachers. For example, only about a third of the education professors surveyed felt it was "absolutely essential" to prepare or train teachers in maintaining classroom discipline. At the same time, an overwhelming majority placed academic learning and achievement at the top of their list of priorities for teachers.[52] A similar deemphasis of discipline holds true in empirical research on school centralization and decentralization. There has been little interest in examining the extent to which teachers control or influence key decisions surrounding behavioral codes and discipline policy, and what the implications are for schools.

In contrast, teachers, administrators, and the public place great importance on these issues. Numerous surveys have found that both teachers and principals feel that promoting good work habits and self-discipline in students is as important a part of schooling as building basic literacy or encouraging academic excellence. Likewise the well-known poll Public's Attitudes toward the Public Schools, conducted annually by Phi Delta Kappa and Gallup, shows that moral and social issues—such as student discipline, lack of respect for teachers, and improper behavior in classrooms—have consistently been among the public's most important educational concerns for decades.[53] Indeed, implicit among those who blame teachers and schools for so many social problems—crime, teenage pregnancy, sexism, the "coarsening" of American society, and so on—is the expectation that teaching values and behavior is a major part of the work of teachers, or that it ought to be. In short, an overwhelming majority of the public feels that an important goal of elementary and secondary schools is and should be to shape conduct, instill motivation, develop character, and impart values, and that an important output is, in plain terms, well-behaved children and adolescents. Teaching "good behavior" is a large part of the job of elementary and secondary teachers—something new teachers quickly learn. The centrality of these issues to their work is also probably something that sets them apart from teachers at the college level.

Given its importance to the public, the dimension of social learning in schools is, not surprisingly, also a major source of conflict among competing school reform movements. As mentioned earlier, conservative Christian groups, for instance, have attacked the school system for a number of years, complaining that public schools teach values and a "religion"—"secular humanism"—that are contrary to their own beliefs.[54] Conservative Christians, in insisting that the inculcation of values is fundamental to schooling are, ironically, in agreement with liberal-left reformers. The latter also criticize the values transmitted in schools, although in their view, the problem lies in the prevalence of class, gender, and racial bias in the social dimension of schooling.[55]

In sum, organization theory suggests that assessments of the distribution of control in schools must focus on who controls the key decisions that affect the content and terms of the work of teachers. In turn, educational theory tells us that the educational work of teachers in schools includes two distinct dimensions—the academic and the social. Research on school organization has shed much light and insight on who controls the former but little on who controls the latter. This is an important limitation. The social side of the teaching job includes some of the most consequential processes taking place in schools. Who controls these issues and what effect does this have on life in schools?

EVALUATING CONTROL IN SCHOOLS

Along with defining the activities on which to focus, a second issue for analysts of control in organizations is deciding the criteria by which to evaluate work settings. Organizational looseness, accountability, coupling, control, centralization, and decentralization are, it must be remembered, relative concepts, and the question must always be posed, compared to what?

Close examination of research on school organization reveals that the two major views on control use very different standards—different yardsticks—by which to evaluate schools. For the disorganization perspective, the point of comparison is the traditional ideal of rational organization. The prototype of this traditional ideal is the bureaucracy, its most extreme embodiment is the modern industrial organization—the factory—and its guiding motif is the smoothly functioning machine. To organization theorists, schools are a key example of organizations that do not fit the classic bureaucratic model; indeed, they have been deemed the epitome of nonrational, debureaucratized, decentralized organizations.[56] Hence, when proponents of this viewpoint conclude that schools are highly decentralized, what they appear to mean is that schools are more decentralized than factories, and teachers are, by implication, more autonomous than factory workers.

Of course, as I noted earlier, organization theorists do not necessarily assume that the structural looseness of schools is inappropriate, inefficient, or unnecessary. But as I also noted earlier, this is less true for educational policymakers and reformers who subscribe to the disorganization view of schools. The assumption often underlying their reform efforts is that hierarchy is functional, proper, and necessary in schools, as it is assumed to be in industry.[57] That is, their assumption is that a distribution of control in which teachers instruct and principals manage is functional, proper, and necessary and that schools' administrative, distributive, and strategic decisions are best left to school officials or external agencies.

The disempowerment perspective compares schools to another traditional ideal, the professional model of work and occupations. This viewpoint also involves a value judgment: it does not assume that a distribution of control in which teachers instruct and principals manage is functional, proper, or necessary; it does not assume that an organization's administrative and planning decisions are simply supportive or "housekeeping" activities, best left to administrators. Proponents of this view explicitly argue that schools ought not adopt the bureaucratic model of organization. The disempowerment perspective seeks to expand the scope of legitimate employee input and influence—the contested terrain[58]—to include organizationwide policy and conditions. In this view, "Teachers are not (but ought to be) treated as professionals; schools are (and ought not to be) top-heavy bureaucracies; and no significant improvements can occur in America's systems of public education unless schools are fundamentally restructured."[59]

Each of these standards for evaluating the distribution of control in schools reflects a different emphasis. One emphasizes the managerial need for accountability; the other emphasizes the employee need for autonomy and input. Thus the two viewpoints, naturally, come to opposite conclusions concerning where schools stand. Given their different assumptions, both viewpoints may well be correct. However, neither actually empirically tests its comparison of schools with professional settings or bureaucracies. Their comparisons are based on hypothetical ideals drawn from occupational and organizational theory. This is understandable. Cross-occupational comparisons are inherently difficult because many issues and decisions are not comparable and the necessary data are rarely available.

Moreover, trying to classify teachers as either professionals or bureaucratic employees may not serve as a useful means of evaluating the degree of centralization or decentralization in schools. The contrast between professionals and bureaucratic employees is a long-standing central theme in the study of organizations and occupations.[60] Traditionally researchers have thought of the two as opposites, and an extensive body of research has focused on the extent to which particular occupations are professionalized or bureaucratized and on the trade-offs between a professional model and a bureaucratic model of organizational control. But insightful analysts have also pointed out that the relationship between the two is complex; they are not opposite ends of a single yardstick, and a simple either/ or dichotomy does not exist between one and the other.[61] Bureaucracy is a mode of administering and organizing large-scale enterprises. Professions are a particular type of occupation, typically characterized by authority, rigorous training and licensing requirements, positive working conditions, an active professional organization or association, relatively high compensation, and high prestige. Many professionals are primarily employed within bureaucracies, and indeed some professions were the creation of bureaucracy. Moreover, the bureaucratization of professional work may or may not lead to disempowerment and proletarianization. In short, determining whether particular types of employees, like teachers, are either professionals or bureaucratic employees may not be a useful means of assessing the degree of control, and I will not adopt such a strategy here. It is, however, possible to move beyond merely asserting that schools are overly centralized or decentralized and empirically ground such an analysis, and occupational and organizational theory offers a means to do so.

From the perspective of the study of occupations and professions, control over the content and terms of work is at the root of the standing and stature of occupations. The relative distribution of control among groups in work settings is a key criterion in the distinction between professions and other occupations and between professionalized and nonprofessionalized employees. Expertise lies at the heart of these distinctions. Professionals are considered not amateurs or dilettantes but experts, and one of the hallmarks of professions is a large degree of self-direction and self-governance. The rationale behind professional control is to place substantial levels of control and discretion in the hands of those who are, presumably, closest to and most knowledgeable about the work.

In an organizational context, what this means is that professionalized employees usually have a great deal of control, both collectively and individually, over the conditions, content, processes, outcomes, and evaluation of their work and jobs. Nonprofessionalized employees usually do not. This control is relative; it is in relation to other groups, primarily managers and, in the case of client-serving work, clients. In the first comparison, professionalized employees usually have control and autonomy approaching that of senior management when it comes to organizational decisions surrounding their work. Academics, for example, often have equal or greater control than university administrators over the content of their teaching and research, over the hiring of new colleagues, and, through the institution of peer review, over the evaluation and promotion of members and, hence, over the ongoing content and character of the profession.[62] In contrast, nonprofessionalized employees usually have far less say over these kinds of issues and decisions. In semi-skilled, nonprofessional occupations within organizations, decisions about the character and processes of the work are more likely to be made by managers and implemented by employees.

Similarly one of the hallmarks of professionals is their degree of control in the professional-client relationship. The underlying assumption is that the expertise level in professions is too high for nonmembers of the profession to decide what is best, and so the relationship between professional and client often is characterized by deference and compliance on the part of clients. Doctors, for example, traditionally have the final say on treatment decisions for clients; the assumption is that those with medical expertise are the best judge of what is medically best for patients. This control is, of course, subject to challenge. Indeed, there has been much criticism that traditional professions, like medicine, have become monopolistic and have too much control in relation to clients and too little accountability to their clients. For example, critics of medicine hold that doctors do not adequately police their own ranks, and that the public has few mechanisms to monitor or sanction incompetent doctors. Some researchers have argued that, partly in response to these challenges, the power of some traditional professions has declined and there has been a trend toward deprofessionalization.[63]

Similarly, some education critics, especially among those who subscribe to the disorganization perspective, hold that the public school system has become monopolistic and the public has too little input into the operation of schools and too few means of holding teachers accountable. As discussed earlier, this demand for more public input is at the root of a wide array of reforms, such as community schools, school choice, vouchers, and charter schools. However, unlike traditional professions, the teaching occupation does have a formal mechanism for collective input from the public—local school boards. The occupations of medicine, law, engineering, accounting, and architecture, for example, do not have equivalent bodies for external, collective public control.[64]

Hence, theory from the study of occupations and professions offers a useful criterion and provides one means of anchoring the debate about the degree to which teachers wield control over their work—the relative control of teachers and school management. That is, which group has more influence over important core teaching and educational activities: school boards and their district-level administrative staffs, school-level administrators, or faculty? What is the hierarchical distribution of control among these groups in schools? In plain terms, who decides what is educationally best for students, and who has the final say over educational and teaching decisions?

MEASURING CONTROL IN SCHOOLS

Along with defining the issues on which to focus and making explicit the criteria by which one evaluates organizational hierarchy, a third issue necessarily arises for analyses of control in organizations—how one actually measures this variable. Analysts of power have long noted the difficulties in adequately conceptualizing and assessing the social and institutional organization of power and control.[65] This is also a problem for research on schools.

Research on control in schools has typically focused on direct, visible, and hence more obvious mechanisms and aspects of employee control, accountability, and influence. Typical of this approach is the influential work of Meyer and Scott. Using data collected by surveys of teachers and administrators primarily from elementary schools in one state, these researchers focused on three means by which school organizations control the work of teachers: through detailed school policies, administrative inspection of teachers at work, and the administrative use of students' examination scores to evaluate the performance of teachers. They found that "schools develop few policies in the areas of greatest significance for their central goals and purposes." Moreover, they found little follow up for those policies that do exist: "Neither teaching nor its output in student socialization is subject to serious organizational evaluation and inspection." Finally, even if there were rules and even if they were monitored for compliance, such control would not be possible, they concluded, because school administrators' "authority to carry out these activities is in fact evanescent."[66]

Policies, inspections, and performance evaluations are all among the most important and most widely used mechanisms of employee control and accountability. Moreover, survey data on school rules and other aspects of organizational accountability can provide a valuable and necessary overview of the forms, distribution, and variations of control in educational organizations. Indeed, one of the strengths of survey data is their ability to provide an accurate picture of variations in organizational structure across many types of schools.

But policies, inspections, and performance evaluations are not the only mechanisms by which control may operate in workplaces. Researchers have insightfully mapped out a whole range of alternative forms by which organizations control their employees. Moreover, some of the most effective forms of organizational constraint, accountability, and control are difficult to capture through survey questionnaires because they require close-up examination of the day-to-day organization of employees' work.

Charles Perrow, for instance, has persuasively argued that far more effective than direct controls, such as rules, regulations, and sanctions, are other types of structural controls wherein the range of behavior and responsibility is restricted by the organization of production and the way jobs and tasks are subdivided.[67] The hierarchical structure of organizations, by definition, delimits the areas in which members have responsibility and power and, hence, functions as a less visible means of both organizational coordination and control.

Besides these structural controls, Perrow also points out the crucial importance of even less visible organizational controls built into the culture of workplaces and organizations. In such cases, behavior is circumscribed by taken-for-granted norms, expectations, and precedents. With both of these less-direct forms of control, an autonomy and independence of employees may appear to exist precisely *because* of the centralization of the power of employers. The absence of obvious controls may be an indicator of the efficacy of these other mechanisms, not of looseness.

Further contributing to a limited understanding of power and control in organizations is confusion surrounding the concept of bureaucracy itself. To many, bureaucracy is synonymous with centralization and, in turn, a lack of bureaucracy is synonymous with decentralization. Like the idea that professions and bureaucracy are opposites, this is a misleading oversimplification. Bureaucracy is only one mode by which individuals may be hierarchically organized in the pursuit of larger goals and tasks. Bureaucratic mechanisms are a means of achieving centralized control in organizations, but they are not the only means of doing so. Moreover, bureaucratization is a variable; there is great variation both within and between organizations in their degree of bureaucratization. Most organizations are a mixture of both bureaucratization and debureaucratization and of both rationalization and nonrationalization. That organizations do not exhibit the characteristics of the rational model does not mean that they lack control and coordination. What distinguishes the bureaucratic mode of control is formalization and standardization. Rather than controlling and coordinating individual members through, for example, personal allegiance or obedience to individuals, bureaucracies emphasize control through impersonal systems of employee selection, standardized training, formal assignment to delimited tasks, standardized operating procedures, routines, written records, and specified salaries.[68]

Bureaucratic modes of control are also not solely applicable to subordinates and lower-level employees. Organizational analysts have observed that the further one goes up the hierarchy in most organizations, the fewer rationalized controls there are.[69] While they are often the first to prescribe routinization for the rest of the organization, those at the top of organizations often staunchly resist rules and regulations for themselves. But the point of standardized regulations is to minimize such exceptions—that is, to try to ensure that no one is above the law, not even the boss or the president. Rules are typically designed to be universalistic and to constrain everyone alike, both subordinates and superordinates.

In a similar vein, some researchers and reformers have assumed that the regulation of administrative prerogative in schools is an impediment to organizational control—almost as if constraints on managers were a wrongful use of bureaucratic rationality. But increased regulation of higher-level managers does not necessarily result in decreased regulation of lower-level employees. Organizational control of school administrators does not result in a lack of organizational control of teachers. For example, some have argued out that the standardization of teachers' salaries and promotions lessens teachers' dependency and thus undermines their loyalty and obedience to particular school administrators.[70] This is certainly true, but it also misses what this kind of rationalization, so fundamental to bureaucracy in general, does provide—the loyalty and obedience of employees to the organization.

As Weber pointed out, the point of formalized organizational regulations is not simply to control employees but to foster their commitment and allegiance to the organization. Regulations and procedures, for instance, that are designed to protect against the arbitrary dismissal of employees, foster fairness, and undermine favoritism and chronyism serve to promote the security and loyalty of employees and, hence, to promote organizational efficiency.[71] In this sense, limitations on superordinate prerogatives are not necessarily a form of decentralization, but can be a different, and innovative, form of centralized control and coordination.

While bureaucratization applies to both superordinates and subordinates, the same is also true for a lack of bureaucratization. By no means can it be assumed that the absence of bureaucracy in organizations is synonymous with organizational decentralization and employee autonomy. Some educational researchers and reformers associate debureaucratization solely with a paucity of rules and regulations for teachers, or with an ability of teachers to bypass rules and regulations. But pockets of nonrationalization and debureaucratization are not limited to subordinates in organizations. Administrators and superordinates may also be subject to too few rules, have inadequate accountability, or enjoy wide autonomy. Or they may also be able to evade, ignore, or resist the rules that do exist—with important consequences for employee control. Indeed, a lack of—or the skirting of—standardized, authorized regulations can be a source of administrative power and organizational centralization, rather than the opposite.

Thus research on work and organizations suggests that to more completely understand the distribution and forms of control in schools, it is necessary to move beyond an oversimple stereotype of bureaucracy and to move beyond examining only the more visible, direct, and obvious means of influence and employee control. This is the strategy I adopted in this research.

3

TEACHERS AND DECISION MAKING IN SCHOOLS

> To the egotistic and asocial being that has just been born, [society] must, as rapidly as possible, add another, capable of leading a moral and social life. Such is the work of education.
>
> —EMILE DURKHEIM, 1911

> Schoolteachers . . . are the . . . proletarians of the professions.
>
> —C. WRIGHT MILLS, 1951

> The one-room country school must have a different social structure from the city high school with five thousand students, but the basic fact of authority, of dominance and subordination, remains a fact in both.
>
> —WILLARD WALLER, 1932

HOW MUCH INPUT do teachers have in determining what is educationally necessary and best for students? And how does the control held by teachers compare with that of school principals, school district administrators, and governing boards? Moreover, do schools vary in their levels of teacher control?

The focus of my analysis is teachers and administrators within schools. However, schools do not operate in a vacuum, and prior to examining the issue of control within schools, it will be useful to describe control as exercised from outside schools and to sketch, briefly, the educational system and the context of state and federal governance within which schools reside.

The Context of School Control

In the United States, the control of elementary and secondary schooling developed in an unusual manner. In contrast to most Western nations, in this country public schooling was originally instituted on a highly localized basis.[1] The framers of the federal Constitution did not include education or schooling among the functions of the federal government, and thus the provision of schooling began as the responsibility of the individual states. The latter in turn delegated control to local, community-based educational authorities. From the early development of public schooling, the operating principal was that the schooling of children should largely be the responsibility of the communities and towns in which the students and their families resided. This doctrine of local control of schooling was, and continues to be, a dominant value in America. The resulting legacy is the current system of almost 15,000 individual public school districts, governed by school boards who hold legal responsibility for the administration and operation of publicly funded, universal, mandatory, elementary and secondary schooling. The history of public schooling in the United States has also, however, been a story of the expansion of the educational system and the erosion of this foundation of local control.

At the turn of the nineteenth century, the education of most children in America primarily took place in one-room schoolhouses and small academies staffed by small numbers of teachers. These schools provided education to about 15 million children, representing about 60 percent of the school-age population. Most attended only elementary school; only about 6 percent of seventeen-year-olds graduated from secondary school. Currently, at the turn of the twentieth century, more than 100,000 schools, employing almost 3 million teachers, provide education to more than 47 million students. In contrast to a century before, almost all of the school-age population now attends secondary school, and 70 percent of seventeen-year-olds graduate with a high school diploma. Moreover, today students are increasingly schooled in large, complex organizations. The average public secondary school has about 700 students and 50 teachers, within a school district of about 2,700 students, 155 teachers, and a nearly equivalent number of administrative and support staff.[2]

Particularly in the second half of the twentieth century, the dramatic increase in the number, character, and size of schools was accompanied by a dramatic increase in the control and influence over these schools exerted by higher levels of government and by a wide array of nongovernmental groups and organizations. Most notably, states themselves have increased their oversight and regulation of a wide range of aspects of schooling, such as the curricula, student graduation requirements, teacher licensing and training requirements, and the funding of education. Especially in the post–World War II period, the role of the federal government also increased. Originally organized as the U.S. Office of Education in the late 1950s, the federal Department of Education was elevated to cabinet-level status in 1979. The nature of the federal role in education has, however, been a source of ongoing disagreement. In particular, there has been much controversy over two issues—the degree of control the federal government ought to have over schooling, and who should be the primary targets or beneficiaries of federal efforts and resources. Education reform movements, such as those outlined in Chapter 2, advocate different and competing notions of both the extent of federal control and the targets of federal initiatives. Perennial conflict arises, for instance, between advocates of "educational excellence" and advocates of "educational equity." The former tend to emphasize programs designed to improve student academic achievement, especially in mathematics and science and especially for high-achieving student populations. The latter tend to emphasize compensatory programs, especially for disadvantaged student populations: low-income and minority students, girls, handicapped children, immigrants, and the rural poor.

By definition, most federal legislative initiatives, whether it's intended or not, have a centralizing influence and result in an increase in external control of schools and districts. The federal government actually provides only a small portion of the total funding required by elementary and second schools. For example, in the 1980s and 1990s the percent of total expenditures in public and private elementary and secondary education provided by the federal government averaged only about 6 percent.[3] Influence is exerted through "strings" attached to the funding of particular federal programs—rules and regulations that determine if and how states, districts, and schools may use federal dollars.

Many have argued that the federal government's actual influence over schooling outweighs its relatively meager budgetary input. One source of influence has been the numerous federal-level judicial decisions in reference to issues such as the role of religion in schools and student entitlements based on disability or disadvantage. The federal government has also exerted its influence through the dissemination of high-profile reports, such as *A Nation at Risk* produced by the federally supported National Commission on Excellence in Education in

1983. Yet another source of influence is the development, in conjunction with state governors, of national standards, as in the National Education Goals Program conceived in the late 1980s.[4]

In addition, the post–World War II period also saw the growth of a bewildering variety of nongovernmental, national, and regional interest groups and organizations that wield increasing influence over schooling through, for example, lobbying efforts directed at local, state, and federal officials. These include philanthropic organizations, such as the Carnegie Foundation; civil rights groups, such as the NAACP; legal organizations, such as the American Civil Liberties Union; teacher unions, such as the NEA; business groups, such as the Committee for Economic Development; teacher associations in particular fields, such as the National Council for the Social Studies; regional accrediting agencies; academic organizations, such as the American Association for Higher Education, the American Council for Education, the American Historical Association, and the American Association of University Women; scientific organizations, such as the National Research Council and the National Academy of Science; parental advocacy groups for particular student constituencies, such as for gifted education; and on and on. All these groups seek to influence how schools are operated.

As a result of this growth in governmental and nongovernmental influence, schools and local school districts in the United States are clearly not the autonomous bodies they once were.[5] They are subject to a wide array of direct and indirect pressures and constraints from without. Many decisions once made autonomously by schools districts and schools are now made in consultation with, or within frameworks mandated by state, regional, or federal agencies.

Despite these changes, however, a number of studies have documented that schooling in the United States remains to a large extent far more localized than in many other nations. One such study was the International Survey of the Locus of Decision-Making in Educational Systems, conducted by the Organization for Economic Co-operation and Development in 1990–1991 and 1997–1998. Its objective was to ascertain how centralized or decentralized are the elementary and secondary education systems in different nations. This survey focused on thirty-five key decisions that could conceivably be made at a local school district or individual school level. It then determined whether these decisions were indeed made by school districts or schools themselves, or whether they were decided at the state/regional or national/federal levels of governance. The decisions concerned key administrative and educational issues. The survey asked, for example, who determines such things as the design of the overall school curriculum; the objectives and content for particular courses; the selection of course textbooks; the methods used to track or group students; the admission, promotion, and dismissal of students; the creation and staffing of new schools; the teaching methods used in classrooms; the criteria and methods used to evaluate the performance of students in courses; the length of the school day; the choice of courses offered in a school; the hiring and dismissal of teachers and principals; the basis for evaluating teachers and principals; the determination of class sizes; the determination of teachers' assignments, workloads, and schedules; the setting of principals' and teachers' salaries; and the allocation and utilization of budgets and resources.[6]

The OECD studies reveal that in the United States an unusually large proportion of important decisions are made at the school-district or individual school level. Indeed, as illustrated in Figure 3.1, of the thirty-five decisions included in the survey, in the United States none was made at the federal level. In only two of thirty-three nations—Finland and Hungary—were more decisions made at the school-district or school level than in the United States. In addition,

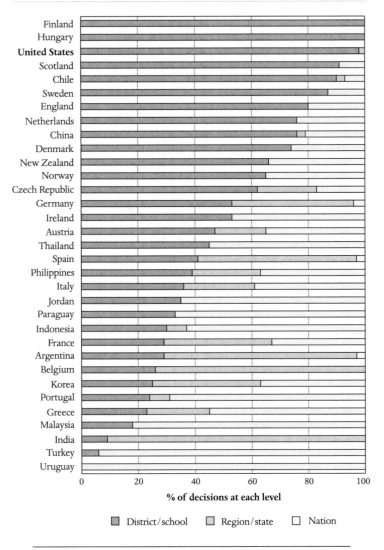

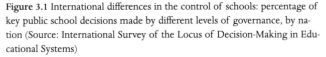

Figure 3.1 International differences in the control of schools: percentage of key public school decisions made by different levels of governance, by nation (Source: International Survey of the Locus of Decision-Making in Educational Systems)

the two cycles of this survey showed that levels of local and school-level control did not change appreciably in the United States during the decade of the 1990s, in spite of the fact that those were years of intense policy and reform debate over the control of schooling. Notably, the survey also distinguished between decision-making control exercised at the school-district level and at the school level, and the data show that in the United States a relatively large proportion of decisions (50 percent) are either strongly influenced or entirely made by the schools themselves.

These data do not of course indicate that, on the one hand, state governments and the U.S. federal government have little or no influence over schooling decisions, nor, on the other hand, do they indicate that districts or schools are autonomous entities that make their own decisions. Indeed, other data from the same survey show that for very few of the decisions examined do schools or districts have complete autonomy. While the federal government does not solely control any of the issues examined, it nevertheless often exerts influence by less direct means. Likewise, many states set parameters, standards, and guidelines within which local districts must operate. However, at a systemic level, the international data do indicate that control of schooling in the United States remains relatively decentralized in comparison with other nations. That is, to a significant degree schooling in the United States continues to be under local control, and many key decisions continue to be made primarily by districts and schools.

This telling fact sheds some light on the debate over how much educational control resides at the different levels of governance. On the one hand, proponents of local community control have argued that education has suffered from far too much government intrusion into schooling affairs and that this has constrained educational flexibility, innovation, and reform. On the other hand, proponents of increased

73

centralized control of schooling have argued that local school districts are far too autonomous and that this is a key obstacle to education reform and progress.[7] The OECD data suggest that there may be some truth to both claims, but resolving these issues requires paying close attention to the level of one's analysis and to the comparisons made. Compared with conditions in the early part of the last century, local school boards and districts no doubt do have less autonomy than they did. However, compared with other nations, these data tell us that the K–12 educational system in the United States is not especially centralized and that much key decision making does take place at the level of districts and schools themselves.

But these data do not shed much light on the debate over who makes these school- and district-level decisions. The data refer to educational systems as a whole, and focus on the balance of power and control among local communities and state and federal governments. They do not and cannot address the question of who controls important decisions *within* schools. That elementary and secondary schooling is relatively decentralized at a systemic level in the United States does not mean, of course, that schools are themselves internally decentralized. In particular, these data also cannot tell us how much control teachers have over their own work. Indeed, it is precisely because of the above findings that this question is both important and a source of debate. Because schooling in the United States remains relatively localized, many high-stakes decisions are made within schools. But who controls these decisions and issues?

How Much Control Do Teachers Have?

To answer this question I examined the degree to which teachers exercise control over a wide range of school decisions, including most of the same decisions examined in the OECD's international survey. I will begin with small-scale data—what I found in my own field research in the four schools I studied in depth (described in Chapter 1)—and then, for comparison, I will turn to national data from the Schools and Staffing Survey.

In my fieldwork, I asked a selection of teachers and administrators how much actual influence they thought teachers had in their school over decisions concerning a selection of key issues.[8] These included both administrative and educational decisions, and the educational issues covered both instructional and social concerns. There were important distinctions among the four different schools I examined, and I will pay attention to those differences later; here I will focus on the common patterns of teacher control.

Consistent with other research, I found academic instruction to be the area in which teachers appear to have the greatest degree of control. As illustrated in Figure 3.2, teachers consistently indicated that they had major levels of control over selecting the particular concepts they taught daily in their classrooms and the particular techniques they used to teach those concepts. Teachers also said they had moderate to major levels of control over the objectives for the courses they taught, over the standards by which they evaluated and graded their pupils, and over how much homework they assigned. However, teachers also consistently indicated they held less-than-moderate levels of power in larger, schoolwide decisions that shaped their instructional program, such as making changes and innovations in the curriculum, choosing their course textbooks, and establishing the overall curriculum for the school.

In contrast to academic instruction, in *none* of the important school administrative and resource allocation decisions did teachers, on average, have even moderate influence (see Figure 3.2). Teachers had little input over decisions about their schedule, their class sizes, the office and classroom space they used, and the use of school funds

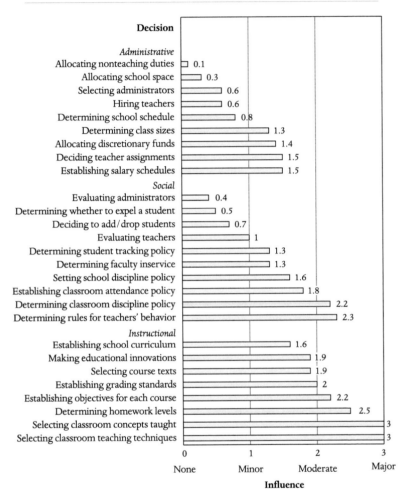

Figure 3.2 Average influence of teachers over key decisions

for classroom materials. Teachers usually had little input into hiring, firing, and budgetary decisions. On average, teachers had very limited control over which courses they were assigned to teach. In other words, teachers had little input in the day-to-day management of their work and their workplace.

A similar account held for teachers' influence over the admission, placement, assignment, and expulsion of students—the all important and consequential gatekeeping and student tracking decisions within schools. Teachers had little influence over the rules and standards for student expulsion. In other words, teachers had little control or choice over what kinds of students were allowed to attend their schools, or not. Likewise, teachers had little say over what kind of student ability grouping the school used and which students were placed into which tracks or ability levels. Teachers indicated they had little say over the consequential decisions surrounding whether to promote particular students or to hold them back to repeat a grade. This is an especially thorny decision when the student has not mastered the required material—the contentious issue of grade retention versus social promotion. The latter has important consequences not only for the student in question but also for the teachers, who must live with the results. On the one hand there are retained students who are must repeat a grade, often with the same teachers as before. On the other hand there are socially promoted students who are underprepared for their new classes, posing a challenge for their new teachers. Teachers also said they had little input into decisions about adding or dropping students from a course—an example of a seemingly mundane decision that, in actuality, is an important part of the sorting of students according to their capabilities. At stake is who controls the assignment or reassignment of students to various levels and courses.

Teachers' levels of control over issues of socialization and the determination of school behavioral and normative standards showed more variation (see Figure 3.2). Teachers reported little input into the means and criteria by which they or their superiors were evaluated. Moreover, teachers had little say in determining the content of their own on-the-job development and training programs, usually referred to as inservice.[9] This is consequential because analysts have often assigned great importance to inservice training and evaluation as mechanisms of socializing and standardizing teacher behavior.[10] In contrast, faculty did indicate a substantial degree of control over behavioral norms for themselves. For instance, most said that the influence of codes for teacher attire and demeanor had diminished in recent decades.

Teacher control over behavioral standards for students was also mixed. Teachers reported little input into schoolwide behavioral rules and standards for students. For example, teachers had little influence over who was enrolled in their courses and did not have the right not to teach particular students. In addition, rarely did teachers have the authority to expel students from their classroom or even to have them temporarily removed. But teachers did report having substantial control over student discipline in their own classrooms. What this often means is that teachers were given responsibility for the enforcement of rules and standards that largely had been established by others—a distinction I will return to in the next two chapters.

Thus I found wide variations in levels of teacher control across different types of activities. Teachers reported substantial control over some issues, mostly in reference to instruction within classrooms. But most teachers had little influence over anything but instructional matters and, among those the issues were confined to their classrooms.

It is also, however, important to acknowledge that my clear analytic distinctions between academic instruction decisions, social decisions, and administrative decisions are often less than clear for particular activities. In practice, different instructional, administrative, and social issues become merged and integrated. For instance, decisions about the methods and standards teachers use to grade students are a matter of academic instruction, as I have categorized them in Figure 3.2. But they also concern the criteria and mechanisms of student ability grouping and thus are related to sorting and tracking—which I categorize as social issues. Likewise, evaluations of principals and teachers are social issues, in that they concern assessing individuals according to particular norms of behavior, and I categorized them accordingly. But they are also an administrative task.

It was also unclear to me how representative my small sample of teachers in four schools would be. Are the patterns I found also to be found elsewhere? To answer this question I examined similar data from the national Schools and Staffing Survey. SASS asked a large sample of teachers across the country to indicate how much influence they have over a selection of important teaching and educational activities, representing both social and instructional issues. For purposes of comparison, I included in my field research all of the same decisions and issues examined in SASS, and so the questionnaires and results were comparable.

The data from SASS show that the findings from my field interviews are highly typical for teachers nationwide. Indeed, it is also immediately apparent from the national data how infrequently teachers hold substantial control over many key educational decisions. For example, as shown in Table 3.1, only about one-third of secondary-level teachers nationwide say they have a great deal of influence in determining their classroom discipline policies, and just 9 percent say the same for schoolwide discipline policies.[11]

Moreover, the national data also reveal how very few differences exist in the amount of power held by different types of teachers.

Table 3.1 Relative influence of different teachers (percentage of teachers with a great deal of influence over key decisions, by type of teacher)

Decision	All	Gender		Field			Experience		Education	
		Male	Female	English	Social studies	Math	Junior	Senior	BA or less	MA or more
Social										
Determining student tracking policy	8	7	8	9	7	9	8	7	8	8
Determining faculty inservice	11	10	12	11	10	10	10	11	11	11
Setting school discipline policy	9	8	10	9	8	7	9	8	9	8
Determining classroom discipline policy	34	29	38	34	31	33	32	34	35	34
Instructional										
Establishing school curriculum	15	14	16	17	12	14	15	16	16	14
Selecting course texts	35	36	34	23	30	24	25	36	35	35
Selecting classroom concepts taught	37	38	36	29	32	24	34	37	37	37
Selecting classroom teaching techniques	64	60	66	64	59	63	62	64	64	64
Determining homework levels	68	65	70	68	65	67	68	68	68	67

Source: Schools and Staffing Survey.

Whether male or female, white or minority, beginner or experienced, in the social studies, English, science, or mathematics departments, more or less educated, similar numbers of teachers reported high influence in reference to both teacher control over schoolwide policies and to teacher control within individual classrooms. The lack of teacher-to-teacher differences in control is especially striking because it contradicts the widely believed notion that some attributes of teachers, especially their gender, experience, subject field, and education, are strongly related to how much power they hold within schools. Some researchers, for instance, have argued that levels of discretion and autonomy vary according to how senior the faculty members are, how much in demand their particular training and areas of expertise are, and their education credentials.[12] Ostensibly, such factors would increase the bargaining power and professional standing of teachers and thus augment their influence over workplace decisions. Moreover, some have argued that, as in higher education, there are large differences in the characteristics and, perhaps, power of different departments within secondary schools: that, for instance, teachers in math departments as a whole might hold more power than those in English departments.[13] No doubt there may be large differences in power between individual teachers and, moreover, between different departments in schools. However, the data indicate that, in general, different kinds of teachers do not vary much in their degree of control—most wield little.[14]

This pattern is not only widespread across schools but also appears to be chronic over time; levels of teacher control and influence appear to have neither increased nor decreased in recent years. Like the international data on school and district decision-making influence, the SASS data show little change in teacher influence levels for these issues across four independent cycles of the survey running from 1987 to 2000. For example, in 1987, 8 percent of secondary teachers said they had a great deal of influence over setting schoolwide discipline policies, while 6 percent said the same in 2000. Likewise, in 1987, 34 percent of secondary teachers said they had a great deal of influence in determining their classroom discipline policies, while 30 percent said the same in 2000. This is especially striking because these were years of intense policy debate over the control of schooling, when great fanfare was attached to numerous reforms aimed at changing the organization and control of schools.

How Do Teachers Compare with School Administrators?

Establishing the set of activities within schools on which to focus, and determining levels of teacher influence over them are necessary first steps in assessing the distribution of control in schools. However, it is also necessary to evaluate these levels. That is, what constitutes a high or low level of teacher control? On what basis is a school labeled centralized or decentralized? The SASS data indicate few teachers report that they have high levels of control over a number of key issues in schools, but how does this compare with other key groups or individuals in schools? Are there some groups who do have high levels of control?

For evaluating teacher control in schools, I used a criterion drawn from the study of occupations and professions in general. A key question is: How much control do teachers have over important school decisions *relative* to the senior management of schools? More specifically, what is the hierarchy of power among teachers, school governing boards, school-district administrators, and school principals?

To answer these questions I turned to the SASS data on the relative control held by school governing boards, public school district administrators, principals, and teachers. SASS asked a large national sample of school principals to evaluate the influence of each of these groups over key decisions in their schools. They included decisions for both administrative and educational issues, and in reference to the latter, decisions regarding both social and instructional issues. Again, the decisions overlap with those I examined in my field research.

The data reveal dramatic differences in the decision-making power of these groups. The lack of control held by teachers over their work stands out in contrast to the control exercised by others. In Figure 3.3, the data present a clear picture of a steep hierarchy of organizational control within schools across the nation. At the top of this hierarchy, for six of the eight important school decisions, are principals. At the bottom of the hierarchy, for five of the eight issues, are teachers. For many key issues, principals view themselves as the most powerful of these groups within schools, and they see teachers as the least powerful within schools.[15] For instance, in the case of determining the school's discipline policy, a crucial part of student socialization, 24 percent of principals perceive their faculties to have major influence, 33 percent perceive their boards to have major influence, but 59 percent perceive themselves to have major influence.

The imbalance of control between teachers and their principals and school boards is also made clear by the issues of teacher hiring and evaluation. The hiring and evaluation of colleagues is an area in which professionals traditionally have a great deal of control. College and university professors, for example, typically have equal or more influence, relative to college and university administrators, over the hiring of new colleagues and the evaluation and promotion of fellow colleagues.[16] This does not hold true for secondary-school teachers. While teachers have little influence over the selection, hiring, and evaluation of their school principals (as indicated earlier, in Figure 3.2), in contrast, principals frequently have a great deal of control over the selection, hiring, and evaluation of teachers. Moreover, prin-

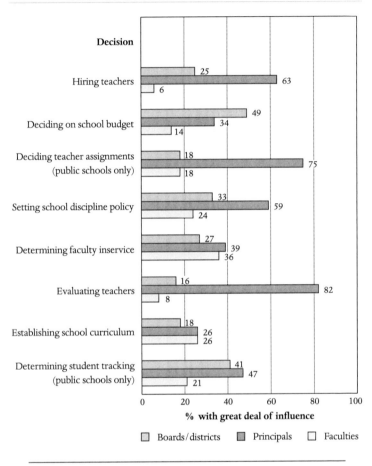

Figure 3.3 Relative influence of school boards, school districts, principals, and teachers (Source: Schools and Staffing Survey)

cipals also have the prerogative to decide teachers' course assignments, that is, to decide which teachers will teach which courses. This issue lies at the heart of the professional status of any occupational group. It is a crucial issue for teachers, because it reveals the extent to which teachers lack control over the content of their jobs and also because of its implications for their degree of expertise. Teacher misassignment—teachers assigned by principals to teach subjects that do not match their expertise—is widespread in the United States—a topic to which I will return in the next two chapters.

Also striking are differences in control over establishing school curricula. This is another issue over which college and university professors typically have equal or more influence relative to college and university administrators. In elementary and secondary schools, it is the domain that researchers have long held to be dominated by teachers, and according to principals, this is one of two areas (along with determining teacher inservice programs) in which the control held by school faculties is akin to that of school principals and higher than that of boards and district administrators. However, the data show that teachers only infrequently exert a high level of control over the instructional program. As illustrated in Figure 3.3, according to principals, only just over one-fourth of secondary school faculties have a great deal of actual influence in decisions concerning the overall school curriculum.

Hence, the comparison of teachers' control with that of their principals and their school boards and district administrators shows that for several key sets of decisions concerned with both educational and administrative activities, schools are highly centralized. It is also clear, however, that evaluating the degree of centralization depends on the groups compared and the level of analysis chosen. Changing one's focus from the school level to the board or district level yields a very different picture. If, in Figure 3.3, we compare the percentage bars for principals with those for governing boards/district administrators, rather than comparing teachers with principals, schools appear quite autonomous. Principals are influential more often than their board or district for seven of eight activities—suggesting a high degree of within-district decentralization—a finding to which I will return in the next section.

Several other points must be stressed concerning these comparative data. First, the rankings are based on the reports of principals, who are, perhaps, in the best position to know how much power these particular groups have. But their reports are, of course, based on their own perceptions and thus could be biased in one way or another. For example, some analysts have found that highly powerful members of organizations can be prone to deny or underestimate their own level of influence because of cultural norms frowning upon the undemocratic aspects of power.[17] If this kind of downward bias is also true for school principals, it suggests that, if anything, schools are even more internally centralized than reported.

Second, there is some discrepancy between the views of principals and those of teachers in these data. A close comparison of principals' reports (as in Figure 3.3) with teachers' reports (as in Table 3.1) indicates that principals more frequently report teachers to be empowered than teachers themselves do. Again, the important point here is relative power. Despite their more rosy picture of teacher control, principals do not find teachers to be as influential as themselves over these activities.

Finally, school governing boards, school district administrators, principals, and teachers are key groups involved with school-level decision-making. But they are, of course, not the only groups and constituencies involved. As discussed earlier, a host of external groups— governmental and nongovernmental agencies, interest groups, and organizations—also influences what goes on in schools. Moreover, within schools themselves there are often different administrative, faculty, and staff groups, cliques, and factions. In secondary schools, teachers are divided into departments, which are often run by chairpersons who may hold an unusual degree of power. Hence, these data do not present a comprehensive portrait of all of the many possible entities, in or out of schools, that exert influence over school issues. What they do is sharpen our understanding of the power held by teachers within schools by comparing their levels of influence with those of several other key groups.

Do Schools Vary in Their Levels of Control?

Assessing the amount of control held by teachers in schools depends on the activities examined and the evaluative criteria used. But one would also expect the distribution of control to depend on the schools investigated. Do teachers usually have more power in some kinds of schools than in others? Are some settings typically more centralized than others?

Research on the organization of schools has shown that there are, indeed, important differences in the organizational character and conditions of schools. These variations depend primarily on the type of school, its community setting, and the type of students enrolled. Differences between public and private schools, in particular, have been the focus of a number of studies of school organization, and researchers have typically concluded that private schools are far more decentralized than public schools.[18]

In background analysis of the SASS data I did find these kinds of factors to be related to school-to-school differences in control. School sector (public or private), in particular, and school size have an effect on both the amount of control held by teachers and the hierarchical ranking of control among boards, administrators, principals, and faculty. I also found that some of these variations run counter to conventional wisdom.

Table 3.2 displays these findings. It lists the same decision categories as in Table 3.1, but it focuses on differences among schools rather than differences among teachers. As shown in Table 3.2, large, public secondary schools occupy one end of the scale. This category represents almost 40 percent of all secondary schools and employs more than half of all secondary school teachers in the United States. At the other end of the scale are small, private secondary schools. This category represents a much smaller number of schools: only 5 percent of secondary schools and only about 5 percent of secondary school teachers in the United States. But it does include almost two-thirds of all private secondary schools.[19]

Large public schools appear to be, for most of the issues, the most centralized of secondary schools. For example, in these schools, only 41 percent of the teachers reported, on average, a great deal of influence over decisions concerned with academic instruction, and just 14 percent of the teachers reported having equivalent control over social decisions.

In contrast, small, private secondary schools appear to be, for many of the issues, the least centralized. It is striking, however, that even in this group, while just over half (51 percent) the teachers, on average, reported substantial control over instructional activities, less than one-fourth (22 percent) of teachers in these schools reported substantial control over social issues. The data clearly show, across a range of schools, that the degree of teacher control depends on the activities examined. As before, a very different picture of teacher control emerges depending on whether one focuses on instructional or social issues. Most important, however, is that, although there were differences between settings, the vast majority of secondary

Table 3.2 Relative influence of teachers in different schools (percentage of teachers with a great deal of influence over key decisions, by type of school)

Decision	All schools	Large public schools	Small public schools	Large private schools	Small private schools
Social					
Determining student tracking policy	8	6	9	13	15
Determining faculty inservice	11	11	13	11	11
Setting school discipline policy	9	7	11	10	18
Determining classroom discipline policy	34	32	37	46	42
Mean % for social decisions	16	14	18	20	22
Instructional					
Establishing school curriculum	15	13	20	20	26
Selecting course texts	35	29	50	48	45
Selecting classroom concepts taught	37	32	48	46	49
Selecting classroom teaching techniques	64	62	67	74	71
Determining homework levels	68	68	70	71	66
Mean % for instructional decisions	44	41	51	52	51

Source: Schools and Staffing Survey.

schools, including small private ones, were highly centralized, especially when it came to social issues.

The hierarchical ranking of teachers, principals, administrators, and boards also differed across these different types of schools, as shown in Figure 3.4[20] and Table 3.3.[21] Particularly striking were the overall differences between public and private schools. In public schools the hierarchical ranking was: principals, boards (including district-level administrators), and then faculty. In contrast, in private schools the hierarchical ranking was: principals, faculty, and then boards. Not only did the rank ordering of these groups differ but also the magnitude of their relative empowerment varied between public and private schools.

In the first place, far more private school principals perceived themselves to be highly influential than did public school principals. For instance, on average, more than three-fourths of the principals in private schools, versus less than half of public school principals, viewed themselves as having a great deal of control over decisions. Second, a primary source of this difference between private and public schools appears to be the relative influence of their school governing boards (and district-level administrators, in the case of public schools). These groups were far more often reported to be influential in the public sector. This seems to be a zero-sum pattern. That is, in schools where principals were more often influential, boards and districts were less often influential, and vice versa. Moreover, the magnitude of the board-to-principal power gap varied; as displayed in Figure 3.4, the gap between private school principals and private school boards was far greater than the analogous gap in the public system.

There were also public-to-private school differences in faculty influence, but these do not appear to be zero-sum.[22] In private schools, where principals were more often influential, teachers were also slightly more often influential, and vice versa. But this also depended

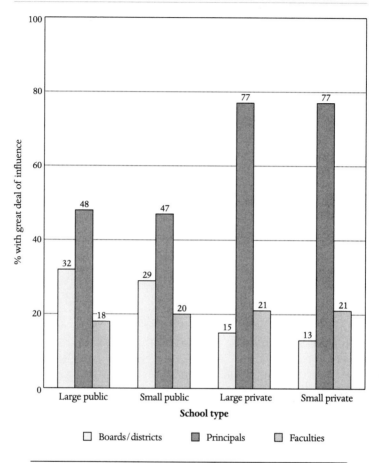

Figure 3.4 Relative influence of school boards, school districts, principals, and teachers in different schools (Source: Schools and Staffing Survey)

Table 3.3 Relative influence of school boards, school districts, principals, and teachers in different schools (percentage of school boards/districts, principals, and faculties with a great deal of influence over key decisions, by type of school)

Decision	Large public schools	Small public schools	Large private schools	Small private schools
Hiring teachers				
Boards/districts	26	27	10	12
Principals	61	57	86	88
Faculties	6	7	4	6
Deciding on school budget				
Boards/districts	47	52	50	40
Principals	36	25	71	59
Faculties	16	15	0	4
Setting school discipline policy				
Boards/districts	40	34	8	11
Principals	54	58	80	83
Faculties	20	27	30	37
Determining faculty inservice				
Boards/districts	34	27	7	2
Principals	33	36	71	79
Faculties	35	36	44	33
Evaluating teachers				
Boards/districts	20	16	4	4
Principals	80	81	88	92
Faculties	8	8	12	10
Establishing school curriculum				
Boards/districts	22	15	9	8
Principals	21	22	67	60
Faculties	25	25	37	37

Source: Schools and Staffing Survey

on the issue examined—over hiring and budgetary decisions, private school teachers were *not* more likely to have a high level of control than were public school teachers (see Table 3.3). Most important, in each of the four types of schools, faculty members were perceived to have substantial control far less frequently than school principals.

That is, although it is true that private school teachers appeared to be more often influential than their public counterparts, they were still, like public school teachers, less often influential than their principals. It is this comparison—the relative control of teachers and administrators—that is important for evaluating the control held by teachers. Focusing on the pervasiveness in both public and private schools of this hierarchical relationship between teachers and principals undermines the widely held view that private schools are highly decentralized places. Indeed, for each of the decisions, the gap between private school principals and private school teachers was either equal to or greater than the analogous gap in public schools (see Table 3.3). That is, *relative to their principals,* the private school teachers were no more empowered than the public school teachers. Public and private, large and small, all secondary schools shared a high degree of within-school centralization for these key activities.

These comparisons also highlight an important distinction noted earlier: assessments of the distribution of control in schools depend on the groups compared and the level of analysis examined. In contrast to the interface between teachers and principals, the interface between districts or governing boards and schools yields a different picture. In other words, in Figure 3.4, if we compare boards/districts with school principals, the data show a great deal of decentralization in both the public and the private sector.

It is true that public schools are more often subject to control from influential boards or districts than are private schools. Unless they are part of a larger collective entity, such as a Catholic church diocese, private schools usually do not have the equivalent of a public school-district administration and thus are subject to less centralized regulation than public schools. (Moreover, private schools are not subject to as many state and federal regulations as are public schools).[23] Nevertheless, public school principals perceive themselves to be in control more often than their boards/districts for most of the key issues examined. The main exceptions are control of budgetary matters and, in large public schools, control of the curriculum and teacher inservice programs. Although public school boards (along with district administrators) are more often influential than their counterparts associated with private schools, for many issues public school principals do not report themselves to be beleaguered, constrained, lower-level managers.

Hence, on the one hand, the data show that both public and private schools are decentralized at the larger interface between schools and their governing boards. This finding is consistent with the international data presented earlier in this chapter showing a high degree of system-level and also district-level decentralization. On the other hand, the data also show that both public and private schools are centralized at the school level, at least for these key issues.

There is another problem with the conventional wisdom concerning private schools. In addition to arguing that they are far more decentralized than public schools and that they have greater school autonomy, proponents of private schools also argue that parents, *individually,* have more influence and input into school decision making in private schools, simply by virtue of the market relationship between client and provider, and their choice to do business with the school or not.[24] There certainly may be some truth to this, but it overlooks an important mechanism of parental and community input into public schooling. Board and district influence over school decision making can be viewed as an example of top-down bureaucratic control, but control by school boards can also be a form of *collective* parental input into the operation of schools. Notably, the data show that this form of collective public and client input is greater in public than private schools.[25]

There are also, the data show, some exceptions to this portrait of centralized control within schools. The data, for instance, do indicate several areas of apparent discretion left open to many teachers in many schools. Teachers often report themselves to have high levels of influence over some classroom instructional tasks and over classroom discipline. Moreover, both the field data and the SASS data also show a clear difference between teachers' control within classrooms and teachers' control over schoolwide policies. Teachers report far higher levels of control at the classroom level.

From the school disorganization perspective, these exceptions would, undoubtedly, be viewed as important evidence of a significant zone of faculty autonomy. Advocates of this view argue that, regardless of school policy, teachers in reality have wide latitude to exercise their discretion over the curriculum within their classrooms. This perspective assumes a sharp separation between classroom and schoolwide activities and that decoupling between the administrative structure and the classroom core results in substantial teacher control over educational processes. That is, from this viewpoint, the data could be interpreted as evidence that behind the closed doors of their classrooms teachers largely teach what they choose.

The data analyzed in this chapter cannot themselves resolve this claim and issue. Numerical data are useful to establish the outlines of teachers' and administrators' relative control over specific decisions. But they do not distinguish between routine and crucial decisions. Nor do they tell us the extent to which decisions are, or are not, connected to one another. For example, it is unclear if and how overall schoolwide policies, such as those concerned with curricula, tracking criteria, attendance requirements, and student disciplinary codes, constrain and influence what teachers actually do in their classrooms. In other words, these data alone cannot tell us to what extent and by what mechanisms the work of teachers is controlled in schools. This is the subject of the next two chapters.

4

RULES FOR TEACHERS

Bureaucracy has a "rational" character: rules, means, ends and matter-of-factness dominate its bearing. . . . This stands in extreme contrast to the regulation of all relationships through individual privileges and bestowals of favor . . . The official [in a bureaucracy] normally holds tenure. Legal or actual life-tenure, however, is not recognized as the official's right to the possession of office, as was the case with many structures of authority in the past. Where legal guarantees against arbitrary dismissal or transfer are developed, they merely serve to guarantee a strictly objective discharge of office duties free from all personal considerations.

—MAX WEBER, 1922

How do schools control the work of teachers? As in any organization, a major task of managers in schools is to direct, supervise, account for the activities of their primary employees—teachers. This is not necessarily an easy nor a straightforward task. This chapter and the next will examine to what extent and by what means this is done.

Analysts of work and organizations have insightfully distinguished and described a wide range and variety of mechanisms by which organizations attempt to coordinate and control their members and employees. On one end of this continuum lie those methods that are more formalized, direct, and obvious. Among these are policies, regulations, requirements, employee job descriptions, and standard operating procedures, typically formalized in employee manuals, contracts, and handbooks. These are hallmarks of bureaucratic organization and the very embodiment of the rational ethos itself. On the other end of the control continuum lie those mechanisms that are less direct and less visible. Some of these less obvious modes of control are embedded in the formal structure of organizations. Others are embedded in the roles that make up the informal, or social organization, of a work setting. Such mechanisms are usually less visible to insiders and outsiders alike because they become institutionalized and, hence, are taken for granted as part of the normal way things are.[1]

Analysts of work and organizations also tell us that any organizational control mechanism must accomplish three tasks in order to be effective. They must define what the employee is to do, they must ascertain whether the employee has done it, and they must sanction or discipline the employee who has not.[2] Each type of organizational control mechanism has its relative advantages and disadvantages in accomplishing these three tasks, depending on the particular kind of work, technology, and skills involved.

In this chapter and the next I move my analysis beyond the examination of decision-making influence to embed my statistical findings in a more full view of the structure of schools and organization of the work of teachers. One might think of the pattern of decision-making influence among teachers and administrators, described in Chapter 3, as a skeletal, preliminary sketch of the distribution of control in schools. The following two chapters fill out this basic portrait by adding features and flesh to the bare bones. My objective is to show the processes by which organizational control actually works (or does not) in schools.

The next two chapters rely far more on material culled from my field research. Through extended interviews with teachers and administrators, I sought to discover what kinds of boundaries may or may not exist for teachers' work and behavior within schools, and to what extent and how these are enforced. I purposely chose to investigate four widely different schools to discover what variations might exist in the degree and character of control. As described in Chapter 1, the first, Catholic High, is a large, urban, less affluent parochial high school. The second, Urban High, is a large, low-income, public high school. The third, Suburban High, is a smaller, more affluent, public high school. Finally the fourth, Friends School, is a small, more affluent, Quaker, combined (elementary and secondary) preparatory school. Where possible, throughout my discussion I try to compare what I found in these schools with representative data from large-scale surveys.

In this chapter I begin my analysis with an examination of the more direct and more visible types of controls. The first section addresses the question: Do schools have rules, policies, and regulations governing the behavior for teachers? The second part of the chapter considers the question: Do schools provide oversight and supervision of the work of teachers? The third section focuses on the question of enforcement: To what extent and by what means are school rules and policies for teachers enforced? In Chapter 5 I will turn to an examination of less direct, less visible, and less obvious mechanisms of control in schools, including the norms and roles for teachers that are embedded and institutionalized in both the structure and the culture of schools.

Do Schools Have Rules for Teachers?

In my field research, I found ample evidence that schoolteachers are governed by numerous official policies, both written and unwritten, concerning a wide range of tasks and activities within schools. I also found that schools vary widely in the depth and breadth of their rules and regulations for teachers. Interestingly, in this regard, among the four schools I investigated there was far more difference between the two private schools than between the two public schools. The private schools appeared to illustrate two extremes in the degree to which teachers are bound by rules. Table 4.1 illustrates the range and variety of rules and policies in the four schools.[3]

The least rule bound of the four sites was Friends School. Friends School was an unusual setting, owing to its faculty-run consensus model for decision making, rooted in its Quaker tradition. Administrators at Friends, for example, typically described themselves as "peers, not masters of the faculty," and teachers at Friends had relatively high levels of influence over most important decisions, including many of the administrative and social issues surveyed in the last chapter. Its faculty, for instance, had a strong voice in hiring both headmasters and teachers, unheard of powers for the faculty in the other schools. In this regard, Friends School is not representative; it is the exception that proves the rule. Indeed, it is clear that it is unusual even among small private schools. Its high degree of teacher control is reflected in its relative lack of rules for teachers. The staff at Friends School prided itself on having few formalized policies and on reversing the burden of justification from the rule followers onto the rule makers. In other words, proponents of new rules had to work hard to justify the necessity of their proposals. This did not mean that Friends School had no rules, only that they were fewer, less codified, and more subject to challenge than in other schools. For in-

Table 4.1 Rules for teachers: the existence of school policies for selected issues, by school (X = rule exists; O = no rule exists)

Issue	Catholic High	Urban High	Suburban High	Friends School
Administrative				
Nonteaching duties (e.g., hall monitoring)	X	O	X	X
Class size levels	X	X	X	X
Use of classroom discretionary funds	X	X	X	O
Setting teacher salary levels	X	X	X	X
Social				
Arrival and departure times for teachers	X	X	X	O
Punishments for students for specific offenses	X	X	X	X
Student dress code	X	X	X	O
Standards for student behavior	X	X	X	X
Standards for student attendance	X	X	X	O
Teacher dress code	O	O	O	O
Standards for teacher behavior	X	X	O	O
Standards for teacher attendance	X	X	X	O
Procedures for teacher evaluation	X	X	X	X
Instructional				
Use of class lesson plans	X	X	X	O
Course textbook selection	X	X	O	O
Use of curriculum guides	X	X	O	O
Standards for student promotion	X	X	O	O
Standards for student grading (A, B, C, D, etc.)	X	X	X	X
Format for student grading (no. of tests, etc.)	X	X	X	X
Class homework levels	X	X	X	X
Total policies (out of 20)	19	18	15	9

stance, of the four sites, Friends was the only school that did not require teachers to fill out and submit verification forms when they were absent from school for illness or other reasons, and the only site that did not spell out the times at which teachers were required to arrive at school and after which they were allowed to depart school grounds.

In stark contrast, the most rule bound of the four schools was Catholic High. A parochial school administered by an urban archdiocese, Catholic High had a highly centralized organizational structure. For example, school administrators were not obligated by school philosophy to include teachers in decision-making processes or even justify their policies to the faculty. Teachers often learned of new school policies after the fact, by formal edict or simply by verbal command. The role of the diocesan and school administrations was to make the key decisions. The role of teachers was to carry them out. Where school administrators at Friends typically described themselves as "peers, not masters of the faculty," school administrators at Catholic High referred to themselves as "shepherds" and to the teaching staff as their "flock." Several teachers at Catholic High used the term "tall children" to describe the way they felt they themselves were seen by the school administration. This distribution of control was reflected in the breadth and depth of rules for teachers at Catholic High.

Many of the rules schools have for teachers are to be found in the faculty handbooks or manuals that are typically presented to new teachers on beginning their employment. Listed inside these handbooks are numerous regulations, directives, and policies concerned with activities both inside and outside of classrooms and for both students and teachers. These manuals formally record some, but not all, of the many standard operating procedures and routines that ostensibly govern life in the organization.

Of the four schools, Catholic High's faculty handbook stood out for its impressively long list of policies for teachers and for their degree of specificity. The rules at Catholic High reflected a relatively coherent school behavioral code, common to Catholic education in general.[4] For example, the manual contained a rule disallowing teachers from eating or drinking in their classrooms, a rule requiring teachers to lead prayers at the beginning of each class, a rule forbidding teachers to use tape on the walls of their classrooms, a rule specifying that teachers not allow the use of their first name in the presence of students, a rule forbidding teachers to discuss maintenance problems with custodians, a rule limiting faculty to the use of particular pay telephones in the building, a rule requiring teachers to report their arrival to and departure from the building, and a rule directing teachers to fill out and submit verification forms when they have been absent from school for illness or other reasons. Moreover, at Catholic there was little sense of what in higher education is called academic freedom; teachers could not openly and without interference express beliefs that did not agree with the norms set by the church administration.

Foremost among the regulations listed in faculty handbooks at all of the schools were rules for the control of student behavior. These rules specify how faculty are to respond to different categories and examples of student misbehavior. The role of the teacher in these cases is usually to implement rules that have been set by others. That is, faculty members are to communicate and enforce the behavioral norms prescribed for students. The different types of student infractions addressed in these faculty manuals can be extensive and include such things as absences from school, lateness to class, being excused from class, loitering in the halls, smoking on school property, student attire, and the use of portable audio players. The work of enforcing rules for such seemingly mundane or trivial issues is neither easy nor peripheral to the central activity of teaching. "Teaching" behavioral norms is intrinsic to the social purpose of schooling, is often a daunting task for faculty, and is often highly rule bound.

Another genre of rules that may be listed in the faculty manuals concerns teachers' nonclassroom responsibilities and nonteaching duties. Typically teachers are assigned "service periods" that involve policing nonclassroom areas of the school: the cafeteria, the study halls, the student restrooms, and the hallways. Teachers are usually assigned to patrol or staff one of these locations during one of the periods each day during which they are not teaching. This aspect of a teacher's job is also neither trivial nor easy. Many teachers heartily dislike these service assignments, and it is for just this reason that some teacher unions have bargained successfully for the elimination of such chores. For instance, at Urban High, faculty were assigned none of these duties because the teacher union had successfully negotiated with the school district to have separate monitors hired, so that "teachers can teach, as they should be doing."

In addition to staff manuals, rules and policies for academic instruction are often embodied in standardized curricula. Like all bureaucratic control mechanisms, standardized curricula are designed to ensure accountability and consistency in the performance of employees and in the delivery of a product. They do this by defining and prescribing the scope and sequence of particular courses. Standardized curricula widely vary in the degree to which they specify what teachers are to teach and how they are to teach it. The most extreme versions are often derisively labeled "teacher-proof" curricula. They consist of step-by-step course programs that are prescribed in such detail that, ostensibly, anyone could teach them, no matter how skilled or unskilled. Different teachers in the same school are all required to teach the same material from the same section of the same textbook during the same week. From an administrative perspective, the advantage of such a program is that it ameliorates differences and inequities in school and teacher quality. Students are provided with the same "product" regardless of which teacher they are assigned or which school they attend.

None of the schools I investigated used this extreme kind of instructional standardization, but both Catholic High and Urban High did prescribe less extreme versions of standardized curricula. At these schools, the instructional content of what teachers taught in their courses was regulated through a curriculum produced by the school district, in the case of Urban High, or by the archdiocese, in the case of Catholic High. This curriculum consisted of written rules, documents, and materials, collected in "curriculum guides," that preset the content and pace of instruction and the methods of evaluating the performance of the students. For each course, the teacher was required to follow the content objectives listed in the course's curriculum guide, to use the prescribed textbook, and to evaluate students with districtwide or diocesewide midterm and final exams. Within this set of boundaries, the curriculum left to the teacher's discretion the concepts and ideas taught on a particular day and the techniques by which this was done. The nature of this division of labor was aptly summarized for me by a school administrator at Catholic High: "Teachers can decide *how* to teach, but not *what* to teach." As one English teacher at Catholic High explained: "Working within those parameters you set the objectives. You teach five novels, as long as they are the five novels prescribed for that year, and track and all of that."

Unlike Catholic and Urban High, Suburban High did not have a standardized curriculum imposed by the school district, and teachers there were relatively unregulated and autonomous when it came to designing the courses they taught. Teachers at Suburban High were responsible for creating their own course objectives and tests, and for selecting the textbooks they used. However, even at Suburban High the faculty handbooks listed extensive guidelines regulating the instructional work of teachers. For example, as at Catholic High and Urban High, policies existed for how many course exams teachers were required to administer to their classes each semester—usually three or four. There were rules requiring the periodic assignment of homework to students and guidelines specifying what proportion of the students' semester and final grades were to be determined by tests, homework, and classwork. Moreover, the relatively high degree of teacher control at Suburban was tenuous and a source of great tension. Suburban High's district administration had recently proposed replacing the faculty-created curriculum that had been used for years with a standard districtwide curriculum. The head of the teacher union described it in this way: "You were free to develop it [a course] in ways that you wanted to within the context of the basic subject of the course. You could make it relevant. People did that. It was an autonomy we prized tremendously here at Suburban High. It made you feel very, very important, as part of that particular department, part of the whole package of what the district was about."

In contrast to the other schools, and on the other end of the spectrum, was Friends School, where there was a far higher degree of professional autonomy surrounding what and how teachers taught. Akin to the model common in much of higher education, as one teacher at Friends put it, there was "maximum freedom for faculty to construct courses they way they want to."

The pervasiveness of extensive policies for teachers is not unique to the schools I investigated, as shown by data from the School Assessment Survey, a large-scale survey of public school teachers conducted by Research for Better Schools, an education policy research center. In this survey teachers were asked about the existence of school policies, either written or unwritten, for fifteen important school activities and issues.[5] It is immediately apparent from these data that most public secondary schools have policies and rules covering a wide range of aspects of the work of teachers.

As illustrated in Figure 4.1, virtually all of the teachers reported that their school had policies concerning their times of arrival and departure; almost all indicated that their school had rules stipulating that they produce daily lesson plans; more than 80 percent reported that their school had rules concerning the choice of texts that they use in their classes; 95 percent said their school issued curriculum guides defining the content of their courses; more than 90 percent said their school had rules defining the standards for satisfactory student academic performance; 94 percent reported that their school had rules defining acceptable punishment for students for specific offenses; more than 90 percent indicated that their school had standards for the assignment of particular grades (for example, A, B, C, etc.) to students; and more than 90 percent noted rules assigning nonteaching service duties to teachers.

Notably, however, some activities and issues were less rule bound than others. For instance, less than half of the teachers reported that their school had a teacher dress code, and less than half reported policies limiting classroom discussion of controversial topics, such as sexuality, political ideology, or religious orientation. These findings are interesting because such issues lie at the heart of the social purpose of schooling—the values, morals, and behavior to be taught in schools. Teachers are important role models for children, and so how teachers behave and the values to which they expose children is a part of their work that has always been of special concern to parents and the public. However, often there is little consensus on the degree to which the personal appearance and values of teachers can and should be controlled. Attempts to implement policies governing teachers' moral codes are often greeted with controversy. For example, the San Francisco public school district made national headlines

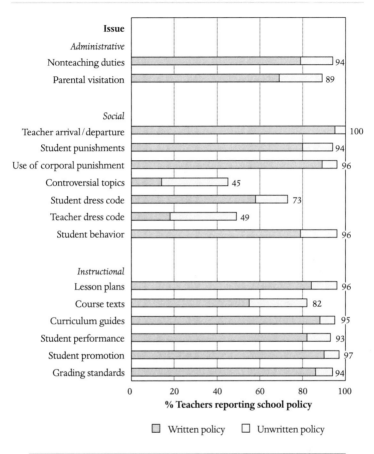

Figure 4.1 Existence of rules for teachers (Source: School Assessment Survey)

and generated much controversy in the mid-1990s by requiring teachers seeking jobs in particular schools to agree to a code of "tenets." Established in response to an antidiscrimination lawsuit filed by the NAACP, these tenets included such broadly liberal notions as "all individuals should learn to live and work in a world that is characterized by interdependence and diversity" and "all individuals learn in many different ways and at varying rates." They also included notions of teacher accountability: "If individuals do not learn, those assigned to be their teachers should accept responsibility for this failure and take appropriate remedial action."[6] Efforts such as these to regulate the values held and modeled by teachers are not, of course, limited to civil rights groups or to those on the liberal left. As noted in Chapter 2, conservative Christian and other like-minded groups have repeatedly sought to ban teachers from discussing in classrooms controversial topics such as abortion, homosexuality, suicide, sex, and drug and alcohol use.[7] The data in Figure 4.1 suggest that these kinds of efforts often have not met with success, at least in recent decades. Moreover, teachers in the survey indicated that policies defining appropriate teacher attire and delimiting the discussion of controversial topics in class were more likely to be unwritten than were policies for other issues.

Bureaucratic regulations, such as those described above, are designed to exert top-down control over school employees, but it is important to note that rules and regulations are not necessarily unwelcome additions to the work lives of teachers. Rules constrain individual discretion, but they can also protect. Such policies clarify the limits of employee responsibility and hence can buffer teachers from pressure exerted by parents and from liability. Such standards and rules can also shield teachers from unfair or arbitrary management practices. Indeed, one of the purposes of bureaucratic standardization is to curb corruption and abuse of power based on "individual privileges and bestowals of favor."[8] For that reason, teachers, like other kinds of employees, have at times favored and even initiated particular rules—an example of the phenomenon known as "bureaucratization from below."[9]

I found several examples of this phenomenon in my field research. The faculties of both Urban High and Suburban High, as in many public school systems, are members of state public teacher unions, which have a long history of making assertive efforts for bread-and-butter issues on behalf of their members. The teacher employment contracts collectively bargained by the unions with the governing boards of these schools contain provisions for standardized teacher salary scales, class size limits, and what is usually referred to as teacher tenure. Teacher salary scales set annual teacher compensation levels, typically based on years of experience, post-secondary degrees, and coursework credits. Class size policies set either recommendations or requirements for maximum class enrollments at different grade levels. Tenure refers to continuing employment contracts granted to teachers after successful completion of a trial period of several years. These kinds of contracts provide an unusual degree of job security because they include legal safeguards and appeal procedures designed to protect teachers from arbitrary firing. Typically, tenure guarantees that teachers must be given reason, documentation, and a hearing prior to being fired. Moreover, in the case of Urban High, a union-initiated seniority system regulates teacher transfers and school-to-school migration within the district. Like many other examples of bureaucratic rules, the above kinds of regulations constrain both school administrators and teachers. But while such regulations tend to be favored more by teachers than by school administrators, this does not necessarily mean that they disempower administrators or that they are not effective mechanisms for organizational control—a point I will return to later in this chapter.

Do Schools Oversee and Supervise Teachers?

The fact that schools have regulations and policies for teachers does not mean, of course, that teachers follow the rules, or that teachers are held accountable if they fail to follow the rules. School directives typically define which staff members are to do which tasks in which situations. But specifying and defining appropriate behavior is only a first step. Inevitably, many rules and policies, especially those less palatable to employees, require at least periodic monitoring in order to be effective. In short, school managers need mechanisms to learn if their teaching employees are actually complying with the policies, rules, routines, and standard operating procedures of the organization.

Perhaps the most common way to assess the performance of employees is to watch them while they are at work. Virtually all public schools in the United States and 90 percent of private secondary schools have formal evaluation programs for teachers,[10] and the most common mode for evaluation is the periodic observation of individual teachers at work in the classroom. In this method, usually referred to as classroom performance assessment, an evaluator, almost always the school principal, typically spends several class periods each school year observing the teacher at work and grades him or her by using a standardized checklist of appropriate teacher practices. These checklists are designed to measure practices and attitudes thought to be associated with effective teaching. Notably, social aspects of the teaching job, such as the teacher's management of student behavior, are as central to these evaluations as are aspects of the job directly related to classroom academic instruction.[11]

I found this type of classroom assessment to be the standard in all of the schools I investigated. In each case, school administrators formally observed and evaluated each member of their faculty in their respective classrooms for a portion of the day. Beginning teachers were evaluated more often than were more senior teachers, and usually their evaluations played a large role in whether they were ultimately promoted to a tenured position. As with all employee evaluation and control mechanisms, there are two often-conflicting purposes underlying teacher evaluations—staff development and staff accountability.

Critics have long questioned the usefulness of formal classroom evaluation for the former purpose, to foster the growth and improvement of individual teachers' skills.[12] Numerous analysts of classroom evaluation have argued that many of the characteristics measured on classroom assessment checklists are trivial and superficial. These critics hold that such checklists do not capture how well the teacher performs many of the most crucial and sophisticated aspects of teaching, such as interacting with parents, constructing tests, establishing appropriate grading criteria, planning lessons, communicating with colleagues, and knowing the needs and capacities of different children.[13]

Moreover, critics have held that for classroom observations, school administrators typically purchase standardized observation forms that, in effect, allow administrators to bypass the time-consuming but all-important preliminary task of defining, with or without the input of those being evaluated, the "effective" teaching practices in their particular schools. Critics term this the "law of the instrument"—the criteria for effective teaching performance are, by default, those underlying the most convenient and readily available measurement forms.[14]

Not surprisingly, teachers are also often unenthusiastic about the developmental benefits of formal evaluations. For instance, in Research for Better Schools' School Assessment Survey, teachers in public secondary schools were asked to what extent they felt the following statement was true: "The information from evaluations is useful for improving my teaching performance." Less than half of teachers perceived their evaluations to be "frequently" useful.[15]

However, I did find ample evidence that formal evaluations do serve their second purpose—control and accountability. Teachers view visits by school administrators as events to be taken seriously. As a senior social studies teacher at Suburban High explained to me, "The general system [of teacher evaluation] works, quote, unquote. It weeds out some who should not be teaching. Is it improving instruction? The answer to that is, probably not. It creates fear among certain people. They always fear the administrator coming into their room." When I then asked if this is also true for tenured and senior faculty, he replied, "Absolutely. Absolutely. It is fear of the unknown consequences. Tenure doesn't mean you can't be moved out. And with the current state of things [fiscal cutbacks], you sure as hell can be."

Like most such bureaucratic procedures, teacher evaluations become official documents and, hence, leave a "paper trail" with a life of its own. Not only do these documents play a key role in determining whether a new teacher receives tenure but also they are placed in teachers' permanent employment files. They can follow a senior teacher in the event of a transfer to another school, and teachers are well aware that a positive recommendation from one's principal can be important for later career moves. Moreover, the manner in which school administrations perform evaluations adds to teachers' sense of vulnerability. In most schools, teachers have little control over who evaluates them, what criteria are used, and the method by which evaluations are carried out (see Figures 3.2 and 3.3).

For instance, at Urban High, Suburban High, and Catholic High, there are two modes of evaluation: announced and unannounced. In the latter case, teachers do not know ahead of time when the visit will occur. This ostensibly produces a more authentic glimpse of a teacher's behavior, but it also adds an element of surprise and anxiety. As one teacher at Catholic High wryly commented, "The best way to make it [teacher evaluation] effective is unannounced. It's dirty pool, but that is the best way. It's rotten and I don't like that idea, but it works." This was in stark contrast to Friends School, where teachers had an unusual degree of input into the assessment and evaluation procedures for both faculty and for administrators. There, evaluations were geared toward staff development rather than being primarily punitive or monitoring devices.

Another method of monitoring and evaluating the behavior and performance of faculty is to use student performance to assess teacher performance. With this method, typically teachers are judged by whether there are gains in their students' academic achievement, as measured on standardized tests. In some settings, such tests are linked to districtwide (or diocesewide) standardized curricula; in other settings they are linked to statewide curriculum requirements. In either case, they can be used to compare the effectiveness of teachers within or among schools.

The use of student test scores to assess teachers has always been an extremely contentious issue. For decades, proponents of the view that schools lack sufficient organizational control have touted them as one of the best means of "weeding out" incompetent teachers and, hence, one of the best methods of ensuring the accountability of teachers.[16] However, the use of student test scores to assess teachers has also been severely criticized for its inability to separate out the portion of student achievement gains that are actually attributable to specific teachers. There are numerous other factors that affect student achievement as well, not least of which are the background, aptitude, attitude, and effort of students. Assessments that do not take account of all these factors can unfairly hold teachers accountable for things out of their control. For this reason, teachers at the elementary and secondary, and also collegiate, levels have long been adamantly opposed to the use of student test scores to assess their performance.[17]

None of the schools I investigated had an official policy to use student scores to evaluate teachers, although some teachers at Urban High claimed that the districtwide tests that came with the school district's prescribed curricula were used informally to identify and pressure teachers whose students scored lower. As a mathematics teacher in Urban High explained: "We have become more computer sophisticated, so that downtown [the school board] produces printouts now. When I was teaching at [another] school, there was a printout that showed the percent of students that I was passing and failing and how that compared with people generally in the city and within my school. If you have a disproportionate number of failures with respect to the rest of the teachers within the school and within your subject, then the question, of course, is brought up as to why . . . To some extent it sends up a red flag as to whether you are doing something different."

The use of student scores as a means of assessment is one of those ideas that come and go with the rise and fall of education reform movements, and the evidence suggests that their use became more widespread in the 1990s, as the movement to increase school and teacher accountability picked up momentum. A 1996 survey of public school teachers found that only 12 percent of teachers reported that student's standardized test scores were used to evaluate their performance, although another 25 percent said they were not sure if administrators used them or not.[18] However, by 1998 a similar survey found that a quarter of public school teachers were evaluated according to how well their students scored on statewide tests alone.[19]

Besides classroom observation and the use of student scores, there were also other formal mechanisms for monitoring teachers' classroom behavior. At both Catholic High and Urban High, new teachers in their first few years were required to submit copies of their class lesson plans to the principal on a weekly basis. These entailed detailed descriptions of the weekly objectives, content, and techniques used in each course the teacher taught. Likewise, in all four schools I investigated official class record books were issued to faculty at the beginning of the year for recording student test and assignment grades. Teachers were required to keep copies of all student tests and assignments with these ledgerlike notebooks. In each school, teachers were required to tally all their students' grades several times during each semester in order to file interim reports on each student's progress and, more specifically, to forewarn parents about those who were failing. Teachers had to file these records with their principal at the end of the year. These records were continually available and could be used as mechanisms of accountability. As one teacher at Catholic High said: "If there is a question about a teacher's reputation or control, I think they [administrators] might glance through their marks [class record] book. And we have had teachers here who have had problems like that, and I have heard principals demand to see their marks book and demand to look at their required three major tests."

There is, however, another, less direct sense in which record keeping serves as a means of organizational control. Writing and filing lesson plans and keeping up-to-date and sufficiently detailed class record books are time-consuming tasks for a teacher and represent one of the most striking aspects of the teaching job—and indeed one of the hallmarks of bureaucratic control—paperwork.

Faculty manuals and handbooks are filled with numerous official forms that must be used for a range of events and activities. For example, at Catholic High, each teacher's day began with filling out standardized forms to compute the overall attendance of students. As part of this chore, teachers had to collect and scrutinize the various forms brought to them by students who had been absent, or who were to be absent. As the day progressed, teachers were responsible for collecting or issuing special passes that controlled the movements of students to and from their classroom and to other "pupil stations." There were different passes for allowing students to use the school elevators, to arrive late to class, to visit the nurse, to be summoned to special meetings, to obtain permission to leave school early, and for being in the school hallways during class periods. There were, in addition, special forms to report when a student had not acted with proper authorization, had been late, or had not attended a class. Finally, there was a general student discipline form on which teachers had to report a range of "conduct violations" to school administrators. Faculty handbooks specified in detail what each of these many passes and forms was for, who had authority to issue them, for what activities each was legitimately used, who had authority to receive them, and what a teacher was required to do upon their receipt.

It is as clear to teachers, as it has been to school researchers, that this paperwork approach often has little intrinsic connection to, or benefit for, the substance of academic instruction in schools. As a seasoned history teacher at Friends School put it: "There are a handful of us who love education, but don't much value schools of education. The education school mentality is a bureaucratic mentality. You solve the problem by writing a memo or developing a new form. That has been the new thing around here the last couple of years. Every time I turn around, somebody's writing up a new form to solve a problem—but it never gets resolved at all. It is just more paper in a file."

A significant portion of a teacher's time and energy is spent issuing, maintaining, and keeping records, and hence not spent providing academic instruction to students. This problem is common to many schools, as documented by data from SASS. In that survey teachers were asked to what extent they agreed with the following statement: "Routine duties and paperwork interfere with my job of teaching." Almost three-fourths of teachers felt there was some degree of interference.[20]

However, because it is sometimes a hindrance to teaching does not mean that the keeping of forms, records, and paperwork is merely a symbolic ritual and does not function as an effective control over teachers' work, as some observers have claimed.[21] One need only spend a short time observing the work of teachers to understand just how intrusive these bureaucratic activities are. Keeping records is a direct means by which organizations coordinate and standardize the activities of employees. Record keeping and paperwork also provide concrete evidence of the extent to which employees are or are not complying with organizational directives. Moreover, although it may have little intrinsic connection to academic instruction, the energy a teacher spends doing paperwork and keeping records has an intrinsic connection to the larger organizational functions of efficiently managing, socializing, and sorting large numbers of children.

The manner by which schools deal with student misbehavior and discipline problems provides a telling example of how these kinds of forms can be used as mechanisms to oversee and evaluate teachers' noninstructional performance. Teachers themselves typically are not empowered to punish students for infractions and disruptive behavior; sanctioning behavioral infractions is usually the responsibility and prerogative of the principal or vice principal. The standard operating procedure requires teachers to "write up" and send to the principal or vice principal a form describing the misbehavior. These forms provide a written record of the number and types of student discipline problems each teacher experiences and, as a result, are a convenient means to formally or informally evaluate each teachers' performance.

However, evaluating teachers' behavioral standards, like evaluating teachers' academic standards, is not straightforward and is open to conflicting interpretations. On the one hand, a teacher who frequently writes up students for misbehavior can be seen as holding his or her students to high behavioral standards, just as a teacher who fails more students can be viewed as holding his or her students to high academic standards. On the other hand, numerous write-ups can be interpreted as evidence that a teacher is "deficient in student behavior management," just as a teacher who fails too many students can be viewed as not doing an adequate job of teaching. How teachers' discipline forms and records are used and interpreted is an important source of administrative discretion and power—a point I will return to later in this chapter.

Teacher's reports of student infractions can also be used in other ways to oversee and evaluate teachers. Several urban school districts made national headlines in the early 1990s by evaluating teachers according to the race of the students they disciplined. For example, the Cincinnati School District responded to racial bias lawsuits filed by civil rights groups, such as the NAACP, by instituting the collection of teacher and student racial data in discipline cases to determine whether white teachers were disciplining disproportionate numbers of black students. The use of these statistics as factors in teachers' annual job performance evaluations was instituted as part of a broad new effort to hold teachers more accountable for the behavior or misbehavior of students.[22]

Finally, besides the use of formal evaluations and records there are also less orthodox, less rationalized means of faculty supervision. For instance, one English teacher reported to me that she had discovered that her principal, with whom she did not get along, had been checking up on her surreptitiously by listening to her classes over the school intercom. Similarly, a social studies teacher claimed that his principal would hover outside his classroom door, out of sight, and attempt to gather information indicating he was an inadequate teacher. Whether these claims were true is less important than their implication for these particular teachers and for fellow faculty to whom they passed on these accounts: they felt themselves to be under surveillance.

Regardless of how frequently or infrequently formal observations or other kinds of evaluations occurred, typically the teachers I interviewed did not feel they were free of administrative surveillance when behind the "closed door" of their classroom. As a teacher at Catholic High indicated: "If school were in session today and you walked down the hall at 12:30 you would know who [of the faculty] had control and who didn't have control. You would know who was teaching their heart out and who was goofing off. It doesn't take any genius to know."

Do Schools Enforce the Rules for Teachers?

The presence of rules and oversight does not, of course, mean that teachers are effectively controlled in schools. Having rules is one thing, enforcing them is another. Analysts of work and organizations tell us that employee accountability can be assured only if those charged with supervising employees have adequate means of enforcement—that is, if there are consequences for noncompliance and if managers have the necessary tools and inducements with which to reward good performance and punish inadequate performance. This is at the core of the ubiquitous problem of accountability for any organization.

From the viewpoint of those who subscribe to the school disorganization perspective, the means to enforce the rules for teachers and the power to motivate teacher performance are precisely what school administrators lack, especially those in public schools. Public school principals not only lack the necessary tools and levers to coordinate and control teachers, these critics argue, but they are also overly constrained by rules and regulations imposed by school boards and school district bureaucrats, often at the behest of teacher unions.[23] Much has been made of the negative effects of, for example, ensuring job protection for teachers through tenured contracts, ensuring automatic annual salary increments through standardized teacher salary scales, and basing staff transfers on seniority systems. Analysts of work and organizations have long held that the power to reward, to remove, and to fire are some of the most important means by which managers can control employees. This is certainly true in schools. I found ample evidence in my field sites that these kinds of rules, regulations, and provisions in schools did, indeed, remove from the hands of school administrators some of the most basic and obvious methods of enforcing employee control.

Especially in the case of senior tenured faculty, administrators cannot assume compliance with school directives. Contrary to popular belief, tenured teacher employment contracts do not mean unsuitable or incompetent teachers cannot be fired. But the legal safeguards and appeal procedures at the heart of such contracts can indeed make firing individual teachers difficult and time-consuming. There are always some faculty for whom, for example, the anticipated threat of a negative annual performance evaluation is of limited significance, because of the legal protection against dismissal that tenure provides. As a vice principal at Urban High noted: "In order to fire someone—because of the rules and regulations established by the [teacher employment] contract, it takes a lot of documentation. It's almost impossible. You have to do something like physically assault a student to get yourself fired from the school system."

Teacher seniority systems, often instituted through collective bargaining by teacher unions, also can sharply curtail school principals' control over staff hiring, transfer, and firing decisions. In big school districts with large numbers of schools, there is typically a great deal of migration of teachers between schools.[24] Districts with seniority rules typically give more experienced teachers priority in cross-school transfers. Seniority systems also come into play when school officials face the need to cut or shift staff as a result of fiscal cutbacks or declining enrollments. In such situations, "last hired, first fired" rules generally require that experienced teachers be given priority. These regulations pose an obstacle to school principals' efforts to pick and choose and thus to control the composition of the teaching staff in their schools. Because of this, seniority rules are often a source of conflict. This was the case at Urban High, where in the mid-1990s a newly hired superintendent for the city school district made elimination of the seniority system a central part of his reform agenda. The superintendent met with a great deal of resistance from the teacher union, and ultimately dropped his effort to eliminate seniority rules.

Teacher salary scales similarly remove another means by which managers control employees. Standard scales typically base teacher compensation solely on years of experience and educational credits, and thus severely curtail the ability of administrators to reward or sanction particular teachers financially for their behavior and performance. This, of course, is why financial incentive mechanisms, such as merit pay, have always been popular with those seeking more accountability in schools. Typically, merit pay programs destandardize annual salary evaluations, and ostensibly teacher performance, rather than experience and credentials, becomes the basis of salary changes.[25] The key source of debate is who controls the teacher evaluation process; that is, who defines "meritorious" performance. Merit pay plans usually put this power into the hands of school principals, allowing them to determine who receives what level of pay increase. Indeed, these plans are often explicitly designed to give administrators more control over compensation, and thus they change the distribution of power between teachers and principals. As a result, merit pay programs are often opposed by teachers and are not widely used. In the 1990s only 12 percent of public school districts used any kind of pay incentives, such as formal merit pay plans in which a teachers' performance was a significant factor in determining his or her compensation. Surprisingly, in the same period only 14 percent of private secondary schools used formal merit pay plans and only 21 percent used pay incentives of any type for rewarding good teachers.[26]

It is important to recognize that while the discretionary power of principals can be curtailed by formal regulations, such as those described above, it can also be curtailed by the opposite—a lack of formalized rules. The ability of teachers to resist administrative pressures may be enhanced if rules are not specifically written into teacher employment contracts or faculty manuals. An example of this was provided to me by a tenured special education teacher, who described his successful effort to resist a unilateral effort by a newly hired school principal to institute a teacher dress code. The incident followed the enthusiastic announcement by the principal of his intention to "upgrade the professional caliber of the faculty" by, in particular, requiring all male teachers to wear ties and jackets while in school. The special education teacher's job involved working either one on one or with small groups of students, and he found that casual attire cultivated a helpful informality with his students. He continued to dress casually and awaited the inevitable "visit" from the new principal. In their ensuing confrontation, the teacher flatly refused to comply, arguing that he felt such clothing would promote just the kind of overly formal relationship with his students that he had long endeavored to overcome. To the teacher's relief, the principal conceded the issue.

The relative lack of bureaucratization and formalization of rules that characterized Friends School provided another example of clear limits on administrative discretion and power. One administrator there described to me how he had difficulty persuading teachers to volunteer for the school's nonteaching duties and chores. As I noted earlier, teachers typically dislike these chores and often view them as contrary to their role as educators. Further regulation was the solution proposed by the administrator: "Everyone knows they are going to have to do more than teach classes. There are clubs, coaching, and clean-up duties. I am proposing to John [the principal], that in the future, the contract the teachers sign include the phrase: 'outside-of-classroom duties will include. . .'" This particular case was also interesting because here was a private school administrator who desired more, not less, bureaucracy.

Even when there are formal rules, regulations, and oversight, teachers may still be able to avoid compliance. One senior social studies teacher described to me how, in compliance with school district policy, he issued to his students the textbooks prescribed for his history course and had the students keep them plainly visible on their desks, in the event of a visit to his classroom by administrators. However, because he felt the text was inadequate and poorly written, he simply never used it and instead constructed his own curriculum from photocopied articles, other books, and group projects.

It is precisely because of these kinds of cases that some researchers and reformers conclude that schools are disorganized and lacking in accountability. In some of these examples, bureaucratization curtails school administrator control. In other examples, a lack of bureaucratization curtails school administrator control. In even other examples, "shirking," or "slippage" between bureaucratic policy and classroom reality, make it difficult for school administrators to ensure faculty compliance.

However, focusing only on examples such as these, which reveal an ostensible autonomy of lower-level employees, is one-sided. Those who subscribe to the disorganization perspective, in particular, sometimes assume that any kind of regulation on administrative prerogatives, such as teacher salary scales, tenure, or seniority systems, is an inappropriate impediment to organizational control—almost as if constraints on managers were a wrongful use of bureaucratic rationality. Certainly some of these forms of standardization do lessen teachers' dependency on, and loyalty to, particular school administrators. But this view misses what these kinds of standardization and formalization, so fundamental to bureaucracy in general, do provide—the dependency and loyalty of employees to the organization.[27]

The character and purpose of tenure, for example, is often misunderstood. For school administrators, tenure regulations concerning termination can be burdensome and hence can make it difficult to push out low-quality employees. But tenure regulations also can make it difficult to push out high-quality employees. Without such job protections it can be very difficult to secure the loyalty and commitment of high-quality employees—something essential to "people-intensive work" like teaching. Historically, tenure rules were instituted precisely because the hiring, promotion, and firing of teachers was rife with patronage, corruption, chronyism, nepotism, and bias. Settings that experiment with radical antibureaucratic decentralization, such as community schools and charter schools, often quickly learn the hard way that bureaucratic regulations and rules do have a purpose.[28]

It is because teachers have had little input into or control over compensation policy, promotion criteria and policy, and transfer policy, that they have supported the bureaucratization of these functions. In this sense, such limitations on school administrator prerogatives are not instances of decreases in centralized control, but are attempts to rationalize an existing centralized structure of control that is at times capricious, personalized, and arbitrary. In other words, these kinds of rules are not so much examples of teacher empowerment as instruments designed to protect teachers *because* of their disempowerment.

There is a second sense in which the disorganization perspective's emphasis on the ostensible autonomy of teachers is one-sided. Bureaucratization applies to both superordinates and subordinates, and the same is also true for a lack of bureaucratization. While having too few rules may curtail administrative control, it can also have the opposite effect. Those who subscribe to the disorganization perspective often see nonrationalization and debureaucratization only among subordinates, the teachers. But administrators may also be subject to a lack of standardization and bureaucratization that results in a high level of autonomy and discretion. Moreover, like their subordinates, superordinates may be able to evade, ignore, or resist the rules that do exist. It cannot be assumed that looseness in organizations is synonymous with employee autonomy and organizational decentralization. Indeed, loose coupling can be an important source of administrative power and centralized organizational control.

What Controls Do School Administrators Have?

Organizational analysts have long shown that power accrues to individuals who control important resources, knowledge, and decisions in an organization.[29] Managers who control key resources have, by definition, a range of inducements, rewards, and punishments with which they can control employees. The control over key decisions provides tools for use in bargaining and negotiation, and hence the ability to shape the behavior of subordinates.

In schools, the highly centralized distribution of decision-making influence (as outlined in Chapter 3) provides a range of levers and tools, both legitimate and illegitimate, rational and nonrational, for the use of administrators. For example, the vice principal at Urban High described some of the numerous ways that administrators like himself can quite effectively exert control over teachers: "We may really need to have something done and we may ask that you [a teacher] pitch in to do it, and you may blatantly, outright refuse. Then later on you may want a piece of something that has some tangible gravy as part of it. I'm of the opinion, at that point, that we basically say, 'Well, remember when we needed your assistance with something and you said no,' and then we say no more. It is a matter of fact that those folks that pitch in . . . are those folks that get the perks."

The "perks" that principals typically control include the distribution of physical space; the determination of each faculty member's daily schedule, teaching assignments, and course load; the distribution of students to courses and teachers; the assignment of nonteaching duties; and the control of the portion of the budget devoted to such things as funding for field trips, projects, and professional development conferences (see Figures 3.2 and 3.3). In concrete terms, this means that principals have discretion over key resources on which teachers are dependent and over key policies and issues that directly affect the jobs of teachers.

In each of the schools I investigated I found, for instance, that it was the principal's prerogative to assign classrooms to faculty and to distribute office and storage space to departments or individuals. The number, size, and attributes of classrooms vary widely, depending on the degree of crowdedness and the age of a building. Teachers spend most of their day in their own classroom, and the quality of this work site is not a trivial issue. Moreover, in some cases of over-crowding, some teachers may not get classrooms of their own but be assigned to rotate daily through a series of different rooms that "be-long" to other teachers—a tiresome, unpleasant, and inconvenient experience. I found that teachers often felt this source of administra-tive discretion was used as an informal, but consequential, means of rewarding some and punishing others. It was also not difficult to find teachers who were suspicious of how rationalized, standardized, or fair these allocations were.

School and staff schedules also provide a source of teacher de-pendency and thus administrative influence. The complicated task of mapping teachers onto courses, time slots, and duties leaves much room for informal discretion on the part of administrators. A teacher's day and week can be quite packed and exhausting, and as a result, during presemester scheduling, there is often considerable jockeying and negotiating for schedules that could make a teacher's day less stressful—a longer lunch, a free or planning period placed at a convenient time, a preferred nonteaching duty.[30] Typically, teachers are allowed to submit a "preference" form spelling out the daily schedule they would like to have for the coming semester, but the principal is in the position to schedule teachers as he or she sees fit. Such decisions may or may not be perceived by teachers as ratio-nal or fair. As a junior teacher at Urban High explained it: "Now, ordinarily we don't have any input into that [the daily schedule]. I can't say, 'I don't want to teach eighth period, give me my prep [nonteaching] period eighth period,' . . . but there are people [who] can say that and get it. I think it is seniority. It is not fair."

Principals also decide which teachers are responsible for which nonteaching duties, such as staffing study halls or policing the cafeteria and student restrooms. This is also not a trivial source of power because, as I said earlier, most teachers heartily dislike these assignments and are quite aware of the deprofessionalizing character of these cost-saving measures. As one veteran English teacher at Catholic High remarked: "I am forty-five years old. I am an intelligent woman. What the hell am I doing down here, pulling french fries off the curtains? I guess there are those who love cafeteria duty or love their service period because they have that cop mentality. I hate it."

An even more potent source of power is the control over who teaches what and to whom. The data show that teachers have little say over which courses they are assigned to teach, and the allocation of teaching assignments is usually the prerogative of school principals (Figure 3.3). As with scheduling, in each of the schools that I investigated teachers may submit a list of their course preferences for the coming semester, but the final decision—except in the case of Friends School—was made by the principal.

Principals not only have the authority to decide who teaches which courses but they also have an unusual degree of discretion in making these decisions. Teaching is subject to an elaborate array of state licensing requirements designed to assure the basic preparation and competence of practitioners prior to employment. However, once on the job there is little regulation or rationalization of how teachers are actually employed and used. One area of loose coupling and principal discretion that has been largely unrecognized by researchers and reformers is the practice of out-of-field teaching—

teachers assigned by their principals to teach subjects that do not match their training or education.[31]

Having the option of teaching subjects for which one has no license or degree can, of course, expand a teacher's utility and versatility within a school and also his or her overall employment opportunities in the labor market, but it poses many problems as well. Teachers, understandably enough, tend to find it less interesting and more difficult to teach subjects they do not know well. For most secondary school teachers, having to cope with out-of-field assignments comes on top of an already burdensome teaching load. And having to teach courses for which they have little formal preparation can also have a negative impact on teachers' sense of efficacy. For all these reasons, the prerogative to decide teacher course assignments is an important and consequential source of discretionary power for principals. Principals are in a position to assign the more desirable courses to those teachers they view as "meritorious" or those they favor for one reason or another. For example, a senior, tenured social studies teacher at Urban High reported that, after having a disagreement with the principal, he had been arbitrarily shifted from teaching in his prime area of expertise—senior world history—which he had taught for twenty years, to teaching seventh-grade geography, a subject he neither knew much about nor liked. Embittered, he shortly thereafter requested a transfer to another school—a blunt indicator of the effective use of administrative power. Indeed this instance is especially telling, because it occurred despite the existence of a seniority teacher transfer system. Notably, in this case the seniority rules did not curtail the principal's ability to be rid of a particular teacher. In stark contrast to the other schools, the assignment of courses to be taught at Friends School was done collectively and collegially by departments, not unilaterally by the principal.

Teachers not only prefer to teach subjects they know and have a background in, but they also often prefer to teach elective courses, as opposed to required ones. Teachers prize elective courses because they involve a modicum of choice for both teacher and student and therefore can generate more interest and enthusiasm from both sides. Consequently, this makes them another valuable and scarce resource and, thus, an effective source of administrative power.

Students themselves are also an important resource that is allocated by the principal. Most teachers readily agree that it is good educational policy to design different curricula for different types and levels of students. But most also would concede that placing students in lower tracks or lower ability-level classes also tends to demotivate and stigmatize students. This in turn can make teaching lower-track courses more difficult for teachers, requiring lower expectations, more patience, different materials, and the time-consuming task of creating individually tailored assignments. In general, I found teachers preferred teaching the more motivated and brighter students, ostensibly to be found in college preparatory, honors, gifted and advanced placement courses. As a result, there is often intense competition over who teaches these courses, which are yet another scarce commodity controlled by the principal. In the minds of many teachers, the "rational" system would distribute desirable and less desirable courses equally among a department's faculty. But this definition of rationality does not always hold sway. To be given the least desirable courses that no one else wants can have disastrous consequences. An inexperienced or new teacher can be overwhelmed by highly disruptive students. I found it to be a typical complaint of many teachers that those favored by the principal were given the lion's share of desirable and higher-level courses. This is consistent with other research that has found that teachers are themselves stratified into tracks parallel to those of their students.[32]

Perhaps the most significant area of vulnerability and dependency for teachers is the key area of student socialization—in particular, the issue of how schools deal with student misbehavior. Teachers have very limited influence over school policy on student discipline, and principals have a great deal of disciplinary influence (see Figure 3.3). As a result, teachers must depend on being "backed up" by their school administrators in cases of student discipline. Some researchers have overlooked the importance of this issue, but being backed up, or not, is one of the most crucial aspects of a teacher's job; indeed, as I will show in Chapter 6, it can be crucial to the likelihood they will even remain in their job.

As I described earlier, in the event of student misbehavior, school policies usually require teachers to report the incident on a discipline form, which is then forwarded to the principal or vice principal. Teachers themselves are rarely allowed to make on-the-spot decisions in their classroom in regard to student disruptions, and they rarely have the authority to punish students. For instance, in most schools teachers cannot simply "throw" a disruptive student out of class on a particular day. Such decisions are the prerogative of the principal (or vice principal), who is responsible for sanctioning behavioral infractions. The latter is cast, quite literally, in the role of judge and jury. Such administrators have a wide degree of discretion over how to interpret and react to teachers' reports of student infractions. They can decide to accept the teacher's claims as stated or to take the student's side, and as a result, teachers are highly dependent on the principal's assessment. A decision against a teacher can make him or her look weak and can also count against the teacher on an annual performance evaluation. In either case, administrators also have a wide range of possible consequences to impose on a student, varying in their degree of harshness.

This relationship of dependency between teacher and administrator can be a great source of anxiety and frustration for faculty. For many teachers, a "good" administrator is one who metes out stern sanctions and masks any disagreement with the teacher over the quantity or quality of the consequences, at least until after the formal part of the disciplinary process is carried out. Especially in schools plagued by high levels of student misbehavior, there is no better way for newly hired principals or vice principals to gain favor with the faculty than to quickly "crack down" on the most visible student offenses, making it clear to a watchful faculty "whose side they are on" and allaying their fear of not being backed up by the new boss.

Teachers who have not been backed up quickly learn the power of this administrative lever. If students conclude that a particular teacher's threats will not be enforced, a spiraling increase in classroom disobedience will most likely follow, making life less pleasant or even intolerable for the teacher. I found most teachers could recount, with sympathy, "war stories" of fellow teachers who "couldn't handle" their classes.

Thus, I found that school administrators do have quite a number of means by which they are able to enforce teacher compliance with school policies. And the pervasiveness of such enforcement is not unique to the schools I investigated. The enforcement of school policies designed to control the work of teachers is widespread, as shown by data from the School Assessment Survey conducted by Research for Better Schools. In this survey, public school teachers were asked about both the existence and enforcement of policies for a series of important educational and administrative issues.[33] Earlier I presented the results concerning the existence of policies for teachers (see Figure 4.1); added here are the data on enforcement of these same policies (see Figure 4.2). These data show that such policies are not only

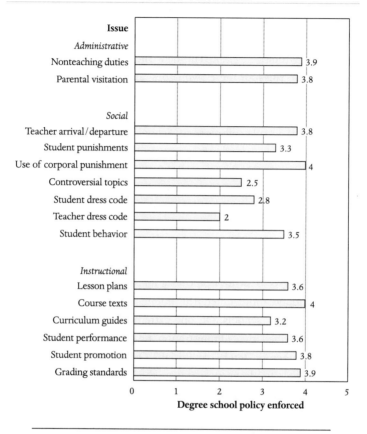

Figure 4.2 Enforcement of rules for teachers (average degree of enforcement of school policies: 0 = never, 1 = almost never, 2 = occasionally, 3 = frequently, 4 = almost always, 5 = always) (Source: School Assessment Survey)

widespread but also usually enforced. As before, the two major exceptions are policies concerning teacher dress codes and teaching controversial topics in class. The data show that schools are least prone to have rules for these two issues, and, moreover, that where there are policies, they are only occasionally enforced.

I also found in my field research that schools vary widely in the character of their rule enforcement. School administrators differed as to whether and which kinds of "carrots and sticks" they used. I found wide variations among schools as to whether the administrators' use of authority was perceived as evenhanded or underhanded, fair or unfair—in other words, how coercive teachers felt administrators were in their wielding of power and control. The style of administration and style in which control was used was related to the distribution and balance of power between administrators and teachers and the overall degree of school centralization or decentralization. Interestingly, I found more difference among the private schools than among the public schools. On one extreme was Catholic High; its teachers described the administration unabashedly and matter-of-factly as "autocratic" and "dictatorial." On the other extreme was Friends School; its administrators were the least coercive in the manner in which they implemented and enforced the rules. At Friends, because the faculty participated in the hiring and evaluating of administrators, the administrators were to a greater degree accountable to the faculty. Moreover, because of mechanisms that allowed a greater degree of shared decision making and widened the range of negotiable issues, teachers there were in a better position to demand and receive what they referred to as "respectful" and "professional" treatment from their administrators.

However, I found that the frequency and style with which administrators sanction teachers is less important than their perceived capacity to do so; the crux of accountability is that teachers believe they will be held accountable and that their behavior is subject to consequences. As analysts of power have long noted, the anticipation of a negative reaction is itself a mechanism of control and serves to discourage challenge and nonconformity.[34] I found this to be the case in the schools I studied. Teachers considered carefully the costs of noncompliance because of the decidedly widespread sense of their dependence on the goodwill and benign judgment of administrators.

5

THE TEACHER IN THE MIDDLE

The foreman feels that he is the guy in the middle. He is
caught between management and the job and must take it
from both sides . . . The foreman feels that he is constantly
faced with demands from his superiors, decisions which they
make that he must carry out. And, yet, in many cases, he feels
that they do not give him the necessary authority and control
over the work situation to get the job done. In some instances, he is being constantly checked by superiors or by
other organizations; he is in a constant state of anxiety and
frustration.

—WILLIAM F. WHYTE AND BURLEIGH GARDNER, 1945

ANALYSTS OF ORGANIZATIONS, occupations, and
work have shown that organizations use a wide variety of mechanisms to coordinate and control their members and employees. Besides the more direct and visible types of controls, such as formal
rules and their enforcement through the use of rewards and punishments, there are numerous other less direct, and often less obvious,
means by which organizations govern the behavior of employees.

Some of these other controls are built into the formal organizational structure of work settings. Others are embedded in the informal organization—the culture, or social organization—of work settings.

These other mechanisms may be less intrusive, and they can be more effective than rules and sanctions if they become "naturalized," or institutionalized. This occurs when processes and patterns become so accepted, so taken for granted, that they function by the weight of precedent alone. Employees simply conform to these norms, rather than rationally and consciously plotting out alternatives. In such settings, a high degree of organizational control may exist in the absence of any apparent mechanisms of definition, supervision, or enforcement. Constraints that become everyday norms for employees are usually more readily complied with, less subject to challenge or resistance, and thus highly effective modes of control.

Analysts have also shown that different work settings vary widely in the kinds of mechanisms they use to coordinate and control their employees, with different degrees of success. The use and effectiveness of particular modes of control depend on a number of organizational characteristics, including the type, number, and nature of the clients or customers served; the objectives pursued; the kinds of products produced; and the technologies or means by which such products are produced.[1]

Who are the "clients" of schools, what are the "products" teachers make, what "technologies" do they use? How is "production" organized in schools? How is the "labor process" of teaching structured? And what implications do these issues have for the control and coordination of teachers' work?

In addition to the rules and sanctions discussed in Chapter 4, does the formal organizational structure of schools itself coordinate, control, and constrain the work of teachers in less direct and less obvious ways? Moreover, how does the informal organization—the workplace culture of teachers—affect the efforts of schools to coordinate and control the work of teachers?

Answering these questions presents methodological difficulties. For the same reason that they can be effective—because they are often taken for granted—such mechanisms of control can be difficult to discern.[2] In my field research and in-depth interviews I spent considerable time pondering and investigating the processes of decision making, the manner in which the day-to-day work of teachers is set up, and the taken-for-granted roles for teachers in schools. My object was to understand what aspects of schools, in addition to policies and sanctions, work to constrain and control teachers, and how this happens. While my field research results are limited to the four school sites I investigated, where possible, throughout this chapter, I also compare what I found in these particular schools with similar data from large-scale surveys.

Teaching as an Unusual Occupation

As introduced in Chapter 2, from the viewpoint of organization theory the teaching occupation is an odd case. The work of teaching involves an unusual combination of "clients," "products," and "technologies" and this has profound implications for its organization and control.[3] In the first place, the clients of teachers are a complex mix—they are at once obligatory, mandatory, multiple, and diverse. Schooling is a mass public service "industry." All school-age members of the public have the right to a publicly funded education. Schools and teachers are obligated to educate all youngsters, regardless of how cooperative, motivated, prepared, or deserving they may be. But all those of legal school age are not only entitled to a tax-paid education, they are also obligated to receive this tax-paid service. Elementary and secondary schooling is mandatory, regardless of whether the student wishes to be in school or not. In short, the relationship between teacher and student is one of "dual captivity"—teachers are public servants who cannot choose not to serve their clients, and their clients are recipients of a public service who cannot choose not to be served.

Additionally, parents and their children are not the only clients of teachers and schools. In a broad sense, the entire society is the client of those public servants delegated the task of preparing future citizens. Regardless of whether they have school-age children or not, all members of the public are financially responsible, through taxes, for the moral, civic, and academic training of the young. The fiduciary responsibility of the general public even extends to students enrolled in private schools. Certain private school expenses, such as textbooks, transportation, and special education, are funded through state and federal taxes. As a result, a wide variety of groups, representing a diversity of interests, see themselves as users of the services provided by schools. This unusual mix of client characteristics has implications for the objectives and expected "products" of these services.

Perhaps the most obvious and straightforward objective of schooling is teaching the young essential academic skills and knowledge, and the most obvious and straightforward product is student academic achievement as measured by test scores. But, as I stress throughout this book, teachers do not simply teach academic subjects. Schools and teachers are also responsible for socializing children, for teaching societal values, behavior, attitudes, mores, and norms—that is, proper behavior. Both implicit and explicit socialization are, of course, important parts of all occupations and organizations. All employees and clients are shaped by the organizations in which they work. But in schools, socialization is not simply a by-product or even a means to an end—it is one of the major "products." Analysts of occupations and organizations have long noted that, as in other kinds of human-services work, such "indeterminate" and "intangible" outcomes present special difficulties for organizational management.[4] For example, a central tension in hospital administration is the difficulty in assessing the quality of nursing, where the major "product" that nurses "make" is patient care. The job and major outcomes of teaching are, however, not simply indeterminate and intangible, they are also a source of conflict. Teaching involves a value-laden social task—the "production" of adults from children—and there is much disagreement over exactly what the end products ought to be.

This unusual combination of clients and products sets schools apart from many other organizations, and teaching apart from many other occupations. But there is an additional and related aspect of teaching that makes it an unusual occupation. Not only are the tasks of schooling important, multiple, contradictory, ambiguous, and contentious, but the process of undertaking and achieving them—the "technology" of teaching—is also both complex and uncertain. In the auto industry a well-developed technology results in the production of automobiles. In contrast, in teaching there is very little consensus as to what the final ends ought to be, very little consensus as to the best process, method, or means of reaching those ends, and, moreover, very little consensus as to how to measure whether those ends have indeed been achieved.

Teaching is interactional work. The production process calls for employees to work not with raw materials or objects, but with other individuals. Moreover, the individuals with whom teachers work are neither mature, socialized adults nor voluntary participants. Indeed, as Willard Waller aptly put it in his classic book on the sociology of teachers, they are "at once the most tractable and the most unstable members of the community."[5] For all these reasons, teaching is an inherently ambiguous, unpredictable, and fluid craft. Teaching requires flexibility, give-and-take, and making exceptions, and it can present formidable and unusual challenges.

The unusual combination of clients, objectives, products, and methods has profound implications for the way in which teaching is organized and controlled in schools. Because of its democratic and mass character and its public funding, the school system is charged with providing a relatively standard and equal service to large numbers of clients in as efficient a manner as possible and at as low a cost as possible. Moreover, because of education's inherent importance and its inherent uncertainties, the public and school administrators have an understandable need to ensure substantial control and accountability over those doing the work—the teachers. Parents, for instance, typically want, and deserve, to know that the quantity and quality of what their child is taught in one classroom or school are similar to what their neighbors' children are taught in other classrooms and schools. All these needs dictate the use of a formalized, standardized, hierarchical—that is, bureaucratic—mode of organization for the provision of school services. And indeed, as summarized in Chapters 2 and 3, beginning in the early twentieth century the American school system quite consciously adopted the bureaucratic mode of organization. As documented in Chapter 4, schools do have many formalized and direct mechanisms designed to coordinate and control the work of teachers. Among these are the policies, regulations, requirements, job descriptions, standard operating procedures, and formal sanctions that are the most obvious hallmarks of bureaucratization. The advantages of these mechanisms should not be underestimated. They foster consistency and predictability and curb arbitrariness, favoritism, and inconsistency, all of which are important and necessary given the particular character of the clients, objectives, processes, and products of schooling. However, bureaucratic mechanisms also have distinct disadvantages for this kind of work, and for the very same reasons—because of the particular character of the clients, objectives, processes, and products of schooling.[6]

Regulations often don't work well for irregular work. Unlike the example of automobile production, much of what teachers do cannot be routinized, that is, it can be difficult to codify and "freeze" the work of teachers into set routines, standard operating procedures, and measurable products.[7] Rules can never cover all the issues and contingencies that arise in work like teaching, where there is little consensus and much ambiguity surrounding means and ends. For each issue governed by rules, there are equal numbers of issues for which no rules exist. It is difficult to significantly reduce uncertainty and ambiguity—the very point of bureaucracy—in work that is inherently uncertain and ambiguous. As a result, rules and standardized procedures are rarely sufficient to establish control in settings such as schools. In short, opportunities and allowances for discretion inevitably arise in teaching, despite the breadth and depth of school rules and procedures.

Moreover, rules can be a relatively costly and time-consuming method of employee control. As shown in Chapter 4, rules are vulnerable to circumvention, and they require continual oversight and enforcement. And even if it were possible to achieve adequate control through the use of rules, such a mode of organizational control can be self-defeating. The advantage of rules—their consistency—can be a decided disadvantage with work that requires give and take. Discretion is not simply inevitable but necessary in the work of teaching. The one-size-fits-all approach of rules can deny teachers the flexibility they need to do their job effectively. For just these reasons, rules can generate resistance. Like all organizations, schools need control, but they also need the consent, goodwill, commitment, and cooperation of their employees. This is perhaps even more true in teaching, because the work involves children and adolescents. If the enforcement of rules and other direct modes of control becomes coercive, it can generate resentment among teachers. The sticks and carrots, described in Chapter 4, may motivate low-performing employees, but they may also demotivate high-performing employees, with detrimental effects for the organization.

For these kinds of reasons, analysts of organizations, occupations, and work have long argued that bureaucratic and direct mechanisms, such as rules and sanctions, are often not the most effective means of ensuring organizational control and accountability in settings such as schools. Schools are likely to rely on other means of control and coordination, and indeed my field research revealed this to be true.

The Division of Labor in Schools

One of the fundamental dimensions of bureaucracy and of all large complex organizations is a structure of hierarchically arranged roles—a division of labor. Within any large organization, productive specialties are typically subdivided into a series of separate decisions, tasks, and steps. These steps are sequential, that is, some tasks and some decisions follow others and are nested within their predecessors, and they are hierarchical, that is, some steps are more consequential and involve more power than others. Moreover, different steps, decisions, and subtasks vary in their degree of complexity and, hence, in the degree of training and skill they require. This hierarchy of steps determines the issues for which employees are responsible and over which they have control. In other words, the distribution or division of labor is a distribution of responsibility and control.[8]

While the hierarchical structure of specialized and circumscribed roles is a universal and fundamental characteristic of modern organization, it varies tremendously in different settings, especially in regard to the degree of control and responsibility held by different employees. Employee discretion and autonomy in regard to their work, for instance, can mean very different things in different kinds of work places. At one extreme, employee discretion may boil down to the execution of simple procedures previously designed by others. At the other extreme, employee discretion may mean having substantial input into complex decisions concerning both the ends and means of their work.[9]

How tight or loose is the division of labor, responsibility, and control in schools? How do these aspects of the formal structure of schools delimit the work of teachers? Precisely how do higher-order decisions made by school administrators affect—widen, narrow, prioritize, or preempt—the decision making of teachers?

A close look reveals that there are numerous ways the division of labor in schools defines and shapes the work of teachers in their classrooms. Daily operational decisions made by teachers are not isolated or independent events, but are nested within a particular kind of highly structured context. One of the best illustrations of this structured context and how the division of labor actually operates in schools can be seen in the crucial social domain of student discipline.

Teachers tell us they have substantial say in decisions surrounding their own morals, values, dress, and behavior. And as also documented in Chapter 3, teachers report that they have substantial say over decisions surrounding students' behavior in the classroom. But they also report that they have little say in or control over schoolwide rules and standards for student behavior. These findings may appear to be contradictory and evidence of a disconnect between school and classroom. This is not the case.

The issue of student discipline is in essence a question of who determines the behavioral standards in the miniature world of the school. This determination, in turn, is very much a function of those moral codes, values, and norms dominant in the larger community setting. Teachers do not set these standards. The role of the teacher is as an agent responsible for the communication and enforcement of these standards. This can be a time-consuming and difficult part of the work of teachers—and one profoundly shaped by the structure of schools.

The conflict between having little say in the substance of student behavioral standards and much responsibility for enforcing them is largely invisible, so long as teacher and school agree on the standards. However, the inherent tension is quickly and starkly revealed in the event that a teacher does not agree with some of the rules he or she is required to enforce. Opportunities to clearly discern this division of labor arise with the advent of new student behavioral and social fads and fashions—a periodic and inevitable occurrence in schools.

For example, during my time at Suburban High I observed a new student fad, the use of portable cassette players with headsets (such as the Sony Walkman). This fad led to the top-down imposition of a new policy banning them from school, which in turn led to a new policing chore for teachers. A veteran teacher described to me his chagrin at this turn of events:

> No Walkmans are allowed in school. Do I think that is a policy that smacks of lunacy? Yes. It's lunacy to try to enforce it. At 2:30 P.M. the students pull them out and walk down the hall—it's after school. Should they be able to have a Walkman? Who cares! It's 2:30 and the day is over. Am I going to run down the hall and confiscate one from everybody? No! I don't need the rules to tell me what is in bounds. Some people get bent out of shape at that. Some people just don't like the idea of students just walking down the hall, because they are not

studying. That is a crazy thing! But the rule is there and I'm confronted with it, and yes I will confiscate these things if I have to.

Because these policing chores can be tedious and time-consuming, the practice of "selective inattention" can be an attractive option for teachers. As a teacher at Catholic High indicated: "There are teachers who will ignore the dress code [for students]. And me, well, there are days I just think I am not even going see it [an infraction] today. I'm going to close my eyes. But then, most of the time I've got to see it, because it is a policy and all that." Even though the enforcement of rules can be an unpleasant chore, there are compelling reasons for faculty to take this responsibility seriously. If students perceive that a teacher does not enforce rules, they will be more likely to disregard that teacher, an attitude that can easily spiral out of control, often with unpleasant consequences for the teacher. The above-quoted teacher from Catholic High went on to describe why consistent and unified enforcement of rules, even those not liked by the faculty, was necessary: "There is a rule now that kids are not to wear their sneakers back and forth to school, and I just don't like it. But you really can't look the other way. If you start looking the other way, chaos will reign. I have seen it happen, and believe me, it is not pleasant. These kids are rough. Once you let it go, you personally pay for it over and over. So I enforce it."

For the same reasons, neglecting enforcement also has collective repercussions. At Urban High a number of teachers, alarmed at an apparent increase in student discipline problems over the course of the year, organized a meeting to address the issue. At the time, several incidents involving physical attacks by students on fellow students and on faculty members had been notorious enough to warrant reports in the city's leading newspapers. The teachers' complaints were, however, not primarily directed at the students, their parents, or school administrators, but at their fellow teachers. Their concern was that some individual teachers were not following through with enforcing school behavior rules for students, and that this had negative repercussions for other teachers. The result was severe collective peer pressure to enforce the rules—rules that teachers had had little input into, and in some instances, rules contrary to a teacher's individual values. Such peer pressure was an effective form of organizational control.

Although teachers' work in loco parentis entails parental-type responsibilities, it does not necessarily entail parental powers. Teachers are far more limited than parents in the tools they may use to ensure compliance on the part of the youngsters in their charge. The process of helping the young to understand and follow social norms can require substantial time and skill, and one-on-one interaction between teacher and student. These resources are often in short supply. Moreover, teachers are highly delimited, sometimes by law, in the kinds of rewards and punishments they may use. For instance, in many schools teachers are not allowed to factor student behavior into academic grades; they are required to evaluate students solely on the basis of academic merit. This situation effectively curtails the power of one of the few levers available to teachers—control over student grades.

Perhaps the most powerful sanction against misbehavior is exclusion—the determination of who does not have the right to participate in a given social situation altogether. I found most teachers able to readily recall instances when they had felt that removing a student from a class would have been a justifiable course to take, but had not been able to do so. As discussed in Chapter 3, teachers have little influence over the expulsion of students from school, nor can they control who enrolls in their courses. And rarely do teachers have the authority to expel students from their classroom or to have them temporarily removed. In other words, teachers rarely have the right not to teach particular students, even if they are disruptive.

This stands in sharp distinction to members of the traditional professions, such as lawyers, accountants, physicians, and psychotherapists. Within the constraints of the market, lawyers, accountants, and psychotherapists can have a substantial degree of choice in whom they serve and may have the option not to work with particular clients.[10]

Upon closer questioning, it became readily apparent to me why teachers are denied the power to pick and choose their students. There are two important sources of opposition to delegating this kind of decision-making control to teachers: parents, who would be inconvenienced and angry if their child were removed from a course, especially one legally required for graduation; and administrators, who would be left to deal with difficult-to-place students. Education is not a privilege; students are both entitled and obligated to receive a tax-paid education. Hence, the needs and power of administrators and parents almost always dominate in the event of a disagreement over a student's expulsion from a important course, as this teacher at Suburban High describes: "In that event, you may be faced with two possibilities. One is to remove the kid from the class, and then he doesn't get credit for the class. Which to the parent is very serious, because he has a legitimate right to an education. So you can't do that! Which means you would have to put him on homebound [individual tutoring in the home]—which costs extra money for the district. It has happened. But don't count on it. Usually after the teacher tries everything—well, the student is still there in the class."

As well as affecting teachers' discretion in disciplinary and behavioral issues, the division of labor and the formal structure of schools also powerfully influence academic instruction in classrooms. Academic instruction appears to be one of the few areas in schools over which many teachers do appear, on average, to have a high degree of autonomy in their work. The data in Chapter 3 indicate that teachers have "major" influence in establishing the objectives of the classes they teach, choosing the methods and techniques by which they teach, deciding the concepts to impart each day, and determining the amount of homework they assign (see Figure 3.2). Of course, in schools like Catholic High and Urban High, this autonomy is curtailed by the use of standardized curricula, which are obvious and intrusive mechanisms of top-down bureaucratic control. But another aspect of the structure of schools—the day-to-day organization of "production"—less visibly defines and constrains the academic work of teachers. A good illustration of this is the manner in which the teachers' workday is set up—an issue over which teachers have little control but that profoundly constrains what they do in their individual classrooms.

A typical workday for a teacher in a secondary school in the United States consists of seven class periods of just less that an hour each, all separated by five-minute breaks, with a lunch period placed in the middle of the day. The average teacher in secondary school teaches classes for five of the seven periods, has one "service" or nonteaching duty period, one "free" or "prep" period, and a twenty-five-minute lunch break. The average class size in secondary schools is about 25 students so hence, each teacher instructs a total of about 125 different students each day. Each teacher's five classes per day involve, on average, two different course subjects or preparations. For example, a typical social studies teacher might teach three classes in history and two classes in civics—which comes to five classes and two preparations—each day. On average, secondary school teachers are required to be at school for about six and a half hours per day, or about thirty-three hours per week. In addition, on average, secondary school teachers spend another thirteen hours per week—after school, before school, or on weekends—on school-related activities, such as coaching, tutoring, attending meetings, class preparation, and grading papers.[11]

What are the implications of this kind of workday structure for the work of teachers and the job of teaching? From the teacher's perspective there is little question that the sheer quantity of students they are assigned to teach shapes what and how they teach. In this regard, teachers commonly talk about class size thresholds—I found the number twenty-eight was often mentioned. Above this threshold, small increases in class size seemed to make a disproportionate difference in the climate of the classroom and the nature of the teacher's job. For just these reasons, class size has long been a source of debate and is a frequent source of complaint among teachers. In the four schools I investigated, either teacher union contracts or informal agreements between administration and faculty stipulated ceilings on class size. These ceilings were usually not exceeded, but they varied significantly among schools: at Catholic High it was thirty-six; at Urban High it was thirty-three; at Suburban High it was twenty-eight; and at Friends School it was twenty.

There are, of course, very good reasons from a management and organizational perspective to have teachers teach large numbers of students. Schools are charged with educating large numbers of students as efficiently and cheaply as is practical. Teacher salaries make up the lion's share of school budgets, and larger classes mean fewer teachers, resulting in considerable savings for tuition payers or taxpayers. Not surprisingly, the smaller class sizes at Friends School come at the price of a relatively high tuition. But this provides a good example of the tension mentioned earlier between the needs to bureaucratize and to debureaucratize. Larger class sizes may be less expensive in some ways, but they are not cost free. The logistics of teaching an average of 125 students per day, every day, pressures teachers to be more impersonal, more formal—that is, more bureaucratic in their relationship to students. The process of helping youngsters to understand classroom material often requires one-on-one interaction between teacher and student. But limitations of time and space place obvious limits on a teacher's capacity to do this. As a teacher in Suburban High concluded: "There is no doubt about it— the less children you have in the class, the more concentrated effort you can put into each child."

Large class sizes make it difficult for teachers to assign and properly evaluate written papers and homework for all their students. The job of English teachers provides one of the more telling illustrations of this kind of organizational constraint. Like other teachers, a typical secondary school English teacher carries a workload of five classes per day, teaching about 125 students per day. But unlike most other teachers, one of the primary tasks of English teachers is to teach writing. Teaching students to write well can require teachers to give ample feedback and can be unusually labor intensive for both teacher and student. I found that teachers in other departments often professed sympathy for the workload of their colleagues in the English department. For instance, if an English teacher assigned all 125 of his or her students to write a short paper and then spent just ten minutes reading and commenting on each student's work, the time spent by that teacher to evaluate just that one writing assignment would come to more than twenty hours.[12]

Criticism of large class sizes—a perennial topic for education reformers—tends to focus on the inevitable problems of an impersonal classroom atmosphere. Only with smaller classes and a less packed daily schedule could a school require, and could teachers realistically provide, a more personal approach to the evaluation of students. The relatively small class sizes at Friends School allowed such an approach. In contrast to the standardized course grade notices issued to students at the end of the semester at most schools, at Friends, teachers were able—and were required—to write detailed "anecdotal" reports on each student's work and behavior.

But there is another consequence of large classes often overlooked by critics—the implications for organizational control. Organizing teachers' workday around large classes has much the same effect as standardizing curricula, but without formal rules and regulations—it standardizes the behavior of teachers. This indirect constraint on the autonomy of teachers within their classrooms was summed up by a veteran teacher at Urban High: "I'm pretty free to do what I want in my classroom . . . but the problem is that there are a lot of things I can't really do when I've got thirty students each hour." Given their workload, many teachers spoke of having insufficient time to design and prepare new and innovative courses or to construct enrichment supplements for their classes, or to participate in school curriculum decisions, even if allowed the opportunity. Indeed, I found that teachers rarely conceived or produced any of the textbooks, tests, and curriculum packages that they used. These were created by those who were provided with the necessary time, resources, and rewards—professors and others employed by the publishers of textbooks and curriculum packages. The result is that, regardless of whether a school actually requires a particular standardized curriculum, standardization takes place because many teachers end up using the most readily available, prefabricated curriculum materials and textbooks. Moreover, teachers commonly turn to other labor-saving devices such as prefabricated tests, also manufactured by textbook publishers. These mass-produced, standardized, short-answer exams influence how teachers teach and evaluate students in a number of subtle but incisive ways. Typically, they emphasize quick recall of facts and deemphasize critical thinking and affective maturity. Hence, they institutionalize a particular definition of what constitutes important knowledge and what constitutes an appropriate level of performance, which sets the parameters within which teachers make their evaluations of students.

The larger organizational imperative to efficiently evaluate, label, and track students in a consistent and thus fair manner also shapes teachers' work in the classroom. There is, for instance, the practice in many schools of grading "on the curve." Many teachers told me they faced pressure to adjust their student evaluation standards up or down so as to produce something close to a bell-shaped "normal" distribution of student scores and grades. In this scheme, regardless of the ability level of the students, the norm was that, in a typical class, a few students would succeed, a few would fail, and most would perform at an average level. I did not find these kinds of standards to be formalized in faculty manuals or curriculum guides, but I did find them to be informal norms and, according to teachers, no less real in their effects and consequences. Teachers who pass or fail an above-average number of students are analogous to what in other occupations are referred to as "rate busters." They ignore organizational norms for the appropriate level of performance and work at their own pace—like factory workers, for example, who produce at higher rates than the norm.[13] Rate busting on the part of teachers poses a threat to prevailing norms about how to conduct the work and can lead to complaints from parents, resentment from other faculty, reprimands from the administration, and, ultimately, forceful demands for restandardization. One administrator at Suburban High explained this concern: "We also hear from parents. They will ask, 'How is it that in this class, there seems to be a larger percent of students failing, as opposed to so-and-so's child, who is with that teacher's class? I know my child is at least as smart as them.' They don't have figures, but they talk among themselves, especially . . . parents of kids in academic programs . . . And in some cases they have a legitimate point."

Teachers who did not conform to these norms learned to be prepared to provide a rationale for their nonrationality, as one teacher explained: "You need to give enough tests in a semester to justify your grading. If you fail a lot [of students] and if somebody came in because you gave their child an F based on three or four grades in a quarter, then they would ask you to justify . . . 'How could you give an F? How could you use that as a reasonable amount?'"[14]

These examples illustrate a basic point: decisions made by teachers concerning daily classroom instruction do not stand alone and are not isolated events. Teachers' classroom decisions about their work are nested within, and highly dependent upon, the larger process of conceiving, planning, and implementing the educational goals of the school, over which most teachers have little influence. Although these mechanisms are less direct and obvious than formal rules and regulations, they are no less real in their impact on what teachers actually do. Indeed, in some ways the pervasiveness of these other kinds of controls make it less necessary for school administrators to implement and require formal regulations, elaborate mechanisms of accountability, and coercive carrots and sticks.

Deskilling

In some kinds of organizations the division of labor is so tightly coupled and the separation of conception and execution is so extreme that it results in the phenomenon that analysts of organizations, occupations, and work refer to as deskilling—the transformation of highly skilled work into highly unskilled work.[15] This concept is useful in understanding how the way production is organized can constrain and control employees in less visible and less direct ways.

Deskilling is the result of an unusually detailed division of labor, when a complex craft or labor process is subdivided and fragmented into its simplest elements. The objective is to eliminate the need for specialized knowledge and expertise from as many steps in the production process as possible, and to the furthest extent possible. In plain terms, the point of this division of labor is to deskill, or "dumb down," complex work. The classic exemplar of this mode of organization is the industrial assembly line. In the typical assembly line, in automobile production, for example, a relatively small number of highly skilled personnel conceive, plan, and design the tasks and the pace of work for a relatively large number of low-skill personnel. The job of the low-skill employees is to execute the prescribed routines.

From the organization's point of view, one of the advantages to deskilling is that it increases productivity and reduces labor costs. It is possible for new employees to quickly become very efficient and "skilled" at simple, repetitive routines. Moreover, undifferentiated employees, that is, "generalists," are more interchangeable and thus can be assigned to a larger range of tasks. In addition, subdividing a craft into simple parts devalues the constituent parts. Knowledge of the production process is distributed on a strict "need to know" basis and becomes unnecessary for the majority of employees. This minimizes the need to employ highly skilled, and hence higher cost, personnel. It also minimizes costly on-the-job training. Finally, deskilling reduces labor replacement costs because unskilled employees are usually more easily replaced than highly skilled ones. Employees know this, and it undermines their ability to speak up—ultimately reducing the threat of employee challenges, resistance, and strikes. Because replaceability is inversely related to power, a final, often unrecognized, advantage comes from deskilling—it fosters organizational control.[16] In short, deskilled employees are inexpensive, easily trained, easily replaced, and have little power.

A disadvantage of deskilling is, of course, is that it can become a self-fulfilling prophecy. Devaluing and degrading the quality of jobs and workers can devalue and degrade the quality of the work performed. In other words, it may be difficult to obtain high-quality performance from low-quality workers in low-quality jobs. Again, the extreme example is the automobile assembly line. On the one hand, the assembly line is the epitome of efficiency. Under Henry Ford's direction, the assembly line became famous for reducing the production costs of automobiles to the point that they became affordable to a large segment of society. But the assembly line has also become the epitome of inefficiency. Since Ford's time, the assembly line has become infamous for mind-deadening work, poor workmanship, and sloppy results.

Not surprisingly, research on deskilling usually focuses on blue-collar occupations and industrial settings organized around mass production and highly routinized work. But the concept of deskilling can be profitably borrowed to illuminate the way in which teachers' work is organized and controlled in some schools. Of course, in many ways the job of teaching is obviously quite unlike that of factory workers. The work of teaching does not entail executing mind-numbing routines, such as tightening bolts or making welds, hundreds of times per day as does the job of an assembly-line worker. The job of teaching entails complex work with children and adolescents. But there are some less obvious similarities between the organization of teachers' work in some settings and that of factory workers.

The act of presenting lessons to students in classrooms is only one step in the complex process that is teaching. Teaching involves a cycle: the planning and design of the curriculum, its objectives, textbooks, materials, lessons, and means of evaluation; the implementation of this curriculum; and then the revision of this curriculum.[17] At a minimum, the work of teaching involves multiple types of expertise: knowledge of state, district, and school objectives and goals; knowledge of the subject (knowing what to teach), skill in teaching (knowing how to teach), knowledge of students, and also a highly specialized expertise: knowing which method to use with particular topics, with particular students, and in particular settings. For just these reasons, as mentioned earlier analysts of work and occupations have traditionally classified teaching as a relatively complex form of work, characterized by uncertainty, intangibility, and ambiguity, and requiring a relatively high degree of initiative, thought, judgment, and skill.[18]

The organizations that make up the education system typically subdivide the complex process of teaching into a series of separate steps that can vary in their degree of complexity, discretion, and control. In the extreme case, teachers are completely separated from the conception, design, and planning of their work, and these steps are carried out by highly skilled outside experts, often college and university professors. In this kind of division of labor, teachers are treated as interchangeable, low-skill technicians, and teaching is reduced to the rote implementation of prefabricated packages designed by the experts.

One example of this deskilled mode of organization in schools is the "teacher proof" curriculum, discussed in Chapter 4. Such curricula consist of step-by-step lesson plans prescribed in such detail that ostensibly anyone could teach them, no matter how skilled or unskilled. Lessons are highly scripted, and teachers read to the students directly from the page. In some programs even praise is scripted. At the end of tasks the lesson prompts the teacher to say: "Good, you did this section correctly."

Such top-down bureaucratic mechanisms have their disadvantages and their critics. By curbing initiative, thought, judgment, and creativity, these programs do away with many of the very things often deemed necessary for high-quality teaching. Moreover, by curbing flexibility these programs have difficulty coping with "client variability"—the fact that children are different.

Of course, reducing uncertainty and ambiguity is the very point of such bureaucratic mechanisms. These minutely standardized curricula are direct, highly visible, and highly intrusive control mechanisms designed to ensure delivery of a standard and consistent product to clients. But these mechanisms also control the work of teachers by devaluing it. Teacher-proof curricula reserve the conceptual portion of the complex craft of teaching—the portion requiring initiative, thought, judgment, and skill—for a small number of highly trained, highly skilled, highly paid outside experts. Reducing the need for skill, knowledge, and training for the majority of inside employees, the teachers, reduces their value and the level at which they should be paid. Moreover, by reducing the need for skill, knowledge, and training, these mechanisms ease the replacement of teachers and can thus reduce the threat of teacher turnover and strikes.

Out-of-Field Teaching as Deskilling

Another aspect of the organization of teachers' work that resembles deskilling is the practice of out-of-field teaching. Chapter 4 introduced out-of-field assignments as an example of the kinds of sticks and carrots principals can use to enforce school rules and hold teachers accountable. But like teacher-proof curricula, out-of-field assignments also can act as a less-direct means of enhancing organizational control. On the surface, out-of-field assignments may appear to be diametrically opposite to teacher-proof curricula. While the latter are highly prescribed and appear to be mechanisms of tight coupling, out-of-field assignments have little prescription and seem to be an example of loose coupling. Teachers are not directed to implement a curriculum conceived and designed by others but are left on their own to teach a subject in which they may have little interest or training. But both practices share common ground—both devalue, deskill, and disempower teachers' work.

Out-of-field teaching provides a unusual window into the internal workings of schools and how schools actually organize and control the work of teachers. It also illustrates how these structures and processes are widely misunderstood. People on the inside of schools have always known about the practice of assigning teachers to teach subjects in which they have little background, but this practice has been largely unknown to outsiders—to the public, to policymakers, and even to many educational researchers.[19] Until recently, almost no empirical research had been done on out-of-field teaching. Indeed, very few studies of school organization have even acknowledged the existence of this practice.[20]

An absence of accurate data on out-of-field teaching contributed to this lack of recognition—a situation remedied with the release of the SASS data beginning in the early 1990s. In my field research, I had come across some teachers who had been assigned by their principals to teach subjects that did not match their training or education—something that I also experienced firsthand during my years as a secondary school teacher. I wondered if this practice were widespread, and if so, why. To answer these questions I analyzed the extensive SASS data on teacher qualifications and assignments.[21]

The data show that out-of-field teaching is, indeed, a common practice; it takes place in well over half of all secondary schools in the United States each year. Most secondary school teachers have a main field or a primary department in which they teach, and most have some kind of credential or qualification in that main field. But about one-fourth of the nation's secondary teachers in any given semester are assigned to teach classes—usually one to three—in other fields or departments. Mathematics teachers, for example, may not simply teach math courses for all five of their daily teaching periods; they may also be assigned to teach a couple of classes in English or another field in which they are not qualified.

There are, of course, different standards by which to define a qualified teacher. School officials tend to define a qualified candidate as someone who has a state-approved teaching certificate (or license) in the fields they teach. Others prefer to define a qualified candidate as someone who has an undergraduate or graduate major or minor in the fields they teach. Regardless of how defined, the data showed significant levels of underqualified teaching. For example, about a third of public secondary teachers who taught math did not have a regular teaching certificate in math. Similarly, the data showed that about a third of all secondary school teachers who taught math did not have a college minor or major in math, math education, or a related discipline such as engineering or physics. About one-fourth of all secondary school English teachers had neither a major nor a minor in English or a related subject such as literature, communications, speech, journalism, English education, or reading education. In science, slightly lower levels—about one-fifth of all secondary school teachers—did not have at least a minor in one of the sciences or in science education. Finally, about a fifth of social studies teachers were without at least a minor in any of the social sciences or in public affairs, social studies education, or history.

The publication of these kinds of data, beginning in the mid-1990s, generated widespread interest.[22] To advocates of raising standards of teacher quality, whether they were teachers, policymakers, or parents of school-age children, high rates of out-of-field teaching were a source of alarm. From their viewpoint, adequately qualified teachers, especially at the secondary school level and especially in the core academic fields, ought to have at least a college minor in the subjects they teach. Common sense suggests that teachers trained in social studies, for example, are unlikely to have a solid understanding of physics, and that for most teachers it is difficult, at best, to teach well what one does not know well.[23] And many empirical studies have borne this out.[24] In short, probably few parents would want their teenagers to be taught eleventh-grade trigonometry, for example, by a teacher who did not have at least a minor in math, no matter how bright the teacher. The data show, however, that in each of the fields of English and math and history, every year well over 4 million secondary-level students are taught by teachers who have neither a major nor a minor in the field.

Some of the most important consequences of out-of-field teaching are probably those not easily quantified. The effects of being taught by a teacher without a strong background in a field may be just the kind of outcome not captured in student scores on short-answer standardized examinations. Teachers assigned to teach a subject in which they have little training are probably more likely to rely heavily on textbooks, and the kinds of learning obtained from textbooks is probably what standardized examinations best capture. One can easily imagine the limitations imposed by a lack of subject background on a teacher's ability to teach for critical thinking and to engage the students' interest in the subject—the kinds of learning not well reflected in standardized tests.

Moreover, teachers who do a lot of out-of-field teaching most likely do not have the opportunity to acquire what is called pedagogical content knowledge—knowing which pedagogy to use with particular subjects in particular settings. Much of what constitutes effective teaching is highly dependent on the specific situation, subject matter, grade level, and type of student. Pedagogical content knowledge is at the core of what teachers must learn and use to teach well; it is the intersection of subject knowledge, teaching skills, and knowledge of learners.[25]

High levels out-of-field teaching can also negatively affect the learning environment for all students in schools, not just those unlucky enough to be taught by out-of-field teachers. Assigning teachers to teach courses in which they have no training can change their allocation of preparation time, decreasing the amount of time they spend preparing for their other courses.

There are, moreover, consequences for teachers to be considered. Having to cope with out-of-field assignments comes on top of an already burdensome teaching load for most secondary teachers. What is the impact on teachers' sense of efficacy of having to teach courses in which they have little formal background? I found in analyses using the SASS data that out-of-field assignments are significantly correlated with decreases in teachers' morale, engagement, and commitment. One might also wonder whether out-of-field teaching has an effect on the legitimacy and authority of teachers, and hence on classroom discipline. For all these reasons, the problem of out-of-field teaching has received a great deal of attention. Nevertheless, the causes behind the problem have been widely misunderstood.

Typically, policymakers, commentators, and researchers have assumed that high rates of out-of-field teaching are due to deficits in the quality or quantity of teachers. For example, many assume that out-of-field teaching is a problem of poorly trained teachers. In this view, the training of teachers in college and university programs lacks adequate rigor, breadth, and depth, especially in academic and substantive coursework, and this results in high levels of out-of-field teaching.[26] Proponents of this viewpoint also typically assume that the problem can be remedied by requiring prospective teachers to complete a "real" undergraduate major in an academic discipline. This explanation for out-of-field teaching, however, is incorrect.

The data show that virtually all teachers in the United States have completed a bachelor's degree; indeed, almost half of all public school teachers have graduate degrees. Moreover, 94 percent of public school teachers and, surprisingly, more than half of private school teachers hold regular state-approved teaching certificates. Many of these teachers, of course, have education degrees and not academic degrees. For example, many of those teaching math have a degree in math education and not in math itself. But having an education degree does not mean a teacher lacks training in a particular subject or specialty. Contrary to popular opinion, most secondary school teachers have completed substantial coursework in an academic specialty. For example, it is common for a degree in math education to require as much coursework in the math department as does a degree in math itself.[27] There certainly have been problems with the depth and breadth of teacher training, and this has been a source of much criticism and reform. But blaming out-of-field teaching on teacher training displays a misunderstanding of the way teachers' work is organized. The source of out-of-field teaching lies not in the amount of education teachers have but in the lack of fit between teachers' fields of training and their teaching assignments. Out-of-field teachers are typically experienced and highly qualified individuals who have been misassigned to teach in fields that do not match their training or education. The key question is not, Why is the training of teachers so inadequate? One must ask, Why is there so much mismatch between the preservice training of teachers and how they are assigned once on the job?

Most commentators and analysts have assumed that the source of this mismatch lies in a lack of teachers, that is, in teacher shortages. In this view, shortfalls in the number of available teachers, primarily due to increasing student enrollments and a "graying" teacher workforce, mean that many school systems resort to lowering standards to fill teaching openings, the net effect of which is out-of-field teaching. For several reasons, this explanation of out-of-field teaching also reveals a misunderstanding of the organization of teachers' work and is also incorrect.

First, shortages cannot explain the high levels of out-of-field teaching in areas such as English and social studies, which have had perennial surpluses. Second, in any given field, even when the rates of student enrollment have been at a peak, only a minority of schools have actually had trouble filling their teaching positions with qualified candidates. Hiring difficulties are a factor, but the data show that, as often as not, out-of-field teaching takes place in schools that have not had problems filling their openings.

The theory of deskilling provides an alternative explanation for the widespread existence of this phenomenon. From the viewpoint of those who seek to raise the quality of teaching, assigning teachers to teach out of their fields may seem like an inefficient and irrational use of an important human resource. But a close examination of the organization of schools reveals some very compelling reasons for its prevalence.

Decisions concerning the hiring of teachers and their course assignments are primarily the responsibility and prerogative of school principals, as documented in Chapter 3. Principals are charged with the often difficult task of providing a broad array of programs and courses with limited resources, a limited budget, and a limited teaching staff. In addition, principals' staffing decisions can be constrained by numerous other factors, such as teacher seniority rules, school district regulations, class-size guidelines, and contractual obligations concerning the number and type of class assignments normally allocated to teaching employees. For example, in a typical secondary school, teacher employment contracts stipulate that full-time teaching staff must be assigned to teach five classes in the normal seven-period day.

However, the data show that within these constraints school principals have an unusual degree of discretion in staffing decisions. Whereas the training of teachers is subject to an elaborate array of state licensing requirements, there is far less regulation of how teachers are used once on the job.[28] Indeed, as noted in the previous chapter, this is an area of loose coupling completely overlooked by analysts of school control and an area in which decisions made by principals are highly consequential for those responsible for carrying them out—the teachers. In this context of many demands, limited resources, and much discretion, principals sometimes find that assigning teachers to teach out of their fields is not only legal but also more efficient, less expensive, and less time-consuming than the alternatives.

For example, rather than trying to find and hire a new science teacher to teach a new state-mandated, but underfunded, science curriculum, a principal may find it more convenient to assign a couple of English and social studies teachers to "cover" a class or two in science. If a teacher suddenly leaves in the middle of a semester, a principal may find it faster and less expensive to hire a readily available, but not fully qualified, substitute teacher than to instigate a formal search for a new teacher. When faced with the choice between hiring a fully qualified candidate for an English position or hiring a less qualified candidate who is also willing to coach a major varsity sport, a principal may find it more expedient to do the latter. If a full-time music teacher is under contract but student enrollment is sufficient to fill only three music classes, the principal may find it both necessary and cost-effective to assign the music teacher to teach two classes in English to make up a regular full-time complement of five classes per semester. Faced with a myriad of such judgments and trade-offs, some degree of teacher misassignment by principals is probably unavoidable. Moreover, the degree to which a school is faced with problems of teacher recruitment or retention may shape the extent to which the principal relies on such options. They are, however, available to almost all schools, and they are used by many.

The contrast with traditional professions is stark. Few employers or organizations would, for example, require cardiologists to deliver babies, real estate lawyers to defend criminal cases, chemical engineers to design bridges, or sociology professors to teach English. Underlying the traditional professions is the assumption that a great deal of skill, training, and expertise are required, and so specialization is necessary. The prevalence of out-of-field teaching suggests that another set of assumptions underlies the work of precollegiate teaching—that school teaching is not especially complex work, that it does not require much skill, training, and expertise, and hence that specialization is less necessary. In the practice of out-of-field teaching, teachers are treated somewhat like interchangeable blocks that can be placed in any empty slot.

In this organizational context, in which teaching is assumed to be low-skill work, misassignment has understandably become an acceptable and common administrative technique. There are good reasons, from an organizational and from a taxpayers' viewpoint, to continue the practice. Treating teachers like low-skill workers makes them more useful to the school administrators as generalists able to teach a wide range of subjects. It justifies less rigorous and less costly preservice training and less extensive and less costly inservice training. Devaluing their complex work justifies lower salaries, and it reduces the cost of turnover by making it easier to replace those who leave. Finally—a point important to my purpose here in understanding how power operates in schools—the ability to easily replace teachers is a significant source of organizational control. Misassigned teachers are expendable, and this undermines their ability to speak up—something I learned firsthand.

At one point in my career I accepted a job at an expensive private boarding school in New England as a history and social studies teacher. Upon arriving at the school I was surprised to find that my job had been changed by the headmaster. For half of my courseload I was assigned to one-on-one teaching of remedial language skills to dyslexic students. I approached the headmaster to ask if he might reconsider, since I had no knowledge of or experience with dyslexia and its remediation. The headmaster was surprised at my response, and it became clear that misassignment was a normal and unquestioned administrative prerogative. The headmaster concluded that I was not sufficiently "committed," was not a "team player," and demanded that I quit or be fired. I quit and was quickly and easily replaced with a new teacher less resistant to misassignment. Although out-of-field teaching was a normal practice at this school, knowledge of it was carefully kept from parents and was of little interest to the relevant authorities. Indeed, when I reported this incident to the regional school accreditation agency charged with overseeing school quality standards, it responded that such "internal management" affairs were not its concern. Again, the contrast with traditional professions is telling—analogous behavior in medicine, law, or engineering could be considered malpractice and subject to litigation or prosecution.

The Workplace Culture of Teaching

The example of out-of-field teaching illustrates one way by which teachers' work can be organized and indirectly controlled. In such a situation, the role of teachers is shaped by mixed and contradictory messages: while teachers have very little control or power over many of the key decisions that determine what they do, they have a great deal of responsibility for implementing those decisions.

This raises several questions: How do teachers respond to and cope with this role, and how does this affect administrative control in schools? Do teachers acquiesce to the mix of demands and constraints put on them, or do they resist? These questions are tied to the fundamental organizational tension between control and consent, introduced in Chapter 2. In the view of those who study organizations, occupations, and work, the reaction of teachers to the way their work is organized is crucial to the success or failure of organizational control in schools. Precisely because of teaching's unusual combination of clients, products, and technologies, schools are unusually dependent on the cooperation, motivation, and commitment of those actually *entrusted* with the work—teachers. What are the attitudes and responses of teachers to the mix of responsibilities and power in their work, and what are the implications of their responses for how organizational control works in schools?

Teachers' attitudes once on the job are shaped by the attitudes teachers hold prior to becoming teachers. This is important to note, because the motives, values, and aspirations of those entering the teaching occupation differ dramatically from those entering many other occupations. Research on occupational choice and values has shown that a unusually large proportion of those entering teaching are motivated by what is called an altruistic or public-service ethic. Such individuals place less importance on extrinsic rewards (such as income and prestige), less emphasis on intrinsic rewards (such as intellectual challenge or self-expression), and more importance on the opportunity to contribute to the betterment of society, to work with people, to serve their community, to help others—in short, to do "good." Those with a public-service orientation prefer careers and jobs with a high "social" content, such as medicine, social work, nursing, and, especially, teaching. Numerous studies over the past four decades have shown that those entering teaching are more likely to value service and less likely to value pecuniary rewards than those entering most other occupations, including law, engineering, natural or social science, sales, advertising, business, architecture, journalism, and art.[29] This continues to be true. For instance, a poll conducted in 2000 by Public Agenda asked a national sample of recent college graduates what they thought about the importance of particular job characteristics, including "that a job contributes to society and helps others." Thirty-nine percent of nonteachers felt this characteristic to be "absolutely essential" in their job. In contrast, almost twice as many teachers—72 percent—believed this to be so.[30]

The workplace culture of teaching is shaped not only by the values of teachers but also, of course, by the way schools are organized and structured. Another aspect of the organization of production in schools is isolation. The organization of teachers' work in schools has often been described as an "egg crate" model. Numerous individuals, separated from one another in classrooms, carry out similar operations, supplied, controlled, and managed by a central office. This aspect of school organization may be advantageous from an organizational viewpoint, but it can also be at odds with the nature of teaching. Teaching may have a high social content, involve extensive interaction with youngsters, require mutual cooperation among those involved, and attract to its ranks those with an unusually strong public-service ethic. But those who do this work—the teachers—often do so in isolation from their colleagues. Schools vary greatly in the degree of communication, support, and collegiality among the teaching and administrative staff.[31] But even in relatively tight-knit workplaces, such as Friends School, "the classroom is a very private place as far as other adults are concerned."[32] Therein lies an irony— teachers serve others and serve society, but they often do so alone. Living with isolation is one of the first and often most painful lessons many new teachers must learn—that being a teacher means being alone with youngsters for most of the day. Although their jobs, responsibilities, and roles, are shaped by decisions made by others, especially administrators, they actually have little contact with, or assistance from, staff, administrators, or other teachers.

Given the combination of a highly altruistic workforce, a highly isolating working environment, and high demands, it is not surprising that one of the most pervasive aspects of the culture of teaching is an ethos of individual responsibility and accountability. This ethos is not universally shared among all teachers, nor does it dominate all schools, but I found it a common theme in the four very different schools I investigated, and it has been noted by other researchers.[33] Alone in the world of their own classroom, it is up to each teacher to make a success or failure of the job. New teachers find themselves suddenly isolated and yet responsible for the operation of their classroom—what many liken to a "sink or swim" situation.

This ethos of individual teacher responsibility is reflected in how teachers and school administrators commonly define the concept of professionalism and what it means to be a professional. As noted earlier, analysts of work and occupations distinguish professions from other occupations primarily by *structural* characteristics. In addition to substantial control over one's work, this includes rigorous training and licensing requirements, positive working conditions, an active professional organization or association, relatively high compensation, and high prestige.³⁴ In contrast, teachers and administrators often define professionals in terms of *attitudinal* attributes. Teachers and administrators commonly use terms like dedication, diligence, caring, warmth, commitment, and engagement to describe professionalism in teaching. From this perspective, a professional is not so much a well-paid, highly respected expert whose job entails good working conditions and substantial autonomy, but rather someone who is personally dedicated to children and who is committed to the needs of individual students. What is revealing about this definition of the proper role of teachers is its emphasis on individual, rather than organizational, responsibility. That is, it implies that the way to obtain success as a teacher is through individual solutions to organizational problems.³⁵

Establishing and maintaining "control" of one's own classroom and one's own students is the first step, and is at the heart of this workplace ethos of individual responsibility and individual success. Almost every teacher I interviewed stressed the necessity of establishing behind the closed door of the classroom, a small universe of control. The creation of an enclave and a stable environment within the classroom is seen as a prerequisite to anything else a teacher does. Success, and even survival, as a teacher depends on creating an orderly climate in the classroom. This characteristic is not unique to the four schools I examined. In the above-described poll by Public Agenda, new teachers were asked about essential characteristics of effective teachers. Ninety-one percent of the teachers felt that "an ability to maintain discipline and order in the classroom" was "absolutely essential" to being a really effective teacher. More teachers scored this characteristic as essential than any other, including in-depth knowledge of the subject, effective teaching techniques, high standards, talent for motivating kids, an ability to work with parents, and being well versed in theories of child development.³⁶

But although teachers agree that this is an obvious and essential prerequisite to success in their job, establishing and maintaining classroom control can be very difficult to achieve. Difficulty in maintaining order varies among schools, among teachers, and among the classes each teacher is assigned. While a basic level of cooperation and civility from clients can usually be taken for granted in many occupations and professions, this is not true in teaching. Few teachers can assume that their students will be cooperative and that basic civility will prevail without effort on their part. A kind of instant accountability pertains to the classroom, because teachers are the first to suffer in the advent of a breakdown of control. A classroom can become surprisingly, quickly chaotic, resulting in a "very long" day for the teacher. Sometimes "just getting through the day" is all a teacher can achieve—what teachers described as "just surviving." The common use of military metaphors by those I interviewed was telling: teachers often referred to classrooms as "battlegrounds" and teaching as "life in the trenches." Another image often conveyed by teachers was of the classroom as "pressure cooker"—to outsiders classrooms may appear calm, but insiders know that under the apparent calm is a simmering mix subject to sudden upset.

The precarious quality of classroom control is not a new or unique finding. In his classic 1930s work on the nature of the teaching job, Willard Waller insightfully described the "perilous equilibrium" common to classrooms. His comments are worth quoting at length:

> It is not enough to point out that the school is a despotism. It is a despotism in a state of perilous equilibrium. It is a despotism threatened from within and exposed to regulation and interference from without. It is a despotism capable of being overturned in a moment, exposed

to the instant loss of its stability and its prestige. It is a despotism demanded by the community of parents, but specially limited by them as to the techniques which it may use for the maintenance of a stable social order. It is a despotism resting upon children, at once the most tractable and the most unstable members of the community . . . There may be some who, seeing the solid brick of school buildings, the rows of nicely regimented children sitting stiff and well-behaved in the classroom or marching briskly through the halls, will doubt that the school is in a state of unstable equilibrium. A school may in fact maintain a high morale through a period of years, so that its record in the eyes of the community is marred by no untoward incident. But how many schools are there with a teaching body of more than—let us say—ten teachers, in which there is not one teacher who is in imminent danger of losing his position because of poor discipline? How many such schools are there in which no teacher's discipline has broken down within the past three years? How many school executives would dare to plan a great mass meeting of students at which no teachers would be present or easily available in case of disorder?[37]

Waller stressed that this instability was not rooted in the inherent qualities of the teachers themselves, but was rooted in the manner in which schools were organized. Teachers were and are vulnerable to student challenges precisely because they can do little about them. As a result, in Waller's analysis the job of teaching involves something of a charade—teachers must put on the appearance of being in control of the classroom. Being considered a "good teacher" means being able to present a convincing appearance of confidence and control. As a seasoned teacher at Suburban High explained: "You have to believe and act as if the classroom is *yours*—you own it and that you belong there—and whatever goes on there is because *you* allow it to."

Success at this performance is measured by what teachers often call "respect"—an important and often scarce resource in schools. It refers to the extent to which students and colleagues accept a teacher's definition of the situation—that the classroom is his or her realm and that he or she is the sole authority in that realm. To respect a teacher is to know he is someone not easily dismissed, that he must be obeyed, that he is not a "pushover." Although it may seem ironic, even students who misbehave usually do not like timidity on the part of teachers and are uncomfortable in classrooms where the teacher is "run all over." Nevertheless, respect's achievement could be a formidable challenge, and possession of respect, I found, could be a source of considerable status and pride for teachers.[38]

This need and struggle for control in one's classroom explains why being "backed up" by administrators is important for teachers, an issue introduced in Chapter 4. It is precisely because they have so little power that teachers are dependent on those who have more power—usually the principal and vice principal. If a teacher is not backed up, especially in disciplinary matters, the power of the teacher is revealed, often painfully, for what it is—a charade—and is vulnerable to challenge by students.

This presents a double bind for teachers. Teachers need support from administrators to establish and maintain control in their classrooms. But the act of asking for this support can undermine a teacher's efforts to establish and maintain control in the classroom. Administrators may frown on requests for help, and the message to teachers is clear, as one principal explained to me: "It is your [the teacher's] job to control your students, and if you can't do it, you

THE TEACHER IN THE MIDDLE

shouldn't be a teacher." Thus, turning to administrators for help with disciplinary concerns can itself be regarded as a sign of weakness—and can be used as evidence that a teacher "can't handle" his or her students. Hence one strategy for success as a teacher is to rely, or appear to rely, on the administration as little as possible. In this view, the key to respect is control, and the key to that is self-reliance and independence from the administration. One senior teacher at Suburban High summed this up: "In my mind, whenever you turn it over to the discipline office . . . you lose . . . You no longer are that authority figure who can handle all problems . . . The kids see that." Or in the words of another veteran teacher, "The best strategy is to shut up and run your own show." Thus, in this kind of organizational context, adopting a highly individualized ethos is a common strategy for success as a teacher.

This climate of individual responsibility can, in turn, foster a certain amount of blaming on the part of both insiders and outsiders. If one assumes that individual teachers are responsible for seeing that classrooms are orderly and students perform adequately, then it is natural also to assume that failure to meet these expectations and responsibilities is also the fault of individual teachers. Those who subscribe to this perspective often blame teachers, for instance, for misbehavior on the part of students. In this view, students are most likely to become disruptive in class if and when teachers fail to engage them adequately. The assumption underlying this view is that "good" teachers are not subject to rude or inappropriate behavior on the part of students, and that "bad" teachers are. Indeed, it almost seems as if proponents of this viewpoint feel that "bad" teachers somehow deserve misbehaving students. This view of the proper responsibilities of teachers is really a variant of the definition of professionalism mentioned earlier that focuses on the degree of caring, enthusiasm, and engagement teachers evince. The implied solution is that if teachers were simply more engaged, and more engaging, then student misbehavior would largely disappear.

This theory of student misbehavior appears to be widely believed. A nationally representative poll of professors of education, conducted in 1997 by Public Agenda, found that nearly two-thirds of the respondents believed that when teachers faced a disruptive class, it probably meant that the teacher had failed to make the lessons engaging enough for the students. This survey result is especially telling, because the respondents—professors of education—represent a large portion of those doing research on schools and also those who teach future teachers.[39] Certainly some teachers lack skill in both teaching and managing large number of youngsters. However, such a view tends to preclude any awareness of the role of the organization and the balance of power in the generation of dilemmas and problems for teachers.[40]

Regardless of whether fair or not, this climate of individual responsibility can be quite successful in fostering effort, engagement, and commitment—the school's version of professionalism—on the part of individual teachers. Indeed, teachers' individual efforts routinely go beyond the official routines of the job. As in any workplace culture, this ethos of individual teacher responsibility is normally invisible and taken for granted. But when challenged, it can become quickly and highly visible. An example of this arises in "work-to-rule" strikes and job actions by teacher unions. In these kinds of collective protests, teachers work, quite literally, according to the formal rules and contractual obligations of their jobs. In concrete terms, what this means is that teachers do not work beyond normal school hours of, typically, 8:30 to 3:30, and do not perform extra and voluntary activities. There are hundreds of such activities: telephoning parents, assigning and grading homework, participating in after-school extracurricular activities, writing college or job reference letters for graduating students, helping students complete college applications, conducting rehearsals, after-school tutoring, helping with holiday programs, sponsoring clubs, serving on committees, chaperoning field trips, and preparing for graduation exercises. In work-to-rule situations, schools quickly cease to function effectively, clearly revealing that what teachers routinely do far surpasses the formal bureaucratic routines and rules. This realization is often a source of both surprise and chagrin to the public, and it is for just this reason that work-to-rule job actions by teacher unions can be a powerful tool for collective bargaining. They bring to attention the fundamental tension between control and consent—the fact that organizations need, and benefit from, the goodwill, commitment, and consent of their employees. Such actions also reveal the limitations of a bureaucratic mode of organization for schools and the extent to which schools both need and benefit from certain kinds of nonbureaucratization. In this case, however, behavior outside of formal guidelines is not a matter of skirting responsibility, or avoiding accountability, as depicted by some critics. Rather it is an example of the opposite—the acceptance of both responsibility and accountability—and it is somewhat akin to one of the classic hallmarks of the traditional professions, pro bono work.

The degree to which these kinds of expectations and responsibilities are both taken for granted and taken advantage of is revealed by the response of critics to work-to-rule job actions. Typically, opponents of these actions argue they are illegitimate because they display a selfishness, a lack of caring, and hence a lack of professionalism on the part of teachers toward children. Underlying this argument is a definition of professions based on attitudinal rather than structural characteristics. Moreover, also underlying it is the assumption that these kinds of tasks are not extra efforts to be rewarded but obligations to be expected. The assumption is that it is teachers, not the organization or the community, who are primarily responsible for the social growth and well-being of the students while in school.[41] Such criticisms can be highly effective in reasserting and reinstitutionalizing these normative mechanisms of control, to the extent to which teachers themselves accept their altruism as a legitimate obligation, as a necessary part of being a professional, and hence feel guilty of shirking their responsibilities. In other words, these kinds of workplace-culture forms of control are most effective when they are accepted by all parties as normal and appropriate. Otherwise, the organization may be pressured to resort to more coercive, more overt measures of control—which is in fact an occasional response to work-to-rule teacher job actions.

Teachers' extrabureaucratic and beyond-the-rule behavior is not limited to pro bono–like efforts. Another indicator of this ethic of responsibility and accountability is teachers' practice of spending their own money on classroom materials. Teachers often find, for a variety of reasons, that their school does not, or will not, provide the curriculum materials and supplies they deem necessary. As the data in Chapter 3 indicate, teachers have little access to or control over school discretionary funds. These monies must be requested through administrative channels, a sometimes frustrating and unsuccessful experience. I found that it is common for teachers to pay for such materials themselves, out of pocket. One teacher told me an especially revealing story of how faculty at his school had to negotiate— at times even plead—with the central office secretary to obtain blackboard chalk, which was carefully rationed to teachers throughout the school year. If a teacher ran out of chalk in the middle of the semester, a not infrequent event, it was his or her responsibility to see that class proceeded, with or without it.

Examples of teachers' backing up their service ethic with out-of-pocket spending are not unique to the schools I investigated. A national survey of public school teachers conducted in 1990 by the Carnegie Foundation for the Advancement of Teaching found that teachers spent an average of $250 of their own money per semester (or about $500 per year) for classroom materials and supplies they felt were necessary to meet the needs of their students. Only 4 percent of teachers reported spending none of their own money for such supplies that year.[42] Similarly, the 1996 Survey on the Status of the American Public School Teacher, conducted by the National Education Association, found that public school teachers had spent, on average, $408 of their own money that year for curriculum materials and classroom supplies.[43] Only 6.3 percent reported spending none of their own money that year for such materials. Notably, this altruism was not merely a matter of youthful idealism; the data show that older teachers spent more of their own money than did younger teachers.

This indicator suggests a remarkable responsibility and accountability on the part of individuals, in the face of a remarkable lack of responsibility or accountability on the part of the organizations that employ them. These nationally representative data suggest that in 1996, a workforce numbering about three million teachers donated a total of well over one billion dollars of educational materials to their schools! This kind of teacher subsidization of the school system also received unprecedented recognition in federal legislation, proposed by the Bush administration in 2001, to provide tax deductions to teachers for their out-of-pocket expenditures for classroom materials.

Teacher subsidization of public schools is all the more notable because teaching is a relatively low-paying occupation. The salaries of new college graduates who become teachers have long been consistently and considerably below those of new college graduates in most other occupations.[44] For instance, the average salary (one year after graduation) for 1993 college graduates who became teachers was almost 50 percent less than the average starting salary of their classmates who took computer science jobs. Moreover, this disparity remains throughout the career span. Comparing total yearly income, teachers earn less than those in many other occupations and far less than most traditional professionals. For instance, data from a 1991 survey show that the average annual earnings of teachers were one-fifth the average annual earnings of physicians, one-third that of lawyers, and were just over half of the earnings of college and university professors.[45] Using these salary data, it is possible to make a crude calculation of equivalent levels of altruistic, out-of-pocket spending for these other occupations. The lower $408 figure reported in the NEA survey represented about 1.5 percent of the average public school teacher's salary that year. Roughly equivalent expenditures for the purchase of materials necessary to serve their clients would come to (in 1991 dollars) about $550 per year for professors, about $820 per year for lawyers, and about $1,400 per year for doctors.

What are the implications of a workplace ethos of individual responsibility and accountability for the focus of this chapter—for understanding how control operates in schools? From the outside, the individualistic ethos may appear to involve a substantial degree of autonomy and discretion on the part of teachers. Although the structure of some schools may isolate and overextend them, teachers do appear to have a wide latitude of choice in how to respond to and cope with the manner in which their work is organized. This interpretation is in keeping with the conventional zone view of the distribution of control in schools. From this perspective, such a workplace ethos could be seen as evidence that behind the "closed door" classrooms are in reality small universes of control, with the teacher solely in command and free to largely do as they please.[46]

Theory from the sociology of organizations, occupations, and work offers an alternative interpretation. From such a perspective, what may appear from the outside to be teacher autonomy and organizational decentralization is actually the opposite—a form of centralized organizational control.

The field of labor process theory, in particular, has shed much light on how organizational control can exist in organizational settings where the work and technology are highly variable, nonroutine, and complex and thus not amenable to rigid, direct, or bureaucratic mechanisms of control and coordination.[47] In these types of settings, managers may find it advantageous to provide employees with substantial control over the pace and details of their workday and, most important, more *responsibility* for successfully completing tasks on time and to specification. In some ways this mode of organizing production is less preferable, from the viewpoint of employees, than highly rule-bound, bureaucratic, and rigid models of work organization. The latter constrain, but they also make the employees' responsibilities clear. But in other ways employees find a less rigid mode of organizing the work is preferable to rigid models of work organization. Employees are often eager to gain more control over their work and often will jump at even a facsimile of empowerment. The result is often prodigious effort on the part of employees to "make out," that is, to meet the goals set for them. By debureaucratizing a work setting traditionally subject to rigid control systems, management can "manufacture consent"—motivate workers to strive to meet organizational goals with less overt regulation and supervision. This mode of control is highly advantageous from the viewpoint of management, because in the course of generating employee commitment, it divests responsibility and diverts vertical conflict (between management and employees) into horizontal conflict (competition among employees), and it does so without sacrificing organizational performance.

The important point from the perspective of labor process theory is that the substitution of greater responsibility and greater latitude for a system of rigid rules and routinized procedures is not necessarily a form of decentralization and employee empowerment, but can be the opposite—an alternative and highly effective, yet highly invisible, form of centralized organizational control. From this perspective, the key distinction is between the delegation of responsibility and the delegation of power. A nonbureaucratic model of organization may grant a great degree of latitude to employees, but this should not be confused with power. Although these kinds of workplaces are less subject to supervision and rules, employees typically do not have more control over key decisions surrounding their work and tasks. Rather, managers have provided employees with "greater quantitative choice, but within ever narrower limits." Ironically, in struggling to successfully balance their mix of demands and constraints, employees can end up easily co-opted—by working hard to make things work in an organization that may have denied them the power, autonomy, and resources to accomplish their tasks adequately in the first place.[48]

The Teacher in the Middle

What, then, can we conclude about the implications for organizational control from this discussion of the structure of schools and the workplace culture of teachers? I have made use of comparisons with factory workers and traditional professionals. In the first case, school workplaces are organized in some ways like industrial factories, and the job of teaching is organized in some ways like that of a disempowered factory worker. But this comparison should not be taken too far. Beyond the obvious differences between these kinds of work and workplaces, there are some less obvious limits to the usefulness of this analogy in understanding organizational control in schools.

In important ways, the roles of teachers and factory workers are fundamentally different. The role of teachers lies in between that of management and the workers. If we think of students as, in some sense, the "workers," then the role of teachers is more analogous to that of supervisors—those directly responsible for the workers below them—rather than that of the baseline workers themselves.

In the same way, there are limits to the usefulness of comparing traditional professionals with teachers to understand organizational control in schools. The role of teachers is distinctly different from that of many professionals. Lawyers, accountants, physicians, engineers, dentists, and psychotherapists all acquire a particular kind of training and licensure to provide a service to clients for remuneration. The client-professional relationship is a market relationship, and the responsibility of the professional to the client is sharply delimited. For example, the role of physicians is to provide diagnosis, prognosis, and prescription to patients for a fee. If patients do not comply with their physician's prescription, the doctor is, usually, not held responsible for the consequences. The boundaries of professional responsibility are, of course, an arena of debate and the subject of both legislation and litigation. However, client compliance is usually assumed to be primarily the responsibility of the client. For another example, the instructional role of professors is, primarily, to present material and evaluate whether students have adequately learned it. If college students do not complete their assignments or fail to come to class, the professor is, usually, not held responsible for the consequences. Less than adequate performance on the part of a student is usually assumed to be the responsibility of the student, not the professor. (Again, this locus of responsibility is the subject of much contention, even litigation; it varies among professors and among colleges and universities.) The contrast with the role of schoolteachers is illuminating. Students are in some ways clients, and their relationship to teachers is in some ways like that of client to professional. But the relationship between student and teacher is not simply a market transaction. Teachers have wide responsibility for the behavior, motivation, attitudes, and performance of their students. Even when elementary or secondary school students do not complete assignments, fail to attend, or disrupt class, teachers may find themselves held responsible for the consequences. Moreover, as we have seen, the authority granted teachers in their relationship with students is not the same as the time-honored autonomy of traditional professionals. The professional is an expert who has a great deal of say over what is best for the client. The teacher is an agent who may be given leeway in carrying out tasks designed by others.

The role of teachers lies in between those of administrators and students and in between those of parents and their children. They do not decide on objectives and tasks, nor do they carry them out; they are responsible for seeing that others do so. Teachers are a good example of the man (or woman) in the middle.

Most work roles and occupations, except of course those at the very top and very bottom, involve being in between two or more groups and both receiving and giving orders. It is when those in the middle are subject to unreasonable, competing, or contradictory demands or are not provided with the necessary power and resources to get their job done adequately that problems arise. In the extreme case, those caught between impossible demands and limited resources illustrate a classic management problem—holding employees accountable for things they do not control. This situation brings to the surface in a compelling way the tension between control and consent and between responsibility and power, and as a result it has long been of interest to analysts of work and organizations.[49]

One of the classic studies that captures the character and tensions of the in-between role was written by William Foote Whyte and Burleigh Gardner. Their research on "men in the middle" is especially useful to illuminate the role of teachers and its implications for organizational control.[50] They focused on industrial settings and the crucial but difficult role of plant foremen caught between the contradictory demands and needs of their superordinates—plant management—and their subordinates—plant workers. Understanding the role and job of foremen, they argued, requires looking both ways, up and down.

On the one hand, foremen are responsible to top management. Management makes commitments to clients, and the foremen are expected to see that those commitments are efficiently met. On the other hand, foremen are responsible for, and—it should be stressed—dependent on, reliable motivation and performance from their subordinates, those who actually do the work.

Those in top management often think and speak of foremen as being part of management and as being the component of management that deals directly with workers and production. But it is more accurate to think of foremen as the agents of management—those who do not participate in, but carry out, the decisions made by management. Indeed, from the viewpoint of management, ideal foremen are not decision makers but "good soldiers" who accept and implement orders without question or criticism.

If those who make decisions do not know much about the process of production and do not communicate with those who do, such as foremen, the demands placed on the foremen may become impractical or may contradict other equally important sets of demands. The foremen's role may suddenly expand to involve responsibility for figuring out how to "make ends meet" and making sure production proceeds as expected. To outsiders this role may appear highly autonomous. But in reality it is often a situation in which the foremen are not given adequate resources and control to get a job done adequately. For example, an essential resource for successful foremen is substantial control over the hiring and firing of those whose performance they are responsible for. Foremen deprived of the right to hire and fire are deprived of a major source of leverage with their subordinates. In this situation, foremen are no longer simply dependent on their superordinates but can become highly dependent on the support, cooperation, and resources of their superordinates *and* their subordinates. They become "bumping posts" beholden to, and battered from, two sides. The imbalance between demands and resources can become especially untenable when the demands placed on foremen increase, such as during economic downturns, or when the resources and control given to foremen decrease, because of, say, demands for increased worker rights.

The similarities between the role of foremen and that of teachers are striking. Teachers are also caught between conflicting demands and are also analogous to men (or women) in the middle. Teachers are the frontline supervisors in schools and are in charge of those who actually do the work of learning—students. As a result, both school administrators and the public often think or speak of teachers as being part of those who are in charge of schools. But it is more accurate to think of teachers as the agents of those in charge. Teachers do not have substantial input into decision making and are not an actual part of school management, but neither are they "hired hands" told simply what to do, without a stake in the outcome. Like foremen, teachers are responsible for and dependent on reliable motivation and performance from their subordinates, students. If students do not behave or apply themselves according to expectations, the students may suffer failure, but it may be the teachers who are blamed.

As with foremen, teachers' in-between role can become especially untenable when unreasonable demands are placed on them or insufficient resources are provided to them. One example of insufficient resources, noted earlier, would be when teachers have no input into the removal of students from classrooms. This is analogous to the ability of foremen to hire and fire—a power crucial to foremen for ensuring the cooperation and discipline of workers. Without this basic lever, foremen can be ill prepared to deal with situations in which an employee does not turn in work on time, sleeps on the job, or is so disruptive that other employees have difficulty doing their own work. The same can be said of teachers dealing with problem students.

The case of out-of-field teaching also provides a good illustration of the tension between responsibilities and resources. In this situation, although teachers may lack a basic resource—knowledge of the subject—this may not diminish their degree of responsibility. Regardless of whether they have expertise in the content or methods of teaching a subject, teachers are nevertheless responsible for seeing that the material is taught.

Teaching a subject well that one does not know well can be very challenging. The SASS data indicate that once teachers are misassigned, they are left to their own devices. Help or support, in the form of effective mentoring, free retraining, or reductions in workload are only infrequently offered by schools or districts. In the absence of such assistance, the misassigned teacher is delegated a great deal of "autonomy" to "figure it out," to "make out" as best she can. As a result, the teacher may become uncomfortably dependent on the cooperation, motivation, and even patience, of her students. Moreover, the data show that beginning teachers are more likely to be misassigned than veteran teachers. Thus, on top of learning how to survive in a new job, beginners often have the added burden of teaching subjects they do not know. There is an irony here: treating teaching as low-skill work creates a situation requiring resourcefulness, initiative, thought, judgment; in short, it turns teaching into highly skilled work. A further irony is that teachers who do work hard to succeed in this role—being responsible for seeing that their students learn a subject that they themselves do not know well—are working overtime to make things work in an organizational setting that may have denied them the power and resources to adequately accomplish their tasks in the first place.

Inventiveness, resourcefulness—a workplace culture of individual accountability—form only one possible set of responses to the teacher's in-between role and the imbalance between responsibility and power. There are other possible outcomes. It is easy to imagine that the pressure to make out could push teachers a different way—toward withdrawal or disengagement rather than commitment and engagement. The teaching job may thrust a great deal of responsibility on teachers, but of course some may not accept it. Unreasonably high demands can backfire, bringing the very thing not wanted—low-quality teaching. Moreover, being caught between unlimited demands and limited resources can foster competition and conflict between teachers and distrust between teachers and administrators. Deskilling could become a self-fulfilling prophecy: treating teachers as low-skill laborers may cut costs and reduce the disruption of teacher turnover by easing replacement, but it could also increase costs and increase disruption by fostering turnover. Thus far we have primarily focused on the distribution of power in schools and the ways in which organizational control operates in schools. The next chapter takes a closer look at outcomes—what are the consequences of the amount of control and power wielded by teachers? What impact does centralization or decentralization have on life inside schools?

6

THE EFFECTS OF TEACHER CONTROL

WHAT DIFFERENCE DOES the amount of control exercised by teachers make in how well schools function? Does the degree of organizational centralization or decentralization in a school affect its performance? Does faculty decision-making influence have a positive or negative impact on life within schools?

Those who study work and organizations have long recognized the important effects that organizational centralization and decentralization and employee input have on the performance of organizations. Educational researchers and policymakers have also long recognized the importance of control in school systems, but, as we have seen, it is a subject marked by substantial disagreement and confusion. The two dominant perspectives on control in schools—the disorganization and disempowerment viewpoints—disagree not only over the degree of organizational centralization and decentralization in schools but also over its consequences for how well schools function.

Although researchers in the disorganization tradition have at times been ambivalent about the advantages and disadvantages of "loose structuring" in schools, this is rarely the case with their counter-parts in the realm of policy and reform. To many educational re-formers, policymakers, and members of the public, inadequate con-trol and accountability are at the root of poor performance on the part of teachers, students, and schools. From this viewpoint, too lit-tle organizational control is tied to a lack of purpose, standards, and coherence—and ultimately to school inefficiency and ineffec-tiveness. Schools with too little accountability are unable to weed out uncommitted, incompetent, or uncaring teachers and unable to reward caring, engaged, committed teachers. Such schools foster alienation and apathy or, alternatively, misbehavior and disruption on the part of students, and generate frustration on the part of the administrators. Accordingly, advocates of this view argue that the solution to problems in education lies in instituting greater account-ability, higher standards, top-down controls, and a "tightening of the ship."

The disempowerment viewpoint argues precisely the opposite—that a surplus of top-down control and accountability in schools are at the root of poor performance on the part of teachers, students, and schools. In this view, too much organizational control, standard-ization, and accountability result in factorylike, overly bureaucratized school systems and, ultimately, school inefficiency and ineffective-ness. Such schools deny teachers the autonomy and authority, and thus the flexibility, necessary for caring, engaged, efficacious, com-mitted teaching. The inevitable result is that such schools deprofes-sionalize and demotivate teachers; foster alienation and apathy or, al-ternatively, misbehavior and disruption on the part of students; and generate frustration on the part of administrators. Accordingly, sup-porters of this view advocate forms of decentralization and teacher professionalization that are designed to increase the control teachers wield over the operation of schools.[1]

Organizational Climate and Performance

Usually when researchers evaluate the quality of schools they examine how well the school's students fare on academic achievement tests. Just as analysts often assume that academic instruction is the primary purpose of schools, many also assume that student academic achievement, as measured on pencil-and-paper, mass-produced, standardized tests, is the best indicator of school quality and the best means to evaluate the effects of school characteristics on educational performance.

This economic-production perspective is certainly a reasonable approach to evaluating school performance, but its shortcoming, I have argued, is that it overlooks some of the most important educational activities transpiring within classrooms and across schools. From a societal perspective, the main purpose of schooling is not simply to impart academic skills and knowledge to children. From a societal perspective, one of the main purposes of schooling is to socialize the next generation. The chief insight underlying this viewpoint is that what students learn in schools has as much to do with the character of relations among and between students and teachers—what is sometimes called the climate of schools—as it does with the content of the academic curriculum.[2]

To be sure, educational researchers have long acknowledged and studied the importance of any number of aspects of the social climate of schools, such as the degree of cohesion and community, student behavioral problems, and staff professional collegiality in schools. But a positive climate in schools is usually assumed to be a prerequisite to a more fundamental outcome—the "real bottom line"—student academic achievement. My point is not that academic instruction and student test scores are unimportant; they are clearly important. Nor I am arguing that they are not integrally related to the social climate in schools. My point is that the academic goals and outcomes of schools and the social goals and outcomes of schools are not the same thing. Positive social relations in schools can themselves be viewed as an important indicator of successful educational performance. Indeed, as numerous polls have shown, from the public's viewpoint and also from the perspective of teachers and administrators, the successful school is not simply a school with high achievement scores but is also a school with positive social relations and a positive climate.[3] Indeed, in recent years increased concern over school violence has made a safe and harmonious environment in schools even more paramount in the eyes of the public. From this viewpoint the "bad" school is characterized by conflict, distrust, and turmoil among students, teachers, and administrators. In contrast, the "good" school is characterized by well-behaved students; a collegial, committed staff; and a general sense of cooperation, communication, and community.

The usefulness of organizational climate as an indicator of organizational performance is not unique to schools. Organization theorists have long held that organizational climate is intimately connected to organizational productivity, especially for those occupations, like teaching, in which interaction among participants itself makes up the "technology" and "product" of the organization.[4] As discussed earlier, in these kinds of settings the "production process" involves individuals working not with raw materials or objects but with other individuals. Because the "technology" often comprises sets of relationships among individuals, such organizations are highly dependent on the mutual cooperation of key groups, such as clients, employees, and management. As a result, organizational analysts have long argued that in such cases, how well the organization's members, units, and levels work together is a critical aspect of organizational performance and is profoundly shaped by organizational structure.

In this view, a positive, cohesive, cooperative climate is not simply a correlate of, or a means to, enhanced productivity but is important in its own right. Indeed, in some fundamental sense, when behavior and interaction are key "products," a cohesive, cooperative organizational climate is a form of high productivity.

The importance of employee commitment and organizational climate has led analysts of work and organizations to pay a great deal of attention to the phenomenon of employee turnover. The rate at which employees leave workplaces and organizations has been the subject of an immense number of studies, because of its significance for and link to both the climate and performance of organizations.[5] On the one hand, the general consensus among researchers is that a low level of employee turnover is normal and efficacious in a cohesive and well-managed organization. Too little turnover can lead to stagnancy in organizations, and effective organizations usually both promote and benefit from a limited degree of turnover by eliminating low-quality performers and bringing in "new blood" to facilitate innovation. On the other hand, most analysts also concur that high levels of employee turnover are both a cause and an effect of a negative climate and low performance, especially in organizations that are dependent on cohesion among clients, employees, and management.

Teacher Control and School Climate

In my research I decided to look at climate as a means to evaluate centralization and decentralization in schools. I asked what effect the control exercised by teachers in schools has on the social climate in schools. Do schools in which teachers hold more control over school activities have more or less positive climates? I focused, in particular, on four indicators related to the social climate of schools: the degree of cohesion or conflict between staff and students, among teachers, and between teachers and administrators, and the amount of teacher turnover.

To evaluate the consequences of the distribution of power in schools, I undertook a series of statistical analyses with the SASS data, focusing on the relationship between the amount of control held by teachers and these aspects of the social climate in schools. One advantage of using a large-scale and comprehensive data source such as SASS for this kind of analysis is that it allowed me to ask progressively more refined questions concerning the extent to which, and the conditions under which, control is or is not linked with the climate in schools. For example, if teacher control is related to school climate, does the effect depend on the type of issue or activity that is controlled by teachers? Is control of some activities more consequential than control over others? In particular, do the effects of teacher control over instructional issues differ from the effects of teacher control over social issues? Does the effect of teacher control on school climate depend on the zone or level at which the teacher control is wielded? More specifically, do the effects of the control exercised by individual teachers in their classrooms differ from the effects of the control exercised by teachers over schoolwide policies? Also, does the effect of teacher control on school climate depend on the groups examined? More specifically, does teacher control differently affect the relationships between students and staff, among teachers, between teachers and principals, or between teachers and schools?

To answer these questions, I used the same measures of teacher control of decision making presented in Chapter 3, distinguishing between the two main types of educational issues (instructional and social), and also between teacher control within classrooms and teacher control schoolwide. From other items in the SASS survey, I also developed three measures of the character of the school climate and of the relations among teachers, students, and principals.

The first measure—conflict between staff and students—focused on the degree to which students are alienated from, do not cooperate with, or actively disrupt the manner in which schools are operated. The second—conflict among teachers—focused on the degree of cooperation and collegiality among teachers. It characterized faculties on a scale from those that function as cohesive teams to those that act as fragmented collections of individuals. The third—conflict between teachers and principals—characterized the faculty-principal relationship along a scale from those exhibiting communication, cooperation, and support to those exhibiting distrust and friction. Finally, I developed a measure of teacher turnover from NCES's Teacher Followup Survey (TFS), a supplementary questionnaire given to all those in the teacher sample who left their teaching job in the year subsequent to the original SASS survey.

Some turnover of teachers is, of course, not directly related to either the commitment of teachers or the character or climate of schools. Teachers, like other types of employees, move from or leave their jobs for a wide variety of reasons.[6] In order to focus on those kinds of departures that were more likely to be related to the character and climate of schools, I excluded from my analysis teachers who departed from their job because of retirement, a layoff, a school closing, or because they were fired. As in organizational studies of employee turnover, the assumption underlying my analysis was that high rates of teacher turnover are of concern not only because they may be an indication of underlying problems in how well a school functions, but also because they can be disruptive in and of themselves, and thus affect the climate in the school.

Public concern over school climate is not misplaced. Like many other studies, the SASS data show that significant numbers of secondary schools have high levels of conflict between staff and students, have high levels of conflict among teachers, and have a high degree of conflict between teachers and principals.[7] In addition, the rate of turnover in teaching appears to be higher than in many other occupations. One of the best known sources of national data on rates of employee turnover, the Bureau of National Affairs, has shown that nationwide levels of employee turnover were quite stable during the 1990s, averaging 11.9 percent per year. The data on nationwide employee turnover provide an overall benchmark, and a comparison with the TFS data suggests that teaching has a relatively high annual total turnover rate: 14.5 percent in 1988–89, 13.2 percent in 1991–92, 14.3 percent in 1994–95, and 15.7 percent in 2000–01.

In other analyses I have found that these relatively high rates of teacher turnover are a dominant factor behind the perennially high demand for new teachers and the chronic difficulties schools encounter in adequately staffing classrooms with qualified teachers. Contrary to conventional wisdom, these staffing problems are not primarily the result of teacher shortages in the sense of an insufficient supply of qualified teachers. Rather, the data indicate that these problems are primarily caused by excess demand resulting from a "revolving door"—the fact that large numbers of teachers depart their jobs well before retirement. Hence, the data suggest a second reason to focus on teacher turnover as an outcome related to school performance. Besides having negative effects on school cohesion, high turnover can also undermine the ability of schools to staff their classrooms with qualified teachers, ultimately undermining school performance.[8]

Not surprisingly, however, while overall levels of school conflict and teacher turnover are high, the SASS/TFS data also show that there are large differences among schools in these conditions and outcomes. This raises a key question: are school-to-school differences in the four outcomes measured (conflict between staff and students, conflict among teachers, conflict between teachers and principals, and teacher turnover) related to the amount of control held by teachers in schools?

There are, of course, numerous factors that could account for school-to-school differences in school climate and also for any apparent connection between teacher control and school climate. It is reasonable to expect that particular kinds of schools have more conflict and turnover than others, regardless of how centralized or decentralized they are. Alternatively, any relationships between teacher control, school climate, and teacher turnover could be spurious, that is, the result of other, more fundamental factors related to both. For instance, the size of a school might account for both its degree of centralization and its climate.

To determine whether there is a relationship between teacher control and the social climate in schools, it is necessary to try to control for, or hold constant, other factors that may be strongly related to school climate and cohesion. Hence, I undertook a series of advanced analyses using the SASS/TFS data to investigate whether the measures of teacher control were statistically associated with school conflict and teacher turnover, while controlling for the effects of a series of teacher characteristics and school characteristics such as school size; student poverty levels; whether a school is in an urban, rural, or suburban setting; and whether it is private or public.

Detailed information on the data used, measures created, the analytic methods employed, and the results I obtained are contained in the Appendix. I will summarize my findings in the following sections of this chapter.

Does Teacher Control Affect Student Behavior?

According to my analysis, the degree of student discipline problems and conflict between students and staff in schools are clearly related to the characteristics of the students and schools. Other factors being equal, faculty report more conflict with students in public than in private schools, in larger than in smaller schools, in urban schools, in schools with more students living at the poverty level, in schools with more minority students, and in secondary schools. These findings are consistent with decades of research showing that poverty and race/ethnicity are among the key sources of tension and large, urban, public secondary schools are among the key sites of conflict.[9]

Beyond these expected findings, the question of particular interest was: Is the amount of control held by teachers also related to student misbehavior, after controlling for the effects of the type of teachers and the type of school?

The results showed that the control held by teachers does indeed have an independent association with student misbehavior. The data clearly showed that there were fewer student behavioral problems in schools where teachers had more control. But I also found that the strength of this relationship very much depends on the type of activities teachers control. The impact of teacher control over instructional issues was overshadowed by the impact of teacher control over social issues, such as disciplinary policy, for decreasing student misbehavior. These differences are illustrated in Figure 6.1. The two graphs display the differences in school conflict associated with differences in the amount of teacher control in schools, after controlling for the background characteristics of teachers and schools. The bottom graph shows that there is almost no difference in staff-student conflict between schools with a high level of teacher control over instructional issues and schools with a low level of teacher control over instructional issues. In contrast, as illustrated in the top graph, schools with a low level of teacher control over social issues had far more student-staff conflict than did schools with a high level of teacher control over social issues.[10] Indeed, I found teacher control

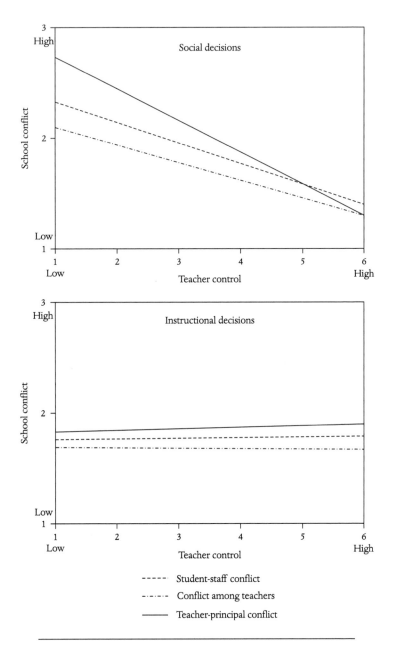

Figure 6.1 Effects of teacher control on school conflict: level of conflict in schools by amount of teacher influence over social and instructional decisions, after controlling for teacher and school characteristics (Source: Schools and Staffing Survey)

over social decisions had a stronger effect on student conflict than *any* of the other variables, including the poverty level of the student population, the size of the school, and whether a school is public or private, urban or suburban.

I also found a similar pattern whether the influence wielded by teachers involved classroom issues or schoolwide issues. Thus the zone in which teachers wield control is less significant than the type of issue teachers control. The effects of teacher classroom control were not very different from the effects of teacher schoolwide control. What was significant was teacher control over social issues, both within classrooms and schoolwide.

Does Teacher Control Affect Relations among Teachers and with Principals?

One interpretation of the above findings on student conflict might be that if teachers are given more leeway to discipline students in their classrooms and schools, students will behave better, or at least teachers will perceive this to be so. However, my analysis of the effects of teacher control on the other aspects of climate suggests that this would be an overly narrow interpretation.

What impact does teacher control over classroom and schoolwide issues have on the degree of solidarity, collegiality, and cooperation among the teachers themselves? Do empowered faculties work better together, or are they more often divided by competition and distrust? Moreover, does the influence and control wielded by teachers have an effect on their relations with administrators? On the one hand, empowered faculties might conceivably challenge, resist, or ignore the decisions of school principals more often than those less empowered, leading to a strained relationship and increased conflict between faculty and administrators.[11] On the other hand, if teachers have an opportunity to influence school decision making, it might result in far more communication with and support from administrators, or at least the perception of it by teachers.

I found that levels of staff conflict, not surprisingly, varied among different types of schools regardless of their degree of teacher control. Other things being equal, teachers reported less collegiality and less cooperation with fellow teachers in public than in private schools, in large than in small schools, and in secondary than in elementary schools, and in high-minority schools. Similarly, teachers reported more conflict with their principals in public schools, in secondary schools, and in high-minority schools.

However, after controlling for these and other teacher and school characteristics, the amount of influence held by teachers also had a substantial connection to staff cohesion and conflict. Schools that delegated more control to teachers had fewer problems among teachers and less conflict between teachers and administrators. Again, however, the strength of this impact depended on which activities and issues were controlled by teachers. There was little difference in cohesion and cooperation among the teachers themselves, and also between the teachers and the principals, in schools where teachers had more say over matters of academic instruction in their classrooms and more influence over the school curriculum versus schools where teachers had little say over instructional issues. But the impact of teachers' controlling social issues, such as disciplinary and tracking decisions, greatly overshadowed that of instructional control, as shown in Figure 6.1. Schools with a high level of teacher control over social issues had far less teacher-to-teacher conflict and faculty-principal conflict than did schools with a low level of teacher control over social issues. Indeed, as before, teacher control over schoolwide discipline and tracking policies had a stronger effect on teacher-to-teacher and faculty-principal conflict than any of the other variables I examined, including the poverty level of the student population, the size of the school, and whether a school was public or private, urban or suburban.

I also undertook a series of background statistical analyses (not displayed here) to see whether teacher control was connected to teachers' sense of commitment, efficacy, job satisfaction, and engagement—qualities considered so important in work with youth. For measures of these qualities I used a number of questions from the SASS survey that asked teachers whether, for example, they felt it was a waste of time to try to do their best as a teacher; if they could go back to college days and start over again, would they become a teacher or not; and whether they felt teacher absenteeism was a problem at their school. The results were very similar to those for school conflict. The control held by teachers in schools was strongly related to these measures of faculty alienation and engagement, after controlling for the characteristics of the teachers and their schools. And, again, the effects of control over social issues completely overshadowed those of control over instructional issues. In schools where the faculty had a high level of control over social issues, teachers on average were far more positive in their answers to these kinds of questions.

Does Teacher Control Affect Turnover?

Given the impact of teacher control on the climate and the degree of conflict in schools, it seems reasonable to expect that teacher control also would have an impact on whether teachers decided to stay with, or depart from, their teaching jobs. The data showed that this was indeed the case.

As before, in my analysis I controlled for the effects of school setting, type of school, and type of teachers on the likelihood of teacher turnover. Beginning teachers were far more likely to depart than experienced teachers, and I also found that school sector and school size, in particular, stood out as key variables. In private schools and in smaller schools, teachers departed at higher rates than in public schools and larger schools. For example, private school teachers were about twice as likely to depart than were public school teachers. Teachers in schools with enrollments of 1,500 students were about 1.4 times more likely to stay with their school than those in schools of 500 students. These are interesting and somewhat surprising findings, because the same data reveal these kinds of schools—small and private—to have less conflict among students, teachers, and principals. The fact that some of the very schools that are more likely to have a positive climate, also have higher teacher turnover is an intriguing finding that is well worth pursuing. However, I will not elaborate on these findings here, because to do so would digress from my primary purpose. Elsewhere I have undertaken the detailed analyses necessary to explore why particular kinds of schools have higher turnover.[12]

The question of particular interest here is: Does the amount of influence and control held by teachers affect the amount of teacher turnover or retention, after controlling for the effects of other factors?

I found that in schools where teachers reported higher levels of control, turnover rates were distinctly lower. But once again, the strength of this impact depended on the activities and issues controlled by teachers. Control over instructional issues made some difference—that is, in schools where teachers had more say over matters of academic instruction in their classrooms and more influence over the school curriculum, teachers were slightly less likely to depart. But the impact of teacher control over social issues, such as disciplin-

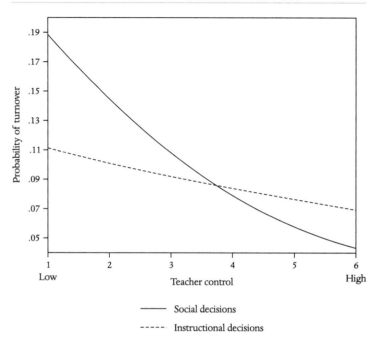

Figure 6.2 Effects of teacher control on teacher turnover: level of teacher turnover by amount of teacher influence over social and instructional decisions, after controlling for school and teacher characteristics (Source: Teacher Followup Survey)

ary and tracking decisions, was far greater than that of instructional control. As illustrated in Figure 6.2, about 1 in 9 teachers (probability of .11) in schools with a low level of teacher control over instructional issues were likely to leave, while slightly fewer—about 1 in 14 (probability of .07)—were likely to leave their jobs in schools with a high level of teacher control over instructional issues. In contrast, the turnover rate was higher—almost 1 in 5 teachers (probability of

.19)—in schools with a low level of teacher control over social issues, while far fewer teachers—only about 1 in 25 (probability of .04)—were likely to depart from schools with a high level of teacher control over social issues.[13] Again, I found the pattern to be similar whether the influence wielded by teachers involved classroom issues or schoolwide issues. The zone in which teachers wielded control was less significant for teacher turnover than the type of issue teachers controlled. What was significant was control over social issues, both within classrooms and schoolwide.

Hence, although much research assumes classroom academic instruction to be the crucial and primary educational activity in schools, and although faculty generally report having greater control (as shown in Chapter 3) over instructional issues (such as the selection of course textbooks, topics, materials, and teaching techniques), teacher control over these kinds of decisions does not have a great impact on school climate and teacher turnover. A lack of teacher control over those decisions that are more fundamentally social—where the educational process involves the selection, maintenance, and transmission of behaviors and norms—shows the strongest association with conflict and turnover in schools. Indeed, teacher control over instructional activities appears to count for little if teachers do not also have some control over socialization and student sorting activities. This pattern holds up across both zones, the classroom zone and the schoolwide zone, and also across all four outcomes I examined—conflict with students, among faculty, and between faculty and principals, and teacher turnover. This finding underlines the value of carefully distinguishing among different educational activities within schools and calls into question the traditional emphasis on classroom academic instruction as the crucial and primary activity in teachers' work. In sum, from the public's viewpoint, the "good" school is characterized by well-behaved students, a collegial, committed teaching staff, and an engaged administration. The data show that the good school also provides high levels of teacher control, especially over social issues.

However, it must be noted that all four sets of analysis accounted for only a portion of school-to-school differences in climate and turnover. This was to be expected. My objective was not to provide a comprehensive explanation of school conflict or teacher turnover. My analysis could include only a selection of the many factors that might conceivably affect the degree of conflict, cooperation, solidarity, engagement, and community in schools. I set out to examine the relative effects of different types of teacher control on school conflict and teacher turnover, while holding constant some of the most important background characteristics of teachers, schools, and students, and I found that teacher control does indeed have an independent effect.

It is important to understand that although the data show that schools with empowered teachers have less conflict, they do not imply that schools with empowered principals will have more conflict. It is often assumed that the distribution of control is a zero-sum issue: if teachers have more control in a school, principals will have less control, and vice versa. Analysts of organizational control have long held that this is not necessarily the case. Some have argued that control in organizations can be a win-win issue; that is, different groups can be simultaneously empowered.[14] Indeed, the data suggest this may be the case in schools. In background analyses (see Chapter 3) of the statistical relationship between the control of teachers and that of principals, I found, depending on the issue, a moderate to strong positive correlation.[15] In other words, schools with higher principal control also had higher teacher control, and vice versa.

In a series of other analyses I also examined the effects on school conflict of the control wielded by school principals and school boards. My objective was to explore whether the control held by principals and boards also had a positive impact on the climate of schools and, if so, whether the impact differed according to the type of issue controlled (social or instructional). I found that increases in both principal control and school board control did appear to be related to decreases in school conflict and, moreover, that control over social issues had more impact than control over instructional issues. But I also found that these effects were weak and often not statistically significant. These results suggest that while school boards and school principals, in particular, have substantial control more often than do teachers, their control is less important for creating a positive climate in schools.[16] However, shortcomings in the data limited my ability to examine conclusively the effects of principal control or board control on school climate, and I will not pursue them here.

The Effects of Teacher Control: An Organizational Explanation

While the data indicate that the amount of influence teachers have is related to the degree of conflict with students, among teachers, and between teachers and administrators, and also to whether teachers decide to stay with their schools, they do not provide an explanation for these relationships. Simply showing a statistical association between variables drawn from large-scale survey data does not tell us how or why something happens.

It is possible, however, to provide an explanation for these findings by again turning to research on control in workplaces and organizations. From the perspective of organization theory, some of the most important influences on the climate and performance of organizations are the degree of centralization or decentralization and the degree of employee input into decision making. Especially insightful and illuminating is Rosabeth Kanter's seminal research on the importance of control and power to the relations between subordinates and superordinates in the corporate world.[17]

Kanter's research centered around the problems encountered by women in supervisory positions in large organizations. One of the problems she examined was the pervasive tendency of employees, of either sex, to report less conflict and fewer problems in their relationships with male supervisors than with female supervisors. Kanter offered an organizational reinterpretation of this long-observed problem. The force of her research was to show that this tension was not due to any intrinsic characteristics of female managers, as commonly depicted in workplace stereotypes. The source of female supervisors' conflicts with their subordinates had to do with the supervisors' levels of control, influence, and power in the organization. She showed that female supervisors, caught between the often contradictory demands of their superordinates and their subordinates, faced the same problems as any man or woman "in the middle," as described in the classic study by Whyte and Gardner that I referred to in Chapter 5.[18]

On the one hand, supervisors, of either sex, who get support and respect from their superiors and have more influence or control over the decisions surrounding those activities for which they are responsible will usually, in turn, garner more respect and cooperation from their peers and subordinates. They also will usually feel more commitment to their job. On the other hand, those supervisors, of either sex, who have little influence or control over the decisions surrounding the activities for which they are responsible will usually command less respect and cooperation from their peers and subordinates. They also will often have less commitment to their job. Kanter argued that female supervisors, in general, often had less upward influence with their superiors and less power in the organization, and hence had less lateral influence with their peers and less downward influence with their subordinates. The attitudes and behaviors stereotypically associated with the "bureaucratic personality" and also with female managers—authoritarianism, rigid rule following, inflexibility, fear of able subordinates—are akin to intervening variables. They result from a lack of power and, in turn, further contribute to problems with subordinates, superordinates, and peers. But, notably, whether a manager is male or female, or has positive relations with her subordinates or not, is less crucial than her level of power and control over the core organizational tasks and issues for which she is responsible. That is, subordinates report better relations with less pleasant but empowered supervisors than with more pleasant but disempowered supervisors, regardless of gender. As summarized by Kanter's variation on Lord Acton's famous dictum: "Powerlessness corrupts. Absolute powerlessness corrupts absolutely."

Although Kanter was specifically interested in explaining gender discrimination in the corporate world, her organizational explanation of the connection between power and conflicts among lower-, middle-, and higher-level organization members can be borrowed and extended profitably to illuminate the conflicts among students, teachers, and principals in schools. Gender is also an issue in school workplaces, and the fact that precollegiate teaching is a predominantly female occupation may well be a factor behind the aggregate powerlessness of teachers in relation to predominantly male school administrators. But the analysis showed, whether a teacher is male or female is less crucial than the teacher's level of power and control. In this sense the parallels between the organizational problems endemic to supervisors and those of teachers are striking. Teachers are also caught between the contradictory demands and needs of their superordinates—principals—and their subordinates—students. Teachers are responsible for the motivation and performance of students, but are also responsible for implementing policies set by the school administration. At the crux of the role—and of the success— of teachers as the man or woman in the middle is the amount of control and power they have over the core organizational tasks and issues for which they are responsible. If teachers have sufficient say over the decisions surrounding those activities for which they are responsible, they will be more able to exert sufficient influence to see that the job is done properly and, in turn, derive respect upward from administrators, laterally from colleagues, and downward from students. If, however, teachers' power and control over school policies are not sufficient to accomplish the tasks for which they are responsible, they will meet neither the administrators' nor the students' needs, and will sour their relationships with both groups. The teacher who has little control and power is the teacher who is less able to get things done and thus is the teacher with less credibility. Students can more easily ignore such a teacher—indeed, a lack of influence and credibility itself invites challenge. Principals can more easily neglect them. Peers may be more likely to shun them. In such cases, teachers may feel they have little choice but to turn to manipulative or authoritarian methods (that is, to adopt the "bureaucratic personality") to get the job done, which may simply exacerbate tensions with students and fellow staff. This, in turn, would likely lead such teachers to feel less commitment to their teaching job or to the teaching career.

From this perspective, conflict between teachers and their students can be seen as a specific instance of a more general phenomenon important in organizations of all kinds: if employees' levels of control are not commensurate with their responsibilities and needs, it can have a negative effect on the relations among those in the workplace and, ultimately, on the performance of the organization.

Why Is Control over Social Issues So Important?

Having control in the workplace promotes employee effectiveness and respect. But why is control over school social issues, in particular, so important to teachers and their relations with students, peers, and principals? Theory from the study of organizations and work can also provide an explanation for this finding. As discussed in earlier chapters, research in this tradition has shown that the effect of the distribution of control and power in workplaces very much depends on the types of activities and issues being controlled.[19] Organizational analysts have long stressed that the power held by particular groups in organizations is a function of the extent to which they influence important activities that affect their work. The importance of decisions and issues derives from their potential impact, and power is, by definition, the control of consequential issues. Having control over less important and less consequential issues is not real power; indeed, the delegation of control over nonessential, inconsequential issues is often used as a form of co-optation and a subtle means of centralizing power. In such cases, employees are led to believe they are participants in the management of the organization, when in fact they are not.[20]

Thus, organization theory tells us that assessments of power in organizations must focus on who controls the crucial and core decisions. Sociological theories of education tell us that the core productive activities in teachers' work are of two distinct types—instructional and social. And my statistical analysis shows us that the degree to which teachers have control over social issues has a significant and overlooked impact on the climate in schools.

Finally, I'll close this chapter with the following anecdote drawn from my fieldwork to illustrate the consequences of a lack of teacher control over a key element of the social domain—school discipline policies in schools. At Urban High I witnessed a conflict that arose over a new student fashion—wearing hats in school. When this particular fad started, it did not actually violate an existing school rule, but it did effectively cross existing boundaries for student attire at Urban High. Hence the school principal decided it was necessary to respond with a new rule explicitly banning the wearing of hats. The administration then arranged a faculty meeting to announce the new rule and request teachers' assistance in enforcing it. At that point, only after the rule had already been conceived, were the teachers asked for their opinions. The resulting problems of enforcement provide a concrete illustration parallel to the above-described statistical relationships between teacher control and conflict among students, teachers, and administrators.

From the beginning, the ban on hats did not have complete support from the faculty. Some strongly favored it; some were willing to go along with it; some opposed it. As a result, many teachers did not enforce the rule, especially those who opposed it. This generated conflict between members of the faculty, between teachers and students, and between teachers and school administrators.

School administrators, now in the position of having to see that all faculty enforced the new rule, resented those who did not. In addition, teachers who did enforce the rule resented those who did not share the burden of enforcement. They were well aware of the problems resulting from inconsistent enforcement. At the same time, those teachers who felt the rule was unnecessary resented being pressured to enforce it. Many teachers felt unsure whether they had sufficient authority or backing to enforce it. In addition, many teachers, whether they supported or opposed the rule, resented the negative consequences that uneven enforcement had on their credibility and their continuing relations with their students—both of which they felt to be crucial to their ability to teach. Finally, the students, sensing a lack of commitment, consensus, and power on the part of the staff, felt more able to resist or ignore the rule. In this case, a situation of top-down control led to increased conflict and discipline problems with students. Teachers' efficacy and performance were undermined by the conflict surrounding the administration's imposition of a social rule. The resulting dissension was unquestionably counterproductive for school life at Urban High.

That conflict and the teachers' lack of control were underscored in remarks by the school vice principal, who was responsible for seeing that faculty enforced the new rule for student attire:

> And we still have staff members . . . I've walked by their rooms and there are kids sitting in there with hats on. Which is totally unacceptable. I just walk in and point to the young man and ask him to remove his hat. The teacher will usually get a memo from me later. I do not embarrass the teacher in front of the students. I feel that is wrong. They are professionals. But I will talk to them later. But then there have been times when I ask the teacher, "Can I see you for a minute out in the hallway?" and I will tell the teacher, "Why is so and so sitting up there with a hat on. You know that is not the policy of the school."

Although he felt that his direct administrative intrusion into the classroom was not counter to faculty professionalism, he did acknowledge the very real frustrations of teachers in regard to their limited role as enforcers of rules they did not set:

> It is a big problem in terms of discipline that there are those faculty who do not follow through with the rules that we have established. Some claim they didn't know of them, although we have a policy and procedures manual that has them listed in there. Some don't feel that the rule is an intelligent one, or they feel that it is not worth their time and energy. I know, [having been] a teacher myself before, that there were times that I would ask myself, "Why am I putting energy into this? I need to be putting energy into what I am doing in terms of education." But I also understood that if I didn't, and everyone else didn't follow through, it wouldn't work at all. In that situation, it would be good to bring it back to the faculty and ask, "Do you want this rule or not?" But you get to . . . whether the principal feels the rule is worthwhile . . . Basically the principal is the overall force of the school, and there are certain things the principal retains.

At first glance, rules for student behavior, like the wearing of hats, may appear to be trivial or atypical. They are, however, central to the mission of schooling. At issue is who decides what the school, and ultimately societal, norms are to be. Such issues are the subject of concern, conflict, and blame. My point is that decisions surrounding such issues as appearance, clothing, and demeanor lie at the heart of teachers' work and that teacher control—or lack of control—over the creation, content, and implementation of such rules is highly consequential. To be sure, neither organization theory, the earlier statistical analysis, nor this anecdote indicate that increasing teacher control over such decisions would eliminate school conflict. But all do suggest that it would reduce school conflict and teacher turnover, and the detrimental impact they have on how well schools function.

7

CONCLUSION

FEW ISSUES IN THE REALM of education have received more attention and are more controversial than the subject of this book—who controls the work of teachers? How much say do teachers have over their work, and how much should they have? Are our schools centralized places with close, top-down control over the work of teachers or decentralized places where teachers work autonomously with little supervision or accountability? And what difference does it make for how well schools function?

Elementary and secondary schooling are universal and mandatory in the United States, and it is into the custody of teachers that children are placed for a significant portion of their lives. The quality of teachers and teaching are undoubtedly among the most important factors shaping the learning and growth of children. Indeed, the work of teachers is fundamental to society; teachers quite literally are entrusted with passing on our way of life and our culture to the next generation. Naturally, who carries out these tasks and how they do it are of great concern and interest. This expectation and concern lie behind the tendency of critics to hold schools and teachers responsible for so many societal problems—American economic competitiveness, crime, teenage pregnancy, juvenile delinquency, sexism, decline in morals, the coarsening of American society, racism, and so on.

Like managers in other kinds of organizations and industries, those who manage schools must confront basic challenges inherent to the coordination and control of large numbers of employees in the accomplishment of large-scale tasks. Among the most fundamental of these challenges is what analysts of organizations refer to as the problem of control and consent: how does one harness the skill and expertise of employees and still ensure the simultaneous need for both organizational accountability and employee commitment? If they are to succeed, organizations must coordinate, control, and hold accountable their individual members, but organizations are also dependent on the cooperation, motivation, and expertise of those same individuals.

It is the task of school managers to exert the necessary coordination and control of teachers and students to ensure that the demands and needs of the public are met. It is also the task of school managers to see that teachers be given sufficient authority and resources to successfully carry out the tasks required of them. On the one hand, too much centralized control of teachers' work may undermine good teaching and demotivate, antagonize, and ultimately drive out teachers. On the other hand, too much decentralization may result in a lack of order, coherence, and accountability. For several reasons, achieving the right balance can be especially difficult for schools.

Schooling is an unusual industry and teaching an unusual occupation. In some ways schools are production-oriented organizations that, like industrial enterprises, must efficiently deliver a product to clients or customers; in other ways schools are social institutions that, like families, are responsible for rearing youngsters. The clients with whom teachers work are unusual. They are, by definition, not mature and at times neither ready nor willing to accept services that they are nevertheless obliged to accept. Moreover, children and adolescents are not the only consumers of education; in a broad sense, the entire society is the client of these societal institutions delegated the task of preparing future citizens. A wide variety of groups, representing a diversity of interests, see themselves as both the benefactors and beneficiaries of the products of schooling. Not surprisingly, this citizenry has many demands for and desires some control over those who actually do the work—teachers.

Teachers are themselves an unusual group. Perhaps because of the importance of the work, those who enter the teaching occupation tend to be unusually likely to have a public-service orientation. They place more importance on helping others and contributing to society, and less importance on material rewards, such as income and status, than those who go into many other occupations and professions. Finally, the work of teaching is itself unusual. There is much agreement that teaching is important work, but much less agreement as to what is the best means of doing it, and much less agreement as to what the final ends of this work ought to be.

This unusual combination of qualities—important tasks; multiple and often contradictory demands; mandatory, obligatory, nonadult clients; altruistic practitioners; ambiguous processes; and, finally, uncertain outcomes—poses unusual difficulties for those who manage and work within schools. The basic organizational tension surrounding the competing needs for control and consent is especially pronounced for the case of teachers' work. In short, because of the unusual characteristics of schooling, organizational control is especially important and necessary, but for the very same reasons, teacher control is also especially important and necessary.

How much control is there over this work? How well is the balancing act managed? Historically, in the United States the control of elementary and secondary schooling developed in an unusual manner. In contrast to most European nations, public schooling in this country was originally instituted on a highly democratized, localized basis. From the early development of public education, the basic operating principal was that communities should themselves be largely responsible for, and have control over, the schooling of the children that reside in their jurisdiction. The resulting legacy is the current system of some 15,000 individual public school districts, governed by local school boards of citizens, each with legal responsibility for the administration and operation of publicly funded, universal, mandatory, elementary and secondary schooling. In addition, a wide array of private schools account for almost one-fourth of all elementary and secondary schools and about one-tenth of elementary and secondary students in the United States.

Local school districts in this country are clearly no longer the autonomous bodies they once were. Particularly since the midtwentieth century, an increasing number of governmental and nongovernmental agencies and organizations have subjected schools and their governing boards to an assortment of direct and indirect pressures and constraints. The result is that many decisions once made autonomously by districts and schools are now made in consultation with, or within frameworks mandated by, state, regional, or federal agencies. Nevertheless, the best international data available indicate that, despite these changes, schooling in the United States remains a relatively local affair in comparison with other nations.

While the U.S. education system is relatively decentralized, schools themselves are not. Most public and private secondary schools are highly centralized internally. Public and private school principals and public school governing boards usually have substantial control over many key decisions that directly affect teachers in schools, while teachers usually do not. As a result, teaching is an occupation beset by tension and imbalance between expectations and resources, responsibilities and powers. On the one hand, the work of teaching—helping prepare, train, and rear the next generation of citizens—is both important and complex. But on the other hand, those who are entrusted with the training of this next generation are not entrusted with much control over many of the key decisions in their work. Perhaps not surprisingly, this is particularly true for those crucial and controversial activities that are most fundamentally social—where the educational process involves imparting values and shaping life chances—that is, in the socialization and sorting work that teachers do with youngsters.

These findings are especially revealing because they were obtained at a time—the late 1980s to 2000—when one would expect teacher control to have been at a relatively high level. Education reform runs in cycles, and it was during this period that proposals and initiatives for teacher empowerment, school decentralization, and school-based management seemed to be at a peak. In other words, even at their highest levels, the power and influence of teachers has been very low.

In my research I spent considerable time examining by what means and mechanisms, if any, administrators exert control over the work of teachers and how they attempt to establish accountability in schools. I found that in schools, as in all bureaucratic organizations, there are numerous rules, policies, regulations, employee job descriptions, and standard operating procedures designed to direct and control the work of teachers. I also found that school administrators have many means, both formal and informal, by which they are able to supervise, discern, and evaluate teachers to determine if they are complying with the rules and policies. In addition, I found that school administrators have numerous mechanisms, both formal and informal, to discipline or sanction those teachers who have not complied with the rules or have not performed adequately. A close look at schools reveals that administrators have a great deal of control over key resources and decisions crucial to the work of teachers, and these provide a range of direct and indirect levers—sticks and carrots—to ensure accountability.

I also found that rules, regulations, supervision, and sanctions were not the only, nor perhaps the most effective, means of controlling the work of teachers. Teachers are also controlled in less visible and less direct ways. Schools have an odd mix of bureaucratic and nonbureaucratic modes of coordination and control. Some of these less visible controls are built into the formal structure of schools and the way the work of teachers is organized. Others are embedded in the workplace culture, the informal or social organization of schools. Although these mechanisms are less direct and obvious than formal rules and regulations, they are no less real in their impact on what teachers actually do. Indeed, in some ways the pervasiveness of these other controls makes it less necessary for school administrators to implement formal regulations and elaborate mechanisms of accountability.

These less obvious controls are reflected in the role of teachers in schools. Teachers are the men and women in the middle. A useful analogy is that of supervisors or foremen caught between the contradictory demands and needs of managers and workers. While teachers are allowed limited input into crucial decisions concerned with the management of schools and their own work, teachers are given a great deal of responsibility for the implementation of these decisions. Like other middlemen, teachers usually work alone and may have much latitude in seeing that their students carry out the tasks assigned to them. This responsibility and latitude can easily be mistaken for discretion and control, especially in regard to tasks within classrooms. A close look at the organization of the teaching job shows, however, that it usually involves little real power.

None of this denies the importance of accountability or the existence of low-quality teachers and teaching. It simply documents the importance of teacher control. The data show that the degree of teacher control does indeed make a difference in how well schools function. From much of the public's viewpoint, the "good" school is characterized by well-behaved students, a collegial, committed staff, and a general sense of cooperation, communication, and community. The data also show that the good school is characterized by high levels of teacher control. Schools with empowered teachers have less conflict among students, faculty, and principals, and less teacher turnover. In other words, decentralized schools appear to have fewer problems with student misbehavior, more collegiality and cooperation among teachers and administrators, and a more committed teaching staff.

However, just as the amount of control held by teachers varies by the type of decision or issue involved, so the effect of teacher control varies by the type of issue involved. Although teachers have more control over instructional issues (such as the selection of course textbooks, topics, materials, and teaching techniques), this appears to count for little if teachers do not also hold control over social issues, such as student discipline and tracking policies. For those activities that are most fundamentally social—where the educational process involves the socialization and sorting of students—a lack of teacher control shows the strongest correlation to increased school conflict, teacher disengagement, and teacher turnover.

While the objective of my research has been to examine the distribution, forms, and effects of control in schools, I have not attempted to explain the causes of centralization and decentralization in schools. Answering that question would probably require a sustained excursion into the history and development of our education system. Certainly, as I have argued, the desire for top-down control, especially in social issues, may partly be traced to the importance of schooling to local communities and parents, but it is unclear that the need for accountability—understandable as it is—entirely explains the overwhelmingly centralized character of schools.

One factor closely tied to the organizational design of schools is the occupational status of teaching in this country. As discussed earlier, one of the most important criteria distinguishing the degree of professionalization and the status of an occupation is the degree of power and control practitioners hold over workplace decisions. Members of low-status occupations typically have little say over their work, and in this country, unlike in many European and Asian nations, elementary and secondary teaching has always been a relatively low-status occupation. This was noted almost three-quarters of a century ago by Willard Waller in his classic work on teaching: "The difficulties of the teacher . . . in maintaining authority are greatly increased by the low social standing of the teaching profession and its' general disrepute in the community at large . . . Concerning the low social standing of teachers much has been written. The teacher in our culture has always been among the persons of little importance and his place has not changed for the better in the last few decades."[1]

One factor closely tied to both the organizational design of schools and to the occupational status of teaching is undoubtedly gender. Teaching is a predominantly female occupation, and some have argued that this is connected both to teaching's low occupational status and to low employee control.[2] But the relationships among gender, occupational status, and organizational control are unclear. Were women disproportionately recruited to teaching because it was relatively low-status work, or has the recruitment of women to teaching resulted in lowering its status? These are good questions worthy of further investigation.

Implications for Theory and Research

The findings from this research have a number of implications for theory and research. One of my objectives has been to resolve the debate between the two prominent and contradictory images of the organization of schools, that schools are the epitome of loosely coupled organizations—that is, highly decentralized settings in which teachers have much workplace autonomy—and that schools are the epitome of top-down bureaucratic organizations—that is, highly centralized settings in which teachers have little workplace autonomy. Both viewpoints have long had substantial support in the realms of research, policy, and popular opinion. The question is, which is correct?[3]

Determining the degree of control in schools depends on where one looks, the evaluative criteria one uses, and how one measures control. The differing conclusions of the two perspectives, I have tried to show, largely derive from implicit differences in their emphasis and their choices concerning how to define the work of teachers and how to evaluate and measure control in schools. Both views give us important insights into the organization of schools, but both are partial and limited. My objective has been to address the limits and build on the strengths of each.

My reexamination of control in schools is not only relevant to theory and research on schools. Along with showing how an analysis of organizational control has something to contribute to our understanding of schools and their problems, it is also my hope that an analysis of control in schools has something to contribute to our understanding of control in organizations, occupations, and work in general. Schools are an important case to organization theorists because they are one of the field's more puzzling anomalies. As I have discussed, numerous organization theorists have concluded that schools are the archetypal loosely coupled systems, the epitome of debureaucratized bureaucracies and nonrational organizations. Over the past several decades this view of schools has been the conventional wisdom among organization theorists. For these reasons schools provide a good case for reexamining the assumptions underlying the study of control and coupling in organizations. If schools, long assumed to be among the most decentralized, loose, and debureaucratized of organizations, are in fact not, this could have implications for how power, control, coupling, and conflict are understood and assessed in other workplaces and organizations. I argue that organization theorists, like analysts of educational organizations, must address three critical issues. First, it is necessary to define the most important decisions, issues, and activities on which to focus in assessing the power of a particular group or groups and the character of an organization's hierarchical structure. Second, one must determine the standards and criteria by which one will evaluate the distribution of control among members of an organization. Third, one must decide how to adequately and confidently measure who controls the issues in question.

DEFINING THE WORK OF TEACHERS

A major theme in this volume is that research on school organization, from either of the two perspectives, has underemphasized the fundamental fact that schools are social institutions. Almost without exception, analysts have assumed classroom academic instruction to be the primary point of teachers' work in schools. In this framework, the objective of schools, like industrial and production-oriented organizations, is to produce outputs from inputs. The product usually is assumed to be student academic learning, as assessed by scores on mass-produced, standardized tests.

In this research I have not attempted to investigate the effects of teacher control on student test scores. These effects are probably complex and not easily ascertained. For example, a top-down, highly scripted system of bureaucratic control, exemplified by teacher-proof curricula, might foster the kind of learning captured on some kinds of tests. In contrast, the positive effects of being taught by teachers who have a lot of control over their work may be just the kind of outcome not well captured on some kinds of tests. Understanding these effects and the relationship between control and academic achievement is certainly worthy of further investigation. But these kinds of effects are not the only important goals and outcomes in schools. A near obsession with test scores has led many to miss some of the most important activities going on in schools and one of the most telling sites of centralized school control—the socializing and sorting work of teachers. These social activities and issues are among the most crucial, the most controlled, and the most consequential aspects of the work of teachers.

Although empirical researchers may lose sight of the fundamental notion that teaching and schooling are more than simply classroom academic instruction, this is not true for teachers, principals, the public, or the education reform groups mentioned earlier. Numerous surveys have found that both educators and the public believe that an important goal of education is and should be to shape conduct, instill motivation, develop character, and impart values and that an important output is, in plain terms, well-behaved children and adolescents. Hence, from much of the public's viewpoint, the good school, is characterized not only, or even primarily, by high student academic achievement, but also by a positive social climate and a sense of community.

EVALUATING CONTROL IN SCHOOLS

EVALUATING CONTROL IN SCHOOLS

A second limitation of much of the research on control in schools is that evaluations of the degree of hierarchy in schools have rarely been theoretically or empirically grounded. The most common yardsticks used to evaluate the degree of centralization and decentralization in schools—the bureaucratic model of organization and the professional model—are largely implicit and hypothetical ideals. In other words, researchers have commonly decided that schools are loose or tight, centralized or decentralized in comparison to their own underlying, theoretical persuasion, rather than through explicit testing.

Drawing from theory in the sociology of occupations and professions, my investigation offers an empirical means of placing schools on a continuum from centralized workplaces to decentralized workplaces—by comparing the relative control held by school governing boards, school district administrators, school principals, and teachers over decisions representing a range of key activities surrounding the work of teachers within schools.

These comparisons draw attention to the ways the distribution of control does and does not vary across different schools. Large public schools are, for example, more frequently characterized by lower levels of teacher control. Smaller private schools are less often so. But even in the latter group, faculty only infrequently report having control equivalent to that of principals over many crucial teaching decisions. The data show that private schools are, in important ways, not particularly decentralized or professionalized settings, in contrast to current perceptions. Only in a very small proportion of schools does the control held by teachers begin to approach that in a decentralized model of organization. The few examples of highly decentralized schools provide the exception that proves the rule; in the majority of schools, both private and public, teachers hold relatively low levels of power compared with boards, district administrations, and principals.

In addition, my comparisons draw attention to the extent to which the distribution of control depends on the level of analysis chosen—distinctions also overlooked in much research. The results show that while public and private schools are highly decentralized at a systemic level, both are highly centralized at the school level.

Finally, distinguishing between the control exercised by teachers and that held by school governing boards, district administrators, and school principals helps clarify the differences among several competing versions of the disempowerment viewpoint. For example, there is little consensus, and much confusion, surrounding the issue of who or which group is most empowered and most disempowered. Does the locus of control over the work of teachers lie with teachers, with principals, with local school districts and school boards, or with some combination of the three? Or, alternatively, does the locus of disempowerment lie with school districts, with teachers, with principals, or with some combination of the three? There are several competing answers to these questions. Usually the answers are couched in terms of public-private comparisons, and typically the public sector is deemed to be the site of greater disempowerment.[4]

One version of disempowerment focuses on the interface between the community and its schools. This view argues that, especially in public schools, the clients of local schools—parents, families, and the public—have little input into the way schools are run. A second version focuses on the interface between governing boards, their district administrations, and principals. It argues that principals, especially in public schools, lack autonomy and are far too constrained by overbearing bureaucratic school boards. Finally, a third version focuses on teachers within schools. It argues that it is primarily teachers, especially those in public schools, who lack control over the educational process.

My primary focus has been on the view that teachers lack control, but the data do have some lessons for the first two views of disempowerment. The data show that the first view—concerned with the interface between the public and schools—misses an important source of public input into schools. In private schools clients may be able to exert individual choice, and hence power, through the marketplace—that is, via the threat of sending their children to another school. Moreover it is probably true that much of the public, as individuals, has little input into the operation of public schools. But the data show that the public collectively, via elected school boards, has substantial input into the operation of schools, and this collective form of client control through school boards is greater in the public sector than the private sector.

The second version of disempowerment—concerned with the interface between governing boards and districts and principals—is also oversimplified in some ways. While it is true that in the public sector school boards do have substantial power relative to teachers, this is far less true relative to principals. Public school principals themselves tell us they have far more control than their boards over many key issues. In other words, although public school governing boards do wield some control, for many issues, public school principals do not report themselves to be the beleaguered, constrained middle managers depicted in many popular accounts.

MEASURING CONTROL IN SCHOOLS

A third limitation of much of the research on control in schools is that few analysts have conducted a comprehensive examination of the possible methods of organizational control in schools. In particular, some researchers have misunderstood the implications of bureaucratization for organizational control. For example, analysts typically assume that rational-bureaucratic controls, such as rules, are primarily designed for lower-level employees and subordinates. Indeed, critics tend to view any kind of regulation on administrative prerogatives as an impediment to organizational control. This criticism arises over standardized teacher salary scales, tenured teacher employment contracts, and seniority rules concerning teacher transfers and assignments. There is no question that these kinds of rules, regulations, and provisions in schools remove from the hands of school administrators some basic managerial tools, and for this reason they are often criticized.

But analysts miss the point of regulations that constrain higher-level managers. Organizational control of school administrators does not result in a lack of organizational control of teachers. Bureaucracy is a form of, not a synonym for, centralization. Indeed, non-bureaucratized settings can be more centralized than bureaucratic settings.

Bureaucracies seek to ensure that superordinates are limited in what facets of their subordinates' behavior they are allowed to control. Bureaucratic forms of centralized control, such as the standardization of salaries, are intended to reduce the discretion of managers and to further the interests of the owners of the organization—the public, in the case of schools. Such rules make it difficult for managers to conduct organizational affairs on the basis of personal, rather than organizational, interests. Tenured employment contracts are, for example, designed to protect against the arbitrary dismissal of employees, ensure fairness, decrease corruption, and undermine favoritism on the part of administrators. Their object is to make it more difficult for the organization to become the personal fiefdom of its top administrators. Historically, these kinds of regulations were pushed through by progressive reformers to counter a surfeit of personal control by administrators. They are intended to promote employee commitment and loyalty not to individual administrators but to the organization, and hence to promote organizational efficiency—a point clearly made by Weber in his classic work on bureaucracy.[5]

School researchers not only often misunderstand the implications of bureaucratization for organizational control but also often misunderstand the implications of debureaucratization. That is, while some analysts misconceive the scope and purpose of bureaucratic mechanisms in schools, they also often misconceive the scope and purpose of their absence. Some researchers assume that debureaucratization is synonymous with a paucity of rules, supervision, and sanctions for teachers and thus is a source of organizational decentralization. There are two problems with this assumption.

First, it overlooks how some kinds of apparent employee autonomy can act as subtle forms of control. As shown in Chapter 5, by delegating a limited autonomy to teachers, school administrators are able to pass on responsibility to teachers without decentralizing control. Indeed, one advantage of partially debureaucratizing the work setting is that it can motivate teachers to strive to meet organizational goals, with less use of overt regulation and supervision.

Second, analysts mistakenly assume that pockets of nonrationalization and debureaucratization are limited to subordinates in organizations. Organization theorists have indeed long noted that the degree of bureaucracy greatly varies within organizations and that, in general, there is less at the top. While they are often the first to prescribe routinization for the rest of the organization, those at the top of organizations often staunchly resist rules and regulations for themselves. Moreover, it is often the case that the further one goes up the hierarchy in most organizations, the fewer rationalized controls there are.[6] Administrators and managers may be subject to few rules, have little accountability, and enjoy wide autonomy, or they may be able to evade, ignore, or resist the rules that do exist. Both situations have important consequences for employee control. Indeed, as shown in Chapter 4, the power that school administrators are able to wield is sometimes a result not of rules and regulations but of the opposite. What researchers often overlook is the extent to which school administrators are either not rule bound or are able to bypass the rules. That is, contrary to conventional stereotypes of debureaucratization, the absence or the skirting of standardized, authorized regulations can be a source of organizational control rather than teacher autonomy.

I have found that organizational control in schools operates in many forms, rational and nonrational, visible and invisible, direct and indirect, coercive and noncoercive. Analysts have tended to focus on concrete, direct controls and explicit decision making in schools. But in schools, highly visible mechanisms like rules and sanctions are not the sole nor even the primary means of controlling the work of teachers. Perhaps the most effective are those least recognized. The source of their effectiveness—because they are institutionalized and taken for granted—can also make it hard for both insiders and outsiders to recognize them. The relative absence of recognition by researchers and reformers alike of the extent to which teachers have so little control over some of the most important, value-laden, and consequential aspects of their work is perhaps evidence of this very phenomenon—teachers' lack of input into what is acceptable student behavior is so taken for granted and assumed so "normal" it has not even been deemed worthy of study or reform.

Research on control in schools has, however, not simply overlooked some key mechanisms of organizational control in schools. Some of the literature has also misconstrued these phenomena. The most telling example of this is the near universal acceptance of the zone view of the distribution of control in schools. Contrary to this conventional wisdom, the classroom is not a separate, inviolate zone of teacher autonomy. It is simply not true that, behind the closed door, classrooms are small universes of control with the teachers in sole command and free to do as they please.

Implications for Policy And Reform

ACCOUNTABILITY REFORM

Findings from this research have implications for policies and reforms concerned with control in schools.[7] To many educational reformers, policymakers, and members of the public, a lack of control and accountability is at the root of poor performance on the part of teachers and many school problems. Since the turn of the twentieth century, this has been a recurrent and popular theme in the realm of educational policy and reform. Inadequately controlled and poorly performing teachers have been blamed by reformers for the bewildering array of societal problems mentioned earlier.

Educational policy and reform proposals and interventions concerned with these social problems, of course, vary greatly. But despite differences, there is some common ground. Most hold that teachers and teaching matter, especially in reference to students' character and values, and that, in one way or another, the teaching force is not doing a very good job, resulting in serious societal problems. All hold that education is far too important to be left to the control of educators, and that it is both necessary and beneficial for concerned citizens and groups to intervene in the work of schools and teachers. Finally, all seek to improve the performance of schools through the imposition of more responsibilities, more demands, more standards, or more accountability on teachers. In other words, such advocates argue that one solution to the problems in schools is to institute more external control on teachers. This desire to increase the control of schooling, often through rules and regulations, resurfaces on a regular basis in a wide range of education reform movements in American education.[8]

There is no question that the public has a right, and indeed an obligation, to be concerned with the performance of teachers. Schools, like all organizations designed to serve the collective needs of the public, need to be accountable to that public. Moreover, there is no question that some teachers are poorly trained, perform poorly, or are inadequate for the job in one way or another. And it is neither convincing nor valid to place sole responsibility for students' educational growth or failure elsewhere—for instance on families. Teachers *are* important, and they do have an effect on students, and hence it is appropriate to hold them accountable.

However, the accountability perspective and many of the reforms that have come out of it suffer from several problems. The first involves understanding and accuracy. Proponents of accountability interventions sometimes lack firsthand experience in, or knowledge of, the settings or groups they wish to change. Despite good intentions, such reforms can be impractical or unfeasible, and often prove frustrating for their proponents.[9]

It is important to ask school reformers if they have taken the trouble to consult those they seek to reform, such as teachers. The data from this research certainly suggest that many top-down school reforms betray a deep lack of understanding of teachers' work and the way schools actually operate. For example, a litany of critics have told us again and again that teachers are disconnected from administrative control and are highly autonomous. This is simply not the case. What the data do show is that schools have a great deal of administrative control and very little teacher control. The data indicate that numerous mechanisms designed to control the work of teachers are in place. Moreover, the data show that the high degree of central-ization in schools—the lack of teacher control, rather than the oppo-site—is often the source of problems in how well schools function. In focusing on teachers, top-down accountability reforms divert atten-tion from the organizational sources of school problems.

A second problem with the accountability perspective is that its reforms are sometimes unfair. It is, for example, common among proponents of accountability reforms to question and criticize the caliber and quality of teachers. Such critics have told us again and again that teachers lack sufficient accountability, engagement, and commitment. But the data suggest that teachers have an unusual de-gree of commitment to public service, compared with others. In-deed, herein lies an irony. While the teaching occupation does not benefit from many of the structural characteristics associated with traditional professions (such as high pay, prestige, authority, and good working conditions), teachers themselves do exhibit high levels of some of the attitudinal attributes associated with professionalism. As pointed out in Chapter 5, researchers have traditionally found teach-ers to score high on measures of public-service orientation—com-mitment and altruism—indeed, higher than members of some of the traditional professions, such as law. Unrecognized and unappreciated by many critics is the extent to which the teaching workforce is a source of human, social, and even financial capital in schools.

Third, accountability reforms often don't work. Too much organi-zational control can deny teachers the very control and flexibility necessary to do their job effectively and can undermine the motiva-tion of those doing the job. Imposing a high degree of organizational control may squander a valuable organizational resource—the un-usual degree of commitment of those who enter the teaching occu-pation. Having little say in the terms, processes, and outcomes of their work may undermine the ability of teachers to feel they are doing worthwhile work—the very reason many of them came into the occupation in the first place—and may end up contributing to turnover among teachers. As a result, such reforms may not only fail to solve the problems they seek to address but also end up making things worse. If top-down policies hold teachers accountable for activities they do not control, they may harm the very thing they seek to improve—teacher performance.

The data suggest that these fears are not exaggerated. For example, NCES's Teacher Followup Survey asked a national sample of teachers in 1995 to indicate their degree of satisfaction or dissatisfaction with twenty-three different aspects of teaching, including salary, school safety, teaching load, student discipline, class size, recognition and support from administrators, opportunities for professional advancement, evaluation procedures, intellectual challenge, and student motivation. Far more teachers indicated they were dissatisfied with "the esteem of society for the teaching profession" (70 percent) than for any other aspect. This also appears to affect potential teachers. A poll conducted in 2000 by Public Agenda of recent college graduates who had not become teachers found that 39 percent had seriously considered entering teaching while attending college. When asked what they felt were drawbacks of teaching as a potential career, 76 percent agreed with the statement: "Teachers today are often made the scapegoats for all of the problems facing education." Only 29 percent said teachers "get the sense they are respected and appreciated." Moreover, as I discussed in Chapter 6, in analyses using the Teacher Followup Survey I have found that teaching has relatively high rates of turnover compared with many other occupations. The data show that this "revolving door" in schools is a primary factor behind the chronic difficulties many school encounter adequately staffing classrooms with qualified teachers—the so-called teacher shortages.[10]

Examples of the problems resulting from top-down reforms are legion and come from both ends of the political spectrum.[11] For instance, there are illustrations of this one-sided approach among the reform movements to eradicate race and gender inequity in schools. In Chapter 4 I described a regulation, proposed by the NAACP in Cincinnati, to collect teacher and student racial data in school discipline cases in order to determine whether white teachers were disproportionately disciplining black students. These statistics were then used as factors in teachers' annual evaluations, as part of a broad new effort to hold teachers more accountable for the behavior or misbehavior of students. The backdrop for this reform was concern over high numbers of student discipline problems in the city's schools.

Student discipline is often a serious problem, especially in poor, urban schools, and concern on the part of reform groups is necessary, appropriate, and beneficial. Also, there is no question that some teachers may be racially prejudiced and should be held accountable for their behavior. But my findings suggest that the proponents of such top-down controls often misunderstand the way schools are organized. The data show that teachers have little control over the existing disciplinary policies in schools, and, needless to say, teachers have little control over the larger societal forces that affect the degree of student conflict in schools. Civil rights activists often make a compelling case that holding students accountable for their academic or behavioral shortcomings is unfair if they are the victims of unequal educational opportunities and resources. But then they apply a different logic to teachers, who, unlike students, are deemed responsible. Holding teachers responsible for student misbehavior is one-sided if attention is not also paid to the larger organizational and societal sources of the problem. Moreover, simply unilaterally imposing more top-down accountability may only make things worse. The data show that in schools where teachers have more say over discipline issues, not less, there are fewer problems with student misbehavior.

Other examples of one-sided approaches can be found among reforms seeking to reduce gender inequity in schools. One of the more significant successes of this movement was the Women's Educational Equity Act, originally passed by Congress in 1974. Among the host of initiatives tied to this legislation and its amendments are funding provisions for the retraining of elementary and secondary teachers to make them more sensitive toward issues of gender equity, and for greater scrutiny of the behavior of teachers in classrooms, in order to curb discriminatory practices. As with racial issues, gender discrimination is a serious problem, and concern on the part of reformers is necessary, appropriate, and beneficial. Moreover, it certainly could be helpful for teachers to learn to be more sensitive to how they treat male and female students. But again, my findings suggest that the proponents of such top-down controls misunderstood the way schools are organized. Feminists have made a compelling case that holding female students accountable for their academic performance is unfair if they are the victims of unequal educational opportunity and resources. But holding teachers responsible for the problem of gender inequity is one-sided if attention is not also given to the larger societal sources of this problem. Indeed, the data suggest that teachers are just as victimized by gender discrimination as female students. Teaching is a predominantly female, low-status, low-pay, disempowered occupation, and the data show that teachers do not design the curricula or tracking systems in their schools. Unilaterally imposing top-down reforms may not only fail to solve gender inequities but also may make things worse for an already disempowered largely female teaching force.

Liberal-left organizations are not the only reformers to promote top-down control and accountability reforms for teachers. As discussed in Chapter 2, conservative groups for decades have blamed teachers for a host of societal ills and have repeatedly called for reform measures in some ways quite similar to those proposed by liberal-left groups. The conservative line of thought appears in newspaper editorials and syndicated columns on a regular basis. Responding to a rampage of vandalism by teenagers that occurred in downtown Philadelphia in the late 1980s, for example, a well-known *Philadelphia Inquirer* columnist, Tom Fox, argued that the underlying cause of that episode, and of teenage crime, in general, was the refusal of teachers to teach values and morals in schools. Like others who share this viewpoint, Fox traced "drug abuse, homicide, promiscuity, vandalism, illegitimacy, alcoholism and a lack of common decency" to teachers' promotion of "values clarification" curricula, wherein children are taught moral relativism. Indeed, echoing some on the liberal-left, Fox argued that the teenage vandals themselves were not responsible for their acts but were "victims" of the "crazies who control the educational establishment." His solution, predictably enough, was to force schools to require courses in character education or moral literacy and to impose behavior codes for teachers and students.[12]

No doubt some teachers may shy away from teaching particular moral values, and no doubt some may err in the direction of lax behavioral standards. However, like other similar proposals, this line of thought displays a lack of understanding of both the way schools are organized and the character of teachers' work. Trying to enforce "proper" behavior is a large part of what teachers do and, as the data show, teachers have always been concerned with behavioral standards and discipline in schools. Indeed, the first to suffer from misbehavior and a lack of discipline are the teachers themselves, who must work closely with such students each and every day. But teachers have little say over the disciplinary codes and standards in schools.

Again, blaming teachers will not only fail to solve any of these societal problems, but also can make things worse by further degrading a job that already suffers from low status and high rates of turnover.

A final example of a one-sided approach to reform can be found in the reforms implemented in response to the problem of out-of-field teaching. With the release of the SASS data, beginning in the early 1990s, this problem began to receive national attention.[13] The findings from my research and that of others captured widespread interest. They were featured in numerous major education reports, widely reported in the media, cited by President Clinton, and debated by state legislatures and U.S. congressional committees. As a result, beginning in the mid-1990s the problem of out-of-field teaching became a real concern in the realm of education reform. However, despite a growing awareness of this problem and its importance, out-of-field teaching has been widely misunderstood. The source of this misunderstanding concerns the question of why out-of-field teaching is so prevalent in schools.

Almost without exception, commentators, researchers, policymakers, and the public have assumed that out-of-field teaching is due to a deficit in either the quality or quantity of teachers. The data show, however, that neither view is correct. As discussed in Chapter 5, out-of-field teaching is not the result of a lack of adequately trained teachers but is, rather, rooted in the way teachers are used and managed once on the job.

The implications of these misunderstandings for reform are crucial. If one assumes that out-of-field teaching is caused by deficits in the quality or quantity of teachers, the policy antidotes are clear: recruit more candidates to the teaching occupation and upgrade their education and training. Indeed, these reforms have been widely proposed and implemented at district, state, and federal levels. Though perhaps worthwhile, none of these reforms will eliminate out-of-field teaching assignments. Recruiting thousands of new candidates into teaching, and mandating more rigorous academic requirements for them, will help little if large numbers of teachers continue to be assigned to teach subjects other than those for which they were trained.

Such reforms reveal a deep unfamiliarity with the way schools are organized and run. Blaming teachers, teacher training institutions, or inexorable forces of supply and demand only diverts attention from the organizational source of the problem. Once again, such reforms not only fail to solve the problem but also can make things worse by contributing to the low esteem in which teachers are held.

EMPOWERMENT REFORM

Findings from this research also have implications for policies and reforms reflecting the disempowerment perspective. In this view, the road to school improvement lies not through decreasing but through increasing delegation, deregulation, and decentralization. However, the wide array of decentralization reforms (such as school restructuring, site-based management, school-based management, charter schools, and school choice) entail different and sometimes contradictory prescriptions, depending on whether their focus is on teacher empowerment, community empowerment, principal empowerment or some combination of the three. As I have shown, some of these reforms have been oversimplified, and this has important implications for their success or failure.

A good example of reform that subscribes to school principal empowerment can be found in proposals from the National Education Summits, which have been bringing together governors, the president, and numerous heads of business and education groups since the 1980s. Prominent members of this group have argued that a major problem with the organization of schools is that school principals, unlike their counterparts in the business world, are overly constrained by school boards and have too little control over budgets, teacher hiring and firing, and school operations in general. Accordingly, their reform proposals typically have sought to give school principals more control over these kinds of decisions. As put by Louis Gerstner, the chair of IBM and the chair of the 1999 summit, accountability goes with power, and the way to improve schools is to "treat principals as managers and leaders."[14]

This view of schools' hierarchy is, however, not consistent with the view held by school principals themselves. As the data clearly show, school principals do not report themselves to be disempowered lower-level managers, as assumed by Gerstner and other business executives at the education summits. Principals tell us that teachers are far more often in the role of beleaguered, overly constrained employees. The reforms the Nation Education Summits have proposed—increasing the control wielded by principals—are one-sided and may simply exacerbate the relative lack of control held by teachers, with negative consequences for school performance.

In fact, the reform measures to come out of this version of school decentralization often look highly similar to those offered by the disorganization perspective and suffer from the same limitations. For example, advocates often call for the removal of standardized teacher salary scales, tenured teacher employment contracts, and teacher seniority rules, because they view these kinds of rules and regulations as impediments to effective school management. However, in the absence of alternative mechanisms to protect teachers from the ill effects of unwise or unfair administrative decisions, reforms proposing the unilateral removal of such provisions can undermine the very thing such initiatives seek—improvements in teacher performance.

The same problems apply to the movement for increased community and parental input into schools. The reforms advocated by this movement, such as community schools, school choice, and charter schools, are often intended to *increase* the accountability of both schools and teachers by shifting substantial power from the education bureaucracy and teachers to parents and communities. Like principal empowerment, this version of school decentralization often advocates reform measures similar to those offered by the disorganization perspective.

School choice reformers usually define choice in terms of the power of individual students and their families to pick and choose among schools. Charter school and school choice reforms are often couched in terms of public-private comparisons, and typically private schools are held up as successful models of deregulation and decentralization to be emulated by public schools. But such public-private comparisons often overlook one of the fundamental differences between public and private schools. In private schools, unlike in public schools, choice runs two ways. Students and their families have the right to pick and choose among schools, but many private schools also have the power to pick and choose among students. Selectivity in student admissions is probably a primary source of enhanced student performance in private schools.

In contrast, in charter school and school choice reforms, rarely is school choice defined as two-sided—that is, rarely do they include the power of schools, and especially teachers, to pick and choose among students. Increasing the control of parents may simply exacerbate the relative lack of control held by teachers, with negative consequences for school performance.

What Is to Be Done?

Accountability and power must go hand in hand; increases in one must be accompanied by increases in the other. Imbalances between the two can result in problems for both the employee and the organization. Delegating power without commensurate responsibility is irresponsible and can even be dangerous and harmful. Likewise, imposing accountability without commensurate power is unfair and can also be harmful. It does not make sense to hold somebody accountable for something they don't control, nor does it make sense to give someone control over something for which they are not held accountable.

The problem with community empowerment and school principal empowerment reforms is not that they seek to increase the power of these groups but that they are one-sided. Many reformers and policymakers appear to assume that the tension between organizational control and employee control is a zero-sum issue—that is, that the two sets of needs are fundamentally incompatible. They appear to assume that giving teachers more autonomy and control cannot coexist with ensuring the administrative and public need for accountability.

Nothing in my research suggests this to be the case. To the contrary, the data analysis in Chapter 6 shows that increasing the control wielded by teachers has a positive effect on relations between teachers and administrators. Schools with more empowered faculties do not have more conflict between the faculty and the school administration. If teachers are given the opportunity to influence school decision making, the result is more communication with, and support from, administrators, or at least the perception of it by teachers. Moreover, the data show a positive correlation between teacher control and principal control; schools with more of one are likely to have more of the other. In other words, the data suggest that it is both possible and beneficial to have empowered teachers and an empowered principal in the same setting.

This is not a new idea. An important stream of applied organizational research has found that effective workplaces carefully maintain a balance between organizational control and employee autonomy.[15] From this viewpoint, there is no reason why school reform could not increase the control wielded, and the accountability required, of all the key parties involved—principals, teachers, and parents. In such an approach, a school-level governing body made up of parents, teachers, and administrators might develop goals and standards for a school, be provided with the necessary resources, and then be held accountable for achieving their goals and meeting their standards.[16]

One essential element of such reform is the need to address the distinction between power and participation.[17] Decentralization reforms often lead to the creation of governance entities, such as committees or panels, which provide input into school curricular, budgeting, hiring, and other similar decisions. Organizational researchers have long noted that if these organizational decentralization entities are to be successful they must have more than an advisory role; they must have actual decision-making power. The capacity to provide advice concerning school decisions is important, but it is not a sufficient substitute for having power over decisions. Indeed, when such programs are simply "window dressing," not only can they fail to generate the engagement of members—their objective—but they can also provoke cynicism, disengagement, and conflict. The history of school decentralization reform is marked by numerous examples of school committees that have little actual power to make or implement changes. The lesson is clear: if reform is to be effective, actual decision-making power must be shared.[18]

Related to this is one of the central findings of this research—that the effects of decentralization and empowerment reforms depend on the task or issue involved. School restructuring and decentralization efforts often focus on expanding teacher input into either instructional activities, such as curricular innovation, or administrative activities, such as teacher hiring and budget allocation.[19] Reforms focus less often on a similar expansion of teacher influence over the social and behavioral issues in schools. The data indicate, however, that improvements in the way schools function depend on increasing teacher control over just those issues.

None of this is meant to suggest that the implementation of effective reforms will be easy. Teacher empowerment, like other forms of empowerment, does not have to be a zero-sum issue; that is, empowering teachers does not have to result in disempowering parents. But increasing teacher control over crucial social issues is difficult and controversial. Giving teachers more control over, for example, policies concerning what is appropriate or inappropriate student behavior can involve a fundamental restructuring of the distribution and balance of control for important social issues. Such restructuring expands teachers' "parenting" role in deciding what is best for children. Moreover, this kind of reform decreases the discretion allowed and increases the accountability required of both parents and students. Ultimately, this restructuring can alter an underlying premise of public schooling—changing it from being an entitlement toward being a privilege. Privileges differ fundamentally from entitlements in that they can be forfeited. The critical question is: How much control do we, as a society, want to give our teachers in the socializing of our youngsters?

To illustrate the kinds of difficulties such efforts encounter, I will close by briefly turning to two specific examples of social reform in schools that touch on crucial and cherished issues. The first are the so-called respect bills—education reform initiatives intended to address student social and behavioral problems in schools. These are state laws that would require public school students to address teachers and other school employees in respectful language, such as saying, "Yes, sir," "No, ma'am," "Yes, Mr. Jones," or "No, Ms. Jones." According to one bill's sponsor, the objective of this legislation is "to encourage courtesy and respect and to help people learn good habits of civility. When you practice the Golden Rule, it becomes a habit."[20]

Respect bills were proposed in numerous states in the late 1990s, but they met with much criticism, and by summer 2000 they had been successfully enacted in only one state, Louisiana. Critics said that they went too far, were too rigid, and undermined the role of families. Proponents countered that their objective was not to impose military values or supplant family prerogatives but simply to reinforce basic manners. Another criticism was that respect bills did not go far enough, were too superficial, and would have little effect on school or societal problems. The response of one teacher and parent summed it up: "I'd rather have a law that gives me more power to discipline." Proponents, typically, agreed with this criticism; they readily acknowledged the limits of their legislation. In their view, ensuring basic manners is only a first step toward making schools better places for young people. Notably, the legislation did not include serious punishment for infractions, resources for resolving underlying problems, or any increase in teacher authority.

An example of school reform legislation that does attempt to more fully address issues of teacher control over student behavior is the Improved Student Learning and Discipline Act, enacted in Georgia at about the time as the respect bills were being debated. In this case, the state mandated a new power for teachers—the ability to remove students from their classrooms for disruption, bullying, sexual harassment, verbal abuse, and so on. The law required schools to replace the structure in which principals have the ultimate authority in deciding what to do with unruly students, including returning such students to classrooms against the wishes of teachers. Under the new legislation, teachers can appeal principals' decisions to a three-member review panel of teachers. In addition, and notably, the law provides counseling, mentoring, and support for both teachers and students in the event of conflicts. In contrast to the respect bills, the Georgia law sought to give teachers far more control over a fundamental social issue—whether teachers should be forced to teach disruptive students.

Not surprisingly, the law faced extensive criticism, and its future is in doubt. State laws allowing schools to identify, suspend, and expel problem students come up against federal laws guaranteeing every student a public education and federal laws restricting the removal of problem children.

These two examples of school reform serve to illustrate a basic truth. Underlying the debate and conflict surrounding these seemingly simple and small changes is the understanding that teachers and schools do make a difference, they do deeply affect our society and its future. For precisely that reason these kinds of reforms inevitably face deep opposition. The public has every right to have high expectations and every right to have a say in such changes. But the public cannot have it both ways. The importance of the task, the height of the public's expectations, and the blame cast are not matched by the tools, and foremost the power, provided to those responsible—the teachers. The data suggest a clear but difficult lesson: If we want to improve the quality of our teachers and schools, we need to improve the quality of the teaching job.

APPENDIX

Research Strategy

Assessing power and control is deceptively simple. The most common method and the one I used in my research is the decisional approach. Rather than inferring organizational hierarchy and the chain of command from written job descriptions and organizational flowcharts, researchers ask members of an organization, either in personal interviews or via questionnaires, who has what levels of influence over which decisions in their organization. Respondents are treated as informants of organizational conditions. Empirical assessments of power face a critical problem, however—accounting for the validity and reliability of the sources of information, the informants. This has been a subject of much insightful debate among those who study power, most notably political scientists.[1] Power is neither a neutral nor a readily accessible phenomenon, and most methods for assessing it in social settings confront questions of both respondent candor and accuracy. Among other reasons, the task of assessing power is difficult because of cultural norms favoring the denial of the undemocratic aspects of power and because of the importance of indirect and latent types of control.

To minimize these limitations, in my research I utilized a "triangulation" strategy.[2] The objective of triangulation is to protect against bias by using multiple methods and acquiring multiple measures. I used multiple indicators of power, representing a large number of organizational issues, and multiple perspectives in the organization—those of both teachers and administrators. But most important, I used two different types of data: quantitative data, obtained from large-scale surveys and analyzed with statistical methods, and qualitative data, collected in fieldwork and analyzed with interpretive methods.

Projects combining quantitative and qualitative data, and statistical and interpretive methods, are unusual. Despite a growing sense among social scientists that these two modes of research are best viewed as natural partners rather than competitors, few researchers actually combine them. This is understandable. The differences between them are more than a matter of deciding whether to display one's evidence as words or as numbers. Each has its own standards of quality and styles of writing and presentation.

After undertaking this research, and despite the difficulties of combining them, I am more than ever convinced of the extent to which the two methods of analysis compliment each other. Using them together allowed me at once to take advantage of the strengths and compensate for the limits of each. In short, I found the result of such a synthesis to be more than the sum of its parts.

In the first place, statistical analysis of survey data from a broad range and large number of school sites was necessary to establish appropriate and generalizable comparisons of organizational power and control in schools and to pinpoint, with confidence, the determinants and consequences of those levels. On the other hand, fieldwork facilitated a grounded interpretation of the survey findings. For example, it allowed me to probe more closely into if and how administrators are able to control and coordinate the work of the staffs in different schools. It helped me to discover the existence of less direct forms of hierarchical control and develop a fine-grained analysis of the social organization of power relationships and processes within schools. This combination of methods enabled the research to be concerned with both general patterns and detailed processes.

The Field Research

My field research allowed me to examine a broader range of school tasks and issues than studies usually include. My interviews included the same questions on teacher control that were used in the Schools and Staffing Survey (SASS) conducted by the National Center for Education Statistics and in the School Assessment Survey, conducted by Research for Better Schools. To these I added a number of original items pertaining to teacher control over activities and issues often neglected in conventional research. This expanded list of questions about teacher control was, moreover, only a starting point. My fieldwork allowed me to examine power and control in more depth and with more specificity than is usually possible. Through intensive interviews I was able to "unpack" the complexities of control in schools and collect concrete details on the mechanisms by which constraint and influence operate in schools. I asked respondents to describe the parameters of their discretion, input, and influence over the widened range of issues and activities. I probed teachers about their frustrations and dissatisfactions with the way schools are run, and whether these are acted on or even raised. Do teachers challenge the decision-making structure? And if not, is this a result of choice or control?

This focus on detail, of course, necessitated limiting the number of schools examined and the number of respondents interviewed. Instead of attempting to obtain a representative sample, I designed my qualitative research component to include principals, or headmasters, and a number of teachers in a broad range of schools. I interviewed respondents in each of four carefully chosen schools in the Philadelphia area—two private and two public schools. Within each sector, I chose schools that varied widely along a number of dimensions: size, setting, socioeconomic status of the student body, and student minority population.

In each school I conducted taped interviews with the building principal and/or vice principal and four teachers. I selected for interviews teachers in the sciences and the humanities in each school. In addition, I endeavored to interview both junior teachers (those with less than four years' total experience) and senior faculty. This was not always possible, because in some school sites little hiring had been done recently. I also attempted to include both female and male teachers at each school. My final sample included: ten science and mathematics teachers and ten humanities teachers; ten female and ten male teachers; fifteen senior and five junior teachers. The interviews averaged one and one half hours each. Before undertaking the in-school interviews, I first tested my interview questions with a half dozen acquaintances who were either schoolteachers or principals. In some instances, I have included material from those prior interviews in this book. My field research took place in the early to mid-1990s.

To maximize the likelihood of obtaining candid responses to sensitive, divisive, and even taboo organizational issues, such as control and conflict, I adopted a scrupulously neutral interview demeanor and designed the interview schedules accordingly. I asked open-ended questions, pledged confidentiality, and permitted respondents to choose their own words in talking about threatening topics. The revealing frankness with which most of my respondents, both administrators and teachers, discussed life within their schools gave me confidence in their candor.

The Schools and Staffing Survey

My primary source of quantitative data in this research was the Schools and Staffing Survey conducted by NCES, the statistical arm of the U.S. Department of Education. This is the largest and most comprehensive data source available on teachers and schools. Indeed, NCES developed the survey to address the paucity of nationally representative data on the staffing, occupational, and organizational aspects of elementary and secondary schools.

SASS gathered a wide range of information on the characteristics, work, and attitudes of both teachers and administrators, and on the characteristics and conditions of schools and districts across the country. It is important to note that it included an unusually wide range of types of schools in both the private and public sectors. Of particular interest for my purposes was its inclusion of a number of questionnaire items tapping both teachers' and administrators' perceptions of the relative levels of decision-making influence of various groups within schools, and their perceptions of levels of a range of problems within schools.

The U.S. Census Bureau collected the SASS data for NCES from random samples stratified by state, school sector, and school level. Throughout my analysis I weighted data to compensate for the over- and undersampling of the complex stratified survey design. I weighted each teacher or school observation by the inverse of its probability of selection to obtain unbiased estimates of the national population of schools and teachers in the year of the survey. My analysis primarily focuses on secondary schools, including both junior and senior high schools, because, as I described in Chapter 1, these have been the focus of much of the debate and concern in regard to both a lack of organizational control and a surfeit of conflict.

Four cycles of SASS have been done: 1987–88, 1990–91, 1993–94, and 1999–2000. I used data primarily from the first three cycles; the last cycle was not officially released until June 2002. Each cycle of SASS constructed and administered separate questionnaires for each school sampled, for the principal or headmaster of each school, for the central district administration for each public school, and for a random sample of teachers within each school. This last sample included on average three to six teachers from each school, depending on school level and sector. The response rates were unusually high for large-scale surveys: on average, about 86 percent for public school teachers, 79 percent for private school teachers, 94 percent for public school administrators, and 79 percent for private school administrators.

SASS has a number of advantages that set it apart from other surveys and made it especially useful for my research. Below I'll briefly describe four: its teacher sample, its school sample, its multiple respondents, and its supplemental followup survey of former teachers.

SASS includes an unusually large and comprehensive sample of teachers. Most other NCES surveys also include teacher samples in their data collection. This is true, for example, for the National Assessment of Educational Progress (NAEP), the National Educational Longitudinal Survey of 1988 (NELS:88), and High School and Beyond (HS&B). However, students are the primary focus of these surveys; information on teachers is included primarily to understand student outcomes, behavior, and achievement. NELS:88, for example, has a large teacher sample (about 45,000 in the base year), but the teacher sample is not representative; students are the representative sample, and teachers were included for each sampled student. Different students could have the same teachers, and thus teachers could be counted more than once. Moreover, NELS:88 focuses on only the eighth, tenth, and twelfth grades.

SASS takes the opposite approach. It was not designed to provide explanations of student academic outcomes, and so it does not include an array of such measures. It focuses on teachers and schools. Other information is included, but only to broaden our understanding of these teachers and schools. Accordingly, the teacher sample is large—about 50,000 teachers. It is also comprehensive—it permits national and state estimates of teachers by any number of characteristics, including their field, race, sex, age, education, experience, and whether they are bilingual.

NCES is, of course, not the only organization that collects national teacher data. Two examples of well-known national surveys of teachers are the Carnegie Foundation for the Advancement for Teaching's The Condition of Teaching: A State by State Analysis and the Metropolitan Life Survey of the American Teacher. Neither of these surveys, however, includes private school teachers. Moreover, although representative, each is based on a small teacher sample—fewer than 2,000 teachers. As a result, neither sample permits extensive disaggregation by social characteristics. In contrast, SASS represents all elementary and secondary teachers in the United States and permits extensive disaggregation.

SASS has an unusually large and comprehensive sample of schools. Most other NCES surveys also include school questionnaires in their data collection, but again, the purpose of school data in most surveys is to provide contextual information for student outcomes, behavior, and achievement.

For example, one of the best known and most commonly used databases on schools is NCES's Administrator-Teacher Supplement (ATS) of the High School and Beyond survey. The ATS represents a subset of the schools in the original 1980 base year of HS&B at which additional information was collected from teachers and principals in 1984.

The ATS was developed specifically to provide national data on the issue of school effectiveness; prior to the ATS, such measures were not available in any national dataset. In particular, the ATS was designed to facilitate research on the relationships between particular school characteristics and student outcomes by linking ATS information to the tenth- and twelfth-grade student achievement data in HS&B.

Much of the best known research conducted since the early 1980s on school effects has been based on the ATS. This has been particularly true for the major studies of the differences between public and private schools. But although the ATS has been used a great deal, it has important limitations. For example, the ATS actually has a relatively small sample of schools—the usable sample size is only about 350 to 400 schools. It does not include elementary schools, and although it includes different types of private schools, only its Catholic school sample is of sufficient size for many analyses of the private sector. Hence, the ATS is an excellent resource for examining the effects of school characteristics on students, but it is less useful for exploring differences among types of schools.

The opposite is true for SASS. It is an excellent resource for examining the range of differences among various kinds of schools, but it is less useful for exploring the effects of schools on students. In contrast to the ATS, the usable SASS sample is very large (it includes about 11,000 schools) and very comprehensive—SASS supports national estimates by any number of different school characteristics, including sector, level, state, percent of minority student population in the school, urbanicity, and school size. Moreover, the SASS sample is capable of providing national estimates for at least eighteen different types of private schools, including several subtypes of

Catholic schools and a range of nonsectarian, independent, and other religious private schools.

SASS has obtained information from a number of different types of respondents at different levels of the school system. Prior to SASS, NCES administered separate surveys at separate times for public and private schools, for districts, and for principals. These were brought together and linked in SASS. As a result, SASS allows examination of the relations between different variables at different levels. Teachers' perceptions, for instance, can be linked to school types, administrator characteristics, or the characteristics of the overall district environment. Having data from multiple respondents also makes it possible to compare and evaluate different types of respondents' views on similar issues.

Each cycle of SASS has included a longitudinal supplement—the Teacher Followup Survey (TFS). The TFS was developed primarily to obtain teacher turnover rates by type of teacher, type of school, and state, and to compare teachers who left teaching with teachers who stayed in teaching. The TFS is administered to a subset from the SASS teacher sample, one year after the administration of the original SASS questionnaire. The TFS includes two separate questionnaires: one for a sample of former teachers and one for a sample of continuing teachers. The TFS has created the best national database available for analyzing determinants of attrition and turnover of teachers.

For detailed discussions of the rationale, conceptualization, and design of SASS, see the original Rand Corporation design report, or the later overview that I wrote.[3] For information concerning technical aspects of the survey design and sample estimation of SASS, see the relevant NCES methodological reports.[4] For extensive summaries of the results from each cycle of SASS, see any of the editions of *Schools and Staffing in the U.S.: A Statistical Profile.*[5]

Multiple Regression Analysis (Chapter 6)

For the multiple regression analysis in Chapter 6 of the effects of teacher control on conflict in schools I used data from the 1987–88 SASS. The analysis was based on a sample of 43,837 teachers from 10,001 schools. The multiple regression analysis of the effects of teacher control on teacher turnover in schools used data from the 1991–92 TFS. This analysis was based on a sample of 5,248 teachers from 4,186 schools. At the end of the Appendix I present the definitions of the measures used in the multiple regression analysis, tables showing background summary statistics of the measures, and tables of the regression models themselves, including the unstandardized coefficients and standard errors.

Because of its size and its wide range of information on school conditions, SASS is an ideal source of information with which to address my research questions. From the SASS questionnaire items concerned with information on control and decision-making influence in schools, described in Chapter 3, I developed four different measures of teacher control that distinguish between the two main types of educational issues (instructional and social) and also between teacher control within classrooms and teacher control schoolwide.

In addition to collecting information on control and decision-making influence in schools, SASS obtained information on the degree of cooperation and consensus or, alternatively, conflict and disorder among students, faculty, and principals within schools. From these items in the survey questionnaire, I developed three measures of the character of the school climate and the relations among teachers, students, and principals.

The first measure—conflict between staff and students—referred to the degree to which students are alienated from, do not cooperate with, or actively disrupt the manner in which schools are operated. The second—conflict among teachers—referred to the degree of cooperation and collegiality among teachers. It characterized faculties along a scale from those that function as cohesive teams to those that act as fragmented collections of individuals. The third—conflict between teachers and principals—characterized faculty-principal relationships along a scale from those exhibiting communication, cooperation, and support to those exhibiting distrust and friction. In addition to collecting information on school climate, SASS obtained information on teacher turnover and retention, through the TFS. From this supplement I drew a measure of teacher turn-over.

The object of my analysis was to weigh the extent to which the above four outcomes, or dependent variables (conflict between staff and students, conflict among teachers, conflict between teachers and principals, and teacher turnover), were affected by the amount of control held by teachers—the independent variable.

There are, of course, numerous factors that could account for school-to-school differences in school climate and also for any apparent connection between teacher control and school climate. Not surprisingly, the SASS data show that the climates of schools vary a great deal among different kinds of schools, and that foremost among these school differences are whether the school is public or private, the size of the school, the socio-economic background of the students, and whether a school is situated in a rural, suburban, or urban setting. Research has shown that, in general, large public schools, especially those serving urban, high-minority, high-poverty communities, are less likely to exhibit a positive sense of community. In contrast, small schools and private schools are more likely to have a coherent and positive climate and sense of community.[6]

To determine whether there was a relationship between teacher control and the social climate and relations in schools, it was necessary to control for, or hold constant, other factors that could be related to school climate and cohesion. By controlling for these others factors, it was possible to discern whether the amount of teacher control itself had an effect on school climate, independent of the particulars of a school and its setting. Hence, in my analysis, in addition to the measures for teacher control, I also included as independent variables background characteristics of the teacher respondents, such as experience, gender, race, and measures for school characteristics, such as sector, size of school, school setting, school level, and the poverty level and race and ethnicity of student populations.

In sum, the analysis examined whether the key independent variables (the measures of teacher control) were statistically associated with the dependent variables (school conflict and teacher turnover), while controlling for the effects of other independent variables (the background characteristics of teachers, of schools, and of their student populations).

The measures used in my regression analyses were couched at more than one level. Some were school-level responses, as in the case of information collected from administrators about schools; some were school-level means, as in the case of the aggregated teacher data on control; and, finally, others were teacher-level responses, as in the case of information collected from teachers about themselves. Over the past two decades, there has been a debate concerning the most appropriate multiple regression method for modeling multilevel data. Accurately predicting an outcome, such as turnover, for members of an organization, such as teachers, while taking into account the characteristics of both the teachers and the organization, is a complex statistical task. Conventional multiple regression techniques, such as ordinary least squares, operate at one level of analysis and, hence, have difficulty properly modeling an outcome that is a product of factors at more than one level. To address this problem, a number of statistical techniques have been developed specifically for modeling multilevel data. In my regression analyses I tried both regular, single-level multiple regression and also multilevel techniques. The coefficients produced by each technique were, of course, different. But the main results were similar. The regression tables at the end of the Appendix display the results from the multilevel procedures. For the multilevel analyses of conflict, I used PROC MIXED (SAS). These analyses test whether the amount of conflict in each school is related to the amount of teacher control in each school, after controlling for other factors. For the multilevel analyses of teacher turnover, I used PROC GENMOD (SAS), a procedure that allowed for logistic regression. These analyses test whether the likelihood of teachers' moving from or leaving their schools was related to the amount of teacher control in each school, after controlling for other factors. Both procedures allowed for the inclusion of design weights. Use of design weights was especially necessary for the turnover analysis, because the

TFS sample was based on the dependent variable—those who departed their teaching jobs—and undersampled those who did not depart. Elsewhere I have published detailed reports of similar analyses.[7]

Measurement and Methodological Issues

Numerous technical issues and problems typically arise in advanced statistical analyses such as those I performed for Chapter 6. Here I will discuss three such issues.

The first issue is *data validity*. In my regression analyses, the school-level measures of teacher control and school conflict are based on the reports of individual teachers. In essence, these measures assess the characteristics of schools indirectly, by aggregating members' perceptions of these structures and conditions. Use of employee respondent perceptions to construct such variables is standard practice in both research on school organization and research on organizations in general. Indeed, the argument is often made that members and employees are in the best position to know what these conditions are. Nevertheless, there are legitimate questions concerning the validity of such measures.

Because such data represent employees' perceptions of school conditions, these responses are, by definition, subjective attributions. It is reasonable to expect that some individuals' reports could be inaccurate because of attribution bias. For example, a highly satisfied teacher might both underestimate the degree of conflict and overestimate the degree of teacher control in his or her school. Alternatively, a highly disgruntled individual could do the opposite. What might appear as a relationship between control and conflict could actually be a spurious effect of the respondent's bias.

In important ways, the data suggest this was probably not a problem in my research. I found that the impact of teacher control is robust—that is, teachers' influence over school issues affects a wide range of dependent variables in a wide range of settings. Moreover, regardless of school climate and regardless of their individual characteristics, respondents do dis-

APPENDIX

criminate among different areas and types of control. For example, teachers do report distinct differences between control over instructional issues and control over other issues. This is reasonable. Whether the conditions in which a teacher works are harmonious or rent with dissension, teachers would know whether, for example, they are able to choose the texts used for their courses, decide how much homework they assign to their students, and have input into the discipline policies in their schools.

Moreover, in a series of background analyses I explored in more detail whether the relationship between teacher control and school conflict could be a spurious effect of the respondents' degree of job satisfaction. To attempt to statistically control for such an effect, I added to the regression models, as an additional independent variable, an item from the teachers' survey that is related to teacher job satisfaction: "If you could go back to your college days and start over again, would you become a teacher or not?" This item was answered on a five-point scale from "certainly would" to "certainly would not."

As expected, this measure of teacher satisfaction had a statistically significant impact on teachers' reports on school conflict. Teachers who reported that, if given the chance to start over again, they would not want to be teachers, also reported higher levels of school conflict. Moreover, the addition of this variable did reduce the amount of variance accounted for by teacher control. However, notably, the association of teacher control with conflict held up even after inserting this control for respondent bias.

In another series of background analyses I explored the possibility of spurious effects by also examining the associations between teachers' reports on conflict and their own scores for each of the four measures of control. I used multilevel analytic techniques to estimate both teacher-level and school-level models of school conflict and substituted teacher-level measures of teacher control and influence for school-level mean measures. In all cases, the relationships with conflict of the teacher-level predictors were significantly smaller than those of school-level versions of the same predictors. This suggested that the attribution bias described above may not be a serious problem in this research. It also provided empirical justification for the use of the school-level measures of teacher control—consistent with the theoretical focus of this research.

In a final series of background analyses, I explored the use of a second version of the measure of teacher control—one based on school principals' reports. In the SASS Administrator Questionnaire, principals were asked to answer two of the same questions asked of teachers: whether faculty had influence over school discipline policy, and whether faculty had influence in establishing the curriculum. These data are presented in Figures 3.3 and 3.4 and Table 3.3. The data indicate that principals and teachers in the same schools often did not agree as to teacher control—principals often reported that faculty had more influence than teachers reported themselves. My analyses of both the qualitative and quantitative data suggest that while the principals' reports were useful to compare the relative influence of the different groups, principals' reports were less valid and less reliable than those of teachers for assessing absolute levels and effects of teacher control. For instance, teachers' mean reports of teacher control were strongly related to both actual teacher turnover and principals' reports of school rates of teacher turnover, while principals' reports of faculty influence showed little relationship to the same outcomes.[8] Hence, in the Chapter 6 regression analyses I used teachers' reports of teacher control.

A second and related issue is *data reliability.* Along with questions of respondent bias, it is also to be expected that different individuals will experience their schools differently and, hence, vary in their reports of school structure and climate, raising the question of reliability. In my investigation I did not assume that schools are uniform entities. As have many previous studies of school organization, in my background analyses I found heterogeneity in the responses of teachers to the questionnaire items on control and conflict, regardless of the conditions of the school in which they taught.

There are several reasons to expect diversity among teachers in their reports on conditions within schools. First, as noted before, respondents' perceptions are by definition subjective, and so could vary according to the perceptions and inclinations of different individuals, regardless of the characteristics of their schools. Second, teachers in different departments and units within schools may have different experiences. Finally, such measures are probably subject to substantial measurement error. That is, it is difficult to precisely measure control and conflict, especially with a survey questionnaire.

My background analyses also indicated substantial variation among schools for the variables of interest here. This suggested that conflict and control are also collective properties of schools. The relationship between these organizationwide properties provides the focus of this investigation.

A third and related issue concerns reciprocal causality, or *endogeneity*. Any analysis of the impact of organizational structure on organizational climate must consider the possibility of the reverse—that it is climate that is affecting the structure. After all, organizational structure, like organizational climate, is really the patterns of relations among organization members; in this case, those of decision-making relationships. This issue is especially pertinent for data, such as those used here, that sample respondents' subjective perceptions of objective organizational conditions and then relate these to the same respondents' subjective perceptions of other organizational conditions. The regression analyses, of course, simply indicate an association exists between teacher control and school conflict and do not substantiate that the latter is a result of the former. It is thus necessary to also ask if levels of conflict in schools might affect teachers' reports of control. For instance, could a highly positive and cohesive organizational climate result in greater delegation of decision-making power to teachers? Or, alternatively, would an adversarial workplace result in the reduction of teachers' input and autonomy? If, for example, school administrators distrust teachers or see them as uncooperative and unmotivated, they may also conclude they are in need of close control and supervision.

Data from Suburban High—one of the four sites I examined in my fieldwork—suggest that this issue of reliability may not be a serious problem for my research. Suburban High was a smaller, suburban school serving a student body that was largely white and affluent. In many respects the school climate and teaching conditions were relatively superior at Suburban High, and the faculty were well aware of this. Suburban's teachers were, for instance, among the highest paid in the state. Student body scores on national standardized tests were routinely in the top percentiles, and the students were relatively well behaved and motivated. The school itself was orderly, well equipped, and graffiti free. Teachers generally respected and got along with the principal. It is thus reasonable to predict that if a reverse effect as discussed above were present, and if a positive school climate resulted in higher reports of teacher control, Suburban High would be a good place to find this effect.

Indeed, Suburban High's faculty did report relatively high levels of control. But rather than finding that the more agreeable school climate led them to either obtain or perceive more power, if anything the opposite appeared to be true. Given their affluent community and high-achieving student body, teachers at Suburban High commonly felt they should be *more* empowered and more professionalized than they were. Higher teacher job satisfaction at Suburban High did not mean that teachers perceived they were delegated more power and control. In this case, a kind of status inconsistency existed in the minds of the teachers, in which good working conditions did not translate into higher teacher control, in perception or fact. From the viewpoint of Suburban's teachers, a more decentralized distribution of control in schools can lead to a more positive climate within schools, but a positive climate does not necessarily cause more decentralization.

Definitions of Measures Used in the Multiple Regression Analysis

DEPENDENT VARIABLES

School Conflict. On a scale from 1 to 4, where 4 indicates a serious problem, the school mean of teachers' reports for three domains of conflict:

Conflict between staff and students: mean of seven items—student physical conflict, robbery, vandalism, possession of weapons, physical abuse of teachers, verbal abuse of teachers, general misbehavior.

Conflict among teachers: mean of two items—faculty consensus about the central mission of the school, cooperative effort among faculty members.

Conflict between teachers and principals: mean of ten items on management of school and the behavior of principals—fairness of evaluation of teachers, principal's expectations communicated, administrative support of teachers, resources available, principal's backing of teachers, frequency of communication about instructional practices, communication about kind of school wanted, recognition of staff, rules versus professional judgment, clarity of goals and priorities for school.

Note: Each of the three school conflict variables is a composite measure derived from factor analysis (with varimax rotation method) of teachers' reports of school conditions and climate. Item loadings of .5 were considered necessary for inclusion in a factor. No items loaded on more than one factor. Each factor had high internal consistency ($a > .7$).

Teacher Turnover. This was a dichotomous variable; $0 =$ currently teaching in same school as previous year, $1 =$ not teaching in same school as previous year. Turnover includes those who moved to other schools (migration) and those who left the teaching occupation altogether (attrition). The measure used in the logistic regression analysis excludes those who departed because of retirement, layoffs, or school closings, or because of being fired or terminated.

Teacher Characteristics.

Teaching experience: total years of teaching experience.

Master's degree or more: a dichotomous variable; 0 = bachelor's degree or less, 1 = master's degree or above.

Math/science: a dichotomous variable; 1 = teachers listed by their principal as primarily teaching secondary math or science, 0 = all other teachers.

Special education: a dichotomous variable; 1 = teachers listed by their principal as primarily teaching elementary or secondary special education, 0 = all other teachers.

Male: a dichotomous variable; 0 = female teacher, 1 = male teacher.

Minority: a dichotomous variable; 0 = white teachers, 1 = nonwhite teacher.

School Characteristics.

Private school: a dichotomous variable; 0 = public school, 1 = private school.

School size: student enrollment of school divided by 100; hence, the estimate represents the effect of a change in school enrollment of 100 students.

Rural school: a dichotomous variable for school location; 0 = urban fringe/large town or central city, 1 = rural/small town.

Suburban school: a dichotomous variable for school location; 0 = rural/small town or central city, 1 = urban fringe/large town.

Poverty enrollment: percentage of students receiving federal reduced-cost or free-lunch program for families below poverty level. Note: this measure was not available for the teacher turnover analysis.

Minority enrollment: percentage of students identified as African American, Hispanic, Asian, Pacific Islander, or American Indian.

Secondary school: a dichotomous variable; 0 = elementary/combined-level school, 1 = secondary-level school.

Teacher Classroom Control. On a scale from 1 (none) to 6 (complete control), the school mean of teacher control over classroom planning and teaching of two types:

Instructional: mean of four items—selecting textbooks and other instructional materials; selecting content, topics, and skills to be taught; selecting teaching techniques; determining the amount of homework to be assigned.

Social: disciplining students.

Teacher Schoolwide Control. On a scale from 1 (none) to 6 (a great deal), the school mean of teacher influence over school policies of two types:

Instructional: establishing curriculum.

Social: mean of two items—setting policy on grouping students in classes by ability, determining discipline policy.

Summary statistics for these measures are found in Tables A.1 and A.2.

Table A.1 Means and standard deviations of measures used in the multiple regression analyses of school conflict

Variable	Mean	S.D.
School conflict		
Conflict between staff and students	1.8	.58
Conflict among teachers	1.8	.67
Conflict between teachers and principals	1.9	.61
Teacher characteristics		
Teaching experience	14	8.62
Master's degree or more	.45	—
Math/science	.10	—
Male	.29	—
Minority	.10	—
School characteristics		
Private school	.11	—
School size	698	548
Suburban school	.31	—
Rural school	.39	—
% poverty enrollment	27	25
% minority enrollment	27	30
Secondary school	.35	—
Teacher classroom control		
Instructional	4.9	.58
Social	4.9	.67
Teacher schoolwide control		
Instructional	3.7	.97
Social	3.5	.89

Source: Schools and Staffing Survey.
Note: Means and standard errors are associated with the teachers in the sample.

Table A.2   Means and standard deviations of measures used in the logistic
regression analysis of teacher turnover

Variable	Mean	S.D.
Teacher turnover	.086	—
Teacher characteristics		
Teaching experience	15	8.99
Math/science	.11	—
Special education	.10	—
Male	.28	—
Minority	.18	—
School characteristics		
Private school	.12	—
School size	687	518
Suburban school	.31	—
Rural school	.40	—
% minority enrollment	28	31
Secondary School	.33	—
Teacher classroom control		
Instructional	4.9	.58
Social	4.9	.66
Teacher schoolwide control		
Instructional	3.8	.97
Social	3.6	.88

Source: Schools and Staffing Survey and Teacher Followup Survey

Note: Means and standard errors are associated with the teachers in the sample. The four
measures of teacher control are all school means of the reports of the total SASS teacher
sample for each school and are not limited to the reports of those in the smaller TFS teacher
sample.

Results from the Multiple Regression Analysis

The results of the analyses of the four outcomes are displayed in two ta-bles—one for the three conflict outcomes (Table A.3) and one for teacher turnover (Table A.4). Each outcome has two models aligned in two verti-cal columns. Each model displays the unstandardized estimates indicating the effects of each independent variable. The top portion for each model shows the estimates for the effects of the various background characteris-tics of teachers, schools and their student populations on the dependent variable. The bottom portion for each model shows the estimates of the effects of the four measures of teacher control on the dependent variable. Because the measures of teacher schoolwide control and teacher control in classrooms are highly interrelated, it is not possible to clearly discern their separate effects when both are included in a single model, hence the need for two separate models for the analysis of each outcome. For each outcome, model 1 focuses on the effects of teacher classroom control, and model 2 focuses on the effects of teacher schoolwide control.

Table A.3 Multilevel multiple regression analyses of variables related to school conflict

Variable	Between staff and students in schools				Among teachers in schools				Between teachers and principals in schools			
	Model 1		Model 2		Model 1		Model 2		Model 1		Model 2	
	(b)	(se)	(b)	(se)	(b)	(se)	(b)	(se)	(b)	(se)	(b)	(se)
Teacher characteristics												
Teaching experience	−.003*	.0003	−.003*	.0003	−.01*	.0004	−.01*	.0004	−.0004	.0003	−.0002	.0003
Master's degree or more	.001	.005	.0003	.005	.06*	.007	.05*	.006	.05*	.006	.05*	.006
Math/science	.01	.008	.01	.008	−.003	.010	−.01	.010	.05*	.009	.05*	.009
Male	.02*	.005	.02*	.006	.09*	.007	.09*	.007	.03*	.006	.03*	.006
Minority	−.14*	.009	−.13*	.009	−.06*	.011	−.06*	.011	−.11*	.010	−.11*	.010
School characteristics												
Private school	−.17*	.011	−.16*	.01	−.22*	.014	−.18*	.014	−.09*	.013	−.04*	.013
School size	.02*	.001	.01*	.001	.01*	.001	.003*	.001	.001	.001	−.002	.001
Suburban school	−.03*	.009	−.02*	.010	−.004	.011	.003	.011	.001	.011	.01	.010
Rural school	−.07*	.009	−.08*	.010	.008	.012	−.004	.011	.05*	.011	.02*	.010
% poverty enrollment	.003*	.0002	.003*	.0002	.0001	.0002	.0001	.0002	.0002	.0002	.0002	.0002
% minority enrollment	.003*	.0002	.003*	.0002	.001*	.0002	.001*	.0002	−.001*	.0002	−.001*	.0002
Secondary school	.20*	.009	.17*	.009	.17*	.010	.11*	.011	.10*	.011	.005	.010
Teacher classroom control												
Instructional	−.002	.006			−.02*	.008			−.02*	.008		

Table A.3 (continued)

Variable	Between staff and students in schools				Among teachers in schools				Between teachers and principals in schools			
	Model 1		Model 2		Model 1		Model 2		Model 1		Model 2	
	(b)	(se)	(b)	(se)	(b)	(se)	(b)	(se)	(b)	(se)	(b)	(se)
Social	−.16*	.005			−.10*	.007			−.18*	.007		
Teacher schoolwide control												
Instructional			−.02*	.004			−.02*	.005			−.02*	.005
Social			−.10*	.005			−.14*	.006			−.21*	.005
Constant	2.3*	.035	2.0*	.0003	2.4*	.042	2.3*	.025	2.8*	.040	2.7*	.023
R^2 (school-level variance)	.51		.51		.25		.35		.21		.38	
Sample size	43,837		43,837		43,837		43,837		43,837		43,837	

Source: Schools and Staffing Survey.

b = unstandardized estimate

se = standard error

* p < .05

Table A.4 Multilevel logistic regression analysis of variables related to teacher turnover from schools

Variable	Model 1 (b)	(se)	Model 2 (b)	(se)
Teacher characteristics				
Teaching experience	−.07*	.008	−.07*	.008
Math/science	.10	.222	.08	.221
Special education	.14	.202	.13	.203
Male	.10	.146	.11	.147
Minority	−.14	.207	−.13	.206
School characteristics				
Private school	.68*	.128	.68*	.125
School size	−.04*	.015	−.04*	.016
Suburban school	.003	.153	.01	.151
Rural school	−.08	.151	−.11	.150
% minority enrollment	.004	.003	.004	.003
Secondary school	−.10	.163	−.17	.165
Teacher classroom control				
Instructional	−.15	.116		
Social	−.25*	.09		
Teacher schoolwide control				
Instructional			−.08	.068
Social			−.17*	.071
Constant	.44	.71	−.62	.385
−2 Log likelihood	1,431,356		1,433,654	
Sample size	5,248		5,248	

Source: Schools and Staffing Survey and Teacher Followup Survey.
b = unstandardized estimate
se = standard error
* p < .05

NOTES

1. Introduction

1. For an especially insightful discussion of this role of schooling, see Grant 1988.
2. See, for example, Elam 1995.
3. For examples or reviews of research on the school disorganization perspective, see Corwin 1981; Bacharach 1981; Hanson 1981; Tyler 1988; Goodlad 1985; Borman and Spring 1984; Wilson, Herriott, and Firestone 1990.
4. For discussion of policies and reforms designed to increase accountability in schools, see Callahan 1962; Wise 1979; Goodlad 1984, 1985; McNeil 1988; Cornbleth 1989; McDonnell 1989; Finn, Kanstoroom, and Petrilli 1999; Fuhrman and Elmore 1990; Wirt and Kirst 1989; Elmore 2000.
5. For examples of this organizational perspective, see Cohen, March, and Olsen 1972; March and Olsen 1976; Weick 1976, 1979, 1984; Meyer and Rowan 1977, 1978; Meyer et al. 1978; Meyer 1984; Meyer and Scott 1983.
6. For a clear set of summaries of this perspective, see Clune and Witte 1990 or Hannaway and Carnoy 1993.
7. For reviews or examples of research in the teacher disempowerment

perspective, see Bacharach, Bauer, and Shedd 1988; Rosenholtz 1989; Corcoran, Walker, and White 1988; Shedd and Bacharach 1991; Johnson 1990; Carnegie Forum 1986; Holmes Group 1986; Weis et al. 1989; Rinehart et al. 1998; Smylie 1994; Hoy and Miskel 1996; Lightfoot 1986; Malen and Ogawa 1988a, 1988b; Midgley and Wood 1993; Blase and Anderson 1995; Short and Greer 1997; Rice and Schneider 1994.

8. For examples of relevant work in this perspective, see Burns and Stalker 1961; Turner and Lawrence 1964; Likert 1967; Porter, Lawler, and Hackman 1975; Kanter 1977; Tannenbaum et al. 1974; Hackman and Oldham 1980; Walton 1980; Whyte and Blasi 1982.

9. See Kirst 1984.

10. See Scott 1987.

11. U.S. Bureau of the Census 1998.

12. Kuhn 1962.

13. My definitions of bureaucracy and organizational rationality follow those of Scott 1987, Perrow 1986, Collins 1975, and Kanter 1977.

14. See, for example, Perrow 1986, Edwards 1979, Burawoy 1979, Frey 1971, and Lukes 1974.

15. See, for example, Kirst 1984, p. 3; Corcoran, Walker, and White 1988; Meyer and Scott 1983, p. 75; Firestone 1985.

16. For details and technical background on the School Assessment Survey, see Firestone and Wilson 1989; Wilson, Firestone, and Herriott 1985.

17. For details and technical background on the International Survey of the Locus of Decision-Making in Educational Systems, see Organization for Economic Co-operation and Cultural Development 1995, 1998.

2. The Debate over Control

1. Perhaps one of the clearest statements of this problem comes from Reinhard Bendix's seminal study of managerial ideologies, authority, and work in industrial societies (Bendix 1956). For other discussions of

the control/consent problem, also see Etzioni 1961, Burawoy 1979, Edwards 1979, Perrow 1986, and Smith 1990.

2. For discussion of organizational control as one of the "primordial" issues, see Selznick 1948, and as the prime "point of convergence," see Hickson 1966. For discussion of organizational decision making, see March and Simon 1958; for centralization, see Blau 1968; for employee compliance, see Etzioni 1961, for types of authority structures, see Meyer 1968; for employee participation, see Berg 1978; for power, see Crozier 1964, Perrow 1986, Pfeffer 1981.

3. For Weber's classic discussion of rational-legal forms of "imperative coordination" and their embodiment in the bureaucratic model of administration, see Weber 1946, pp. 196–244, and 1947, pp. 324–341.

4. My necessarily brief sketch here of organizational theory, the study of bureaucracy, and Weber's concept of rationality draws from Scott's standard text (1987). It is important to recognize that in the context of bureaucratic organizations, the term *rationality* is used in the narrow sense of formal or technical rationality. This refers to the rationality not of the goals but of the means by which they are achieved. In contrast to formal rationality, substantive rationality is concerned with how sensible and valuable the goals of the entity are. It is, of course, possible to use rational means to obtain nonrational ends. Weber, for instance, pointed out that regardless of the degree of formal rationality, whether observers find organizations to be characterized by substantive rationality depends on what values and standards the observers themselves hold (Weber 1947, pp. 185, 215).

5. Theory in this field has been marked by the development of numerous parallel analytic dichotomies—organic/mechanical, open/closed, informal/formal, natural/bureaucratic, institutional/organizational, professional/bureaucratic—all of which touch upon, in one way or another, variations in this tension within and between organizations. For useful reviews of the literature on the limits of the bureaucratic model, see Zey-Ferrell and Aiken 1981, Corwin 1981, Pfeffer 1982.

6. The ideas of this perspective have generated a great deal of interest in the sources, forms, and variations of organizational looseness and tightness. The result is a body of research that is highly varied, depending on the units and levels of analysis chosen and the definition of loose coupling used. Some analysts, for example, focus on the connections among individuals within organizations; others focus on the degree of coupling among organizations; even others focus on linkages among sectors or populations of organizations. This body of work is actually made up of several different streams of thought and research: "garbage can" theory (see, for example, Cohen, March, and Olsen 1972; March and Olsen 1976); the organizational social psychology of Karl Weick (1976, 1979, 1984); and institutional theory (see Meyer and Rowan 1977, 1978, Meyer et al. 1978, Meyer 1984, Meyer and Scott 1983). While it shares an emphasis on loose coupling, institutional theory is a distinctly different approach to organizational analysis from that of Weick and March. Moreover, institutional theory is not one theory but rather several theories and approaches that are not entirely consistent or cohesive. For reviews of this genre, see Zucker (1987, 1988) and Scott (1988). My discussion here refers to that branch of institutional theory associated with the work of Richard Scott, John Meyer, and their associates. Its contribution has been to transcend traditional task-oriented explanations of organizations and resurrect and reconstruct Philip Selznick's (1949) notion of institutionalization as the driving force shaping organizational order and disorder. Indeed, this variant of institutional theory is often credited (e.g., Dreeben 1994) with providing an intriguing explanation of the anomaly of loosely coupled organizations: tight coupling at the interorganizational level leads to loose coupling at the intraorganizational level.

The image conveyed by institutional theories is one of form over substance—a presentation of engineered impressions by organizations, which are themselves the actors. Such outward conformity is all important; "organizations that do so increase their legitimacy and their survival prospects, independent of the immediate efficacy of the acquired practices and procedures" (Meyer and Scott 1983, p. 21). Institutionalization is, however, a source of both legitimacy and internal looseness. Because such organizations must pay close attention to a range of pressures from important environmental constituencies, they "decouple"—that is, intentionally neglect to adequately supervise, coordinate, and control their workers and productive activities. This is a useful strategy for three reasons. First, it serves to hide inconsistencies and inefficiencies—in short, poor performance—that might undermine public faith in the organization. Second, internal decoupling allows local input into organizational processes without disrupting the outward public face of the organization. Third, the autonomy associated with decoupling generates commitment and job satisfaction on the part of employees. But, of course, although loose coupling aids the legitimacy and survival of the organization, it can also lead to poor performance and organizational inefficiency. For a more detailed summary and critique of theory and research on loosely coupled systems, see Ingersoll 1993.

7. See Aldrich's summary of research on organizational coupling. In it, he notes that "the major determinant of coupling [is] the degree of hierarchical control by a central authority" (1978, p. 52).

8. For insightful discussion of this tension, see, for example, Block and Hirschorn 1987.

9. See, for example, Weick 1976; Meyer and Scott 1983; Corwin 1981; Tyler 1985, 1988.

10. Ouchi, in his review of organizational culture analysis, went so far as to claim that "it was the resistance of school systems to bureaucratic interpretation that brought to an end the study of formal organization structure." See Ouchi and Wilkins 1985, p. 467.

11. See Meyer and Scott 1983, p. 48. For examples or reviews of research finding that schools are overly loose, see Corwin 1981; Bacharach 1981; Hanson 1981; Tyler 1988; Goodlad 1984, 1985; Borman and Spring 1984; Wilson, Herriott, and Firestone 1990.

12. Among the most representative studies in this line of research are

Dewey 1974 (1902); Waller 1932; Becker 1953; Bidwell 1965, 1970; Lortie 1969, 1973, 1975, 1977; Dreeben 1973, 1976. In particular, my summary draws from two classic pieces: Bidwell's 1965 review of the formal organization of schools, and Lortie's 1969 article on the organizational control of teachers.

13. See, for example, Lortie 1969, pp. 9, 14; 1977, p. 30.

14. The more recent work of Bidwell has insightfully elaborated the sources and variations of looseness in schools. He and his associates developed a typology of mechanisms by which the work of teachers is organizationally controlled across different kinds of schools. In their model, organizational-control systems in schools vary from top-down, highly bureaucratized, highly centralized to loosely coupled, highly debureaucratized, highly decentralized, depending on the size of the school and the socioeconomic status of the school community. Their focus is on the different forms of workplace control in schools, how these are embedded in the social organization of school workplaces, and how these affect a range of student outcomes. See Bidwell and Quiroz 1991, and Bidwell, Frank, and Quiroz 1997.

15. As noted earlier, Bidwell, Lortie, and their associates, for instance, argue that structural looseness in schools, while perhaps dysfunctional in some ways, is, nevertheless, an inevitable, necessary, and functional condition of schools. By granting faculty an unusual degree of discretion over classroom instructional matters, administrators are able to harness the skills and expertise of teachers and generate their consent in organizational arrangements.

Likewise, as also noted earlier, Meyer, Scott, and their associates have argued that loose coupling has mixed consequences for schools. Although they found loose coupling to promote inefficiency and ineffectiveness with regard to teachers' and students' productive activities, these analysts also held that looseness serves to mask these inefficiencies and ameliorate potential tensions with staff, thus ensuring long-term organizational stability and survival (Meyer and Scott 1983, pp. 50–51, 57).

For discussions of the negative implications of loose structuring from the viewpoint of the movement to improve school standards and accountability, see Hannaway and Carnoy 1993, Elmore 2000, Barth 1985.

16. See Levin 1998 for an insightful review of this movement and these arguments.

17. See, for example, Bennett 1993, Murray and Herrnstein 1992, Hirsch 1987, Josephson 1992, Crawford 1980, Kellman 1982.

18. See Etzioni 1996.

19. For criticism of increasing student standards and accountability, see, for example, Bourdieu and Passeron 1977, Bowles and Gintis 1976, Giroux 1981, Darling-Hammond 1994.

20. See, for example, Rist 1970; Haycock 1998; Hull 1994; Bennefield 1997; Urban League 1999; Stevens 1993; Herndon 1968, 1971; Kozol 1967. Criticisms of the role of decentralization in racial disparities in educational resources are, of course, not limited to the problems of teacher quality. For example, another prominent set of criticisms of school decentralization focuses on funding inequities inherent in the system of local control of schooling. Proponents of this view typically call for top-down intervention from the state or federal level. See, for example, Kozol 1991.

21. See Associated Press story by Shepard, February 19, 2000.

22. See, for example, Sadker and Sadker 1994.

23. It is important to acknowledge that the initiatives proposed by these reform groups do not always begin as more top-down control. For example, unlike many of the reform reports of its type, *A Nation at Risk* recommended that teachers themselves be given more decision-making influence in order to achieve the new standards and goals proposed. I will return to these reform differences in the concluding chapter.

24. For insightful discussion of state education reforms and the power relations between states, school districts, and schools, see, for examples, Theobald and Malen 2000, Hannaway and Talbert 1993, Hannaway

1993, Hannaway and Carnoy 1993, Fuhrman and Elmore 1990, Anyon 1997.

25. See National Education Goals Panel 1997.

26. See, for example, Coleman and Hoffer 1987; Chubb and Moe 1990; Bryk, Lee, and Holland 1993.

27. For a historical perspective on this movement, see Katz 1972, 1987.

28. For discussion of this viewpoint, see Rogers 1968; Ravitch 1974; Fantini, Gittell, and Magat 1979; Borman and Spring 1984.

29. See, for instance, Neill 1960; Kozol 1967; Herndon 1968, 1971.

30. For summaries of this perspective, see Clune and Witte 1990.

31. For discussion of this perspective, see, for example, Rogers 1968; Borman and Spring 1984; Chubb and Moe 1990; Finn, Kanstoroom, and Petrilli 1999.

32. See McPherson 1972, chap. 5; Waller 1932; Tyack 1974.

33. Reviews or representative examples of this literature and research include: Conley and Cooper 1991; Conley 1991; Corcoran, Walker, and White 1988; Rosenholtz 1989; Sergiovanni and Moore 1989; Bacharach, Bauer, and Shedd 1988; Bacharach, Bamberger, and Conley 1990; Shedd and Bacharach 1991; Johnson 1990; Rinehart et al. 1998; Smylie 1994; Hoy and Miskel 1996; Lightfoot 1986; Malen and Ogawa 1988a, 1988b; Blase and Anderson 1995; Short and Greer 1997; Rice and Schneider 1994.

34. For summaries of this reform stream, see, for example, Cornbleth 1989; Weis et al. 1989; David 1989; Cistone 1989; Hannaway and Carnoy 1993; Midgley and Wood 1993.

35. For representative statements by teacher union presidents, see Shanker 1989, and Futrell 1988.

36. Among the most relevant works in this area of organizational research are Burns and Stalker 1961; Turner and Lawrence 1964; Likert 1967; Porter, Lawler, and Hackman 1975; Kanter 1977; Tannenbaum et al. 1974; Hackman and Oldham 1980; Walton 1980; Whyte and Blasi 1982.

37. Freidson (1973), for example, distinguishes between control over the content of work (the what and how of tasks) and control over the larger terms of work (the organizational and social context that defines and regulates the work). Groups that control important parts of the larger terms of their work are, in turn, likely to have substantial control over the content of their work. For a useful review of the sources of workplace control, see Simpson 1985. For other work on organizational control, see, for example, Crozier 1964, Perrow 1986, Kanter 1977, Pfeffer and Salancik 1978, Thompson 1967, Selznick 1949, Pfeffer 1981, Tannenbaum et al. 1974, Hinings et al. 1974.

38. See Selznick 1949.

39. For discussion of the zone view, see Lortie 1969, 1975; Barr and Dreeben 1983.

40. See Parsons 1960 for an early discussion of this model.

41. See, for example, Meyer and Scott 1983, Firestone 1985.

42. Disempowerment analysts typically advocate examining decision making in a wide range of domains, such as personnel, curriculum, student life, and budgetary matters (Rinehart et al. 1998). See, for example, Rosenholtz 1989; Bacharach, Bauer, and Shedd 1988; Conley and Cooper 1991; Shedd and Bacharach 1991; Firestone and Bader 1991.

43. Conley 1991, pp. 237–238.

44. See Durkheim 1961 (1925); Sorokin 1928; Dewey 1974 (1902), 1934; Waller 1932; Parsons 1959; Henry 1965; Dreeben 1968; Jackson 1968; Katz 1972; Bowles and Gintis 1976; Bourdieu and Passeron 1977; Apple 1982; Giroux 1981; Grant 1988; Kirst 1989; Schneider and Stevenson 1999; Goodman 2001.

45. See, for example, Coleman and Hoffer 1987 and Coleman 1987.

46. It is necessary to recognize that although Coleman and others emphasize academic test scores, they do not totally ignore nonacademic outcomes. Some, of course, do examine dropping out, delinquency, alienation, and so on as valid outcomes of schooling.

47. See Murray and Herrnstein 1992 for a discussion based on the assumption that student assessment scores are evidence of moral learning and character development.

48. Like the concept of bureaucracy, the term *institution* is defined and used in numerous ways. Some, for instance, use it to refer to organizations, others to a normative principle behind organized behavior. There is a long tradition in organizational theory concerned with the distinction between organizations and institutions. Following Selznick (1957) and Scott (1987), by institution I mean an entity that is "infused with value beyond the technical requirements at hand." A formal organization refers to a rational tool geared to specified goals; an institution refers to a more natural, more normative, less technically oriented collectivity.

49. For a review of the vast sociological research on educational stratification, see Bidwell and Friedkin 1988.

50. Using this broader view of discipline, in his classic treatise on education Durkheim makes a compelling case that a "spirit of discipline" is *the* basic element of the moral and social order transmitted in schools (see, for example, Durkheim 1961 [1925], chaps. 2 and 3). By discipline Durkheim is not referring to the inculcation of specific moral precepts, nor to a temporary constraint imposed to prevent misbehavior. He views discipline in the general sense of a necessary adherence on the part of students to social norms. He writes: "Through it and by means of it alone are we able to teach the child to rein in his desires, to set limits to his appetites of all kinds, to limit and, through limitation, to define the goals of his activity. This limitation is the condition of happiness" (pp. 43–44).

51. See Brint, Contreras, and Mathews 2001 for an insightful study of whose values are emphasized in public schools.

52. Data on the views of professors of education are from a 1997 survey conducted by Public Agenda, an education-oriented public opinion research group based in New York. The sample size was 900 college and

university professors. For details on the data and survey see, Farkas, Johnson, and Duffett 1997.

53. For SASS data on teachers' and principals' views of the most important goals of schools, see Choy et al. 1993b. For the Phi Delta Kappa survey data, see Elam 1995.

54. Crawford 1980, Kellman 1982.

55. See, for example, Haycock 1998, Sadker and Sadker 1994, Urban League 1999.

56. See Scott 1987 for a discussion of the bureaucratic model.

57. For instance, when Weick (1984, p. 397) describes loose coupling as disconnection "between headquarters and the field," he is referring to the control of teachers by administrators, not vice versa.

58. See Edwards 1979.

59. Shedd and Bacharach 1991, p. 1. For examination of the degree of professionalism in teaching, see, for example, Firestone and Bader 1991 or Talbert and McLaughlin 1994.

60. For examples and discussion of the extensive literature on professionals versus bureaucratized employees, the trade-offs between professional and bureaucratic control, and the characteristics that distinguish professions from other kinds of occupations see, for example, Hall 1968; Parsons 1960; Mills 1951; Perrow 1986; Simpson 1985; Scott 1987; Kohn and Schooler 1983; Freidson 1973, 1984, 1986; Larson 1977; Abbott 1988; Vollmer and Mills 1966.

61. For an early insightful article that made these points, see Freidson 1970.

62. For discussion of the characteristics of the work of professors and of the academic occupation, see, for example, Mills 1951, Krause 1971, Clark 1987, Grant and Murray 1999.

63. See, for example, Starr 1982; Freidson 1973, 1984, 1986; Larson 1977.

64. How much collective public control over schooling is actually wielded by local school governing boards and school district administrative staffs is the subject of much debate. For review of the argument that

layperson control can be inversely related to professional control, see Lortie 1969 and Clark 1987. For an insightful discussion of school boards as instruments of client control, see Tyack 1999. For a review of the functions and powers of school boards and school districts and their power relationship with states, see, e.g., Campbell, Cunningham, and McPhee 1985; Hannaway and Carnoy 1993; Fuhrman and Elmore 1990; Hannaway and Talbert 1993.

65. See, Lukes 1974; Gaventa 1980; Pfeffer 1981; Frey 1970, 1971, 1978; Simpson 1985; Edwards 1979.

66. See Meyer and Scott 1983, pp. 50–51, 57–58, 74–75, 84; Dornbusch and Scott 1975.

67. Perrow 1986.

68. Weber, for instance, described two less-rationalized modes of authority: that based on personal loyalty to a leader and that based on taken-for-granted norms and tradition. For an insightful discussion of these issues, see Perrow 1986, especially chap. 1.

69. For insightful discussions of the point of limiting the discretion of higher management, see, for example, Caplow 1954, p. 66; Kanter 1977, pp. 73, 118; Kohn and Schooler 1983, chap. 2.

70. See, for example, Lortie 1969, 1975.

71. See Weber 1946, p. 202; Kohn and Schooler 1983.

3. Teachers and Decision Making in Schools

1. For histories of schooling in the United States, see, Tyack 1974, Cremin 1964, Kirst 1984.

2. Data on student enrollment, attendance, and graduation are from the 1995 Common Core of Data Surveys and are published in Snyder, Hoffman, and Geddes 1997, p. 50. Data on districts, schools, and teachers are from the 1993–94 SASS.

3. Snyder, Hoffman, and Geddes 1997, p. 36.

4. See National Education Goals Panel 1997.

5. For discussion of the decline in local control, see Walberg and

Walberg 1994, Fuhrman and Elmore 1990, Hannaway and Carnoy 1993.

6. The International Survey of the Locus of Decision-Making in Educational Systems was conducted by the Indicators of Education Systems (INES) project of the Center for Educational Research and Innovation of the OECD. The data represent public schools at both the elementary and secondary level. The 1990–91 cycle of the survey included fourteen nations, and the 1997–98 cycle included thirty-three nations. The data in Figure 3.1 are from the 1997–98 cycle of the survey. For further information on the 1990–91 survey, see OECD 1995. For details on the 1997–98 survey, see OECD 1998.

7. For a set of insightful papers on these debates, see Theobald and Malen 2000.

8. The data in Figure 3.2 represent the means of respondent scores from all four school sites. My field interview sample was twenty-two respondents. In my field research I examined teacher control and influence over a total of twenty-seven issues, including both administrative and educational decisions and, in reference to the latter, for both social and instructional issues. These decisions included most of the same issues examined in the OECD survey and all the issues examined in NCES's Schools and Staffing Survey. Moreover, in my interviews I intentionally used wording similar to that used in the SASS questionnaires; for example: "At this school how much actual influence do you think teachers have over school policy in . . .?" I used a standard four-point scale: "none, minor, moderate, major."

The results of fieldwork and qualitative research usually come in the form of detailed accounts of how individuals in a certain setting make sense of their world and their lives. Typically, this mode of research provides the reader with a series of real-life instances and illustrations of the phenomena under study. In this way, the researcher is able to take advantage of one of the strengths of fieldwork—its *depth* of fine-grained detail. To this end, I will later describe in some detail how teachers' jobs are organized and how control is achieved within the four different schools studied. In this chapter, however, I present the results of the fieldwork in an alternative manner. I adopt the unusual step of quantifying my qualitative data. My objective is to take advantage of a second strength of my fieldwork—its *breadth*. Intensive interviews provide an opportunity to examine a broad number of issues, thus compensating for the limits inherent to large-scale survey questionnaires. Quantifying the results of my interviews allows me to reveal the commonalities in control among the four different types of schools.

There is, in addition, a second advantage to summarizing respondents' accounts in numerical form. Throughout this study I attempt to take advantage of the relative strengths of each type of data and method in order to speak to the question of validity—asking, can we trust these data, especially for measuring phenomena as complex and sensitive as power? To this end I analyzed and will present in this chapter both field interview data and survey data to provide a means of checking the validity of each and of the patterns I found.

9. Preservice is the training teachers receive prior to employment. In contrast, inservice is the formal training and retraining teachers receive once employed. It typically involves workshops, seminars, and conferences on teaching issues, provided to teachers by the school or district one or more times during the school year.

10. See, for example, Lortie 1975.

11. The data in Table 3.1 are from the teacher questionnaire of the 1990–91 SASS. The sample size was 29,890 secondary-level teachers. For a detailed and parallel analysis using the 1987–88 SASS, see Ingersoll 1994. SASS asked about teachers' perceptions of their influence over decision making for a number of education issues within schools. The questions focused on two units of analysis: the amount of faculty influence over schoolwide issues and the amount of the teacher respondent's control over classroom issues.

For the school level, teachers were asked, "At this school, how much influence do you think teachers have over school policy in each of the areas below: determining discipline policy; determining the content of inservice programs; setting policy on grouping students in classes by ability; establishing curriculum." For these items the questionnaire used a six-point scale from "none" to "a great deal."

For the classroom issues, teachers were asked, "At this school, how much control do you feel you have in your classroom over each of the following areas of your planning and teaching: selecting textbooks and other instructional materials; selecting content, topics, and skills to be taught; selecting teaching techniques; disciplining students; determining the amount of homework to be assigned." These questions used a six-point scale from "none" to "complete control."

The data in Table 3.1 present the frequency of teachers reporting themselves to have "a great deal" of influence or "complete control" over each of these decisions. I defined teachers as having a "great deal of influence" or "complete control" if their score was equal to six on a scale of one to six, where one equals "none" and six equals "a great deal" or "complete control." I also grouped the decisions into two categories, social and instructional. In Table 3.1 junior teachers are those with less than four years of total teaching experience. Senior teachers are those with four or more years.

It is revealing to recognize the extent to which the survey's questionnaire design itself reflects the conventional zone view of the distribution of control in schools. The items are divided between classroom and schoolwide zones, instruction is equated with the classroom zone, and, in addition, that domain is disproportionately weighted; more than half of the total decisions concern instructional matters. The fact that the questionnaire primarily focuses on the control of classroom instruction illustrates the assumption that teachers' primary task and realm of decision-making control is classroom academic instruction. Consequently, any overall aggregate score would be effectively biased.

12. See, for example, Lortie 1977.

13. See, for example, Talbert and McLaughlin 1994. For higher education, see Salancik and Pfeffer's (1974) classic study of power differences among departments and schools within the University of Illinois.

14. Of course, particular types of teachers may be clustered in particular types of schools, and so teacher-to-teacher differences in teacher control could be confounded by school-to-school differences in teacher control. To find out if this is the case, I conducted within- and between-school analyses of the relationships between teacher control and both teacher and school characteristics. The data confirmed a lack of correlation between teacher types and teacher control.

15. The data in Figures 3.3 and 3.4 and Table 3.3 on discipline, hiring, and curriculum are from the school administrator questionnaire of the 1990–91 SASS. The sample size was 4,110 secondary schools. The data on the budget, teacher evaluation, and inservice are from the school administrator questionnaire of the 1993–94 SASS. The sample size was 4,031 secondary schools. I calculated standard errors for all of the SASS estimates in the tables and figures. Because of SASS's large sample sizes, differences between estimates were invariably statistically significant at a high level of confidence (above 95 percent), even if they were not of substantive significance. Hence, in my discussion I will focus on the latter. For a detailed and parallel analysis using the 1987–88 SASS, see Ingersoll 1994.

    In SASS questionnaires, principals (or headmasters in some private schools) at each school were asked, "Using the scale 1–6 [or 0–5 in the 1993–94 SASS], indicate how much actual influence you think each group or person has on decisions concerning the following activities— setting discipline policy; hiring new full-time teachers; establishing curriculum; evaluating teachers; determining the content of inservice programs; deciding how the school budget will be spent." The groups evaluated were school governing boards, school principals, and school faculties. In the 1993–94 questionnaire, school district staff were also included as a group, and I counted them with school governing boards. The questions used a six-point scale from "none" to "a great deal." In Figures 3.3 and 3.4, and Table 3.3, I defined the groups as having a "great deal of influence" if they had the highest score (six in the 1990–91 and five in the 1993–94).

The data on teacher assignment and student tracking in Figure 3.3 are from the 1993 Survey of High School Curricular Options, conducted by NCES. This survey was a supplement based on the 1990–91 SASS sample, but it was much smaller and only for public schools. Like the SASS administrator questionnaire, the Survey of High School Curricular Options asked principals about the influence of different groups on several school decisions, but the questions were worded slightly differently and used a slightly different scale. The questions used a four-point scale from "not at all" to "a great extent." In Figure 3.3, I defined the groups as having a "great deal of influence" if their score was four. The sample size was 912 public secondary schools. For the item on student tracking, the groups evaluated were school governing boards, school principals, and teacher department heads (not all teachers). For the item on teacher assignment, the groups evaluated were school district administrators, school principals, and teachers. Because these data were not collected for private schools and were not available for disaggregation, they are not included in Table 3.3. For more details on this survey, see Carey and Farris 1995.

16. For discussion of the case of higher education, see, for example, Mills 1951, Krause 1971, Clark 1987, Grant 1999.

17. See, for example, Frey 1970, Lukes 1974, Gaventa 1980.

18. For research on school differences in organizational characteristics, see Chubb and Moe 1990; Pallas 1988; Bidwell and Quiroz 1991; Bryk, Lee, and Smith 1990; Coleman and Hoffer 1987.

19. See n. 11, above, for information on the questionnaire items used in Table 3.2. As in Table 3.1, the data in Table 3.2 are from the teacher questionnaire of the 1990–91 SASS. I defined teachers as having "a great deal of influence" or "complete control" if their score was equal

to six on a scale of one to six, where one equals "none" and six equals "a great deal" or "complete control." In Table 3.2, small school size refers to those schools with student enrollments of less than 351. Large school size refers to schools with student enrollments greater than 650. The middle size category is omitted. The teacher sample sizes in Table 3.2 are: large public—14,738; small public—5,622; large private—478; small private—1,106.

20. The data in Figure 3.4 represent simple means, for each type of school, of the influence of each group for the six issues in Table 3.3. Refer to n. 15, above, for details.

21. See n. 15, above, for information on the questionnaire items. In Table 3.3, small school size refers to those schools with student enrollments of less than 351. Large school size refers to schools with student enrollments greater than 650. The middle size category is omitted. The school sample sizes in table 3.3 for the 1990–1991 data are: large public—1795; small public—975; large private—81; small private—261. The school sample sizes in table 3.2 for the 1993–1994 data are: large public—1849; small public—896; large private—108; small private—278.

22. In background analyses of the statistical relationship between the control of teachers and that of principals, I found, depending on the issue, a moderate to strong, statistically significant, positive correlation between principals' reports of their own control over decisions and both principals' reports of teachers' control and teachers' reports of teachers' control over decisions. In other words, schools with higher principal control also had higher teacher control, and vice versa. At the same time, I found either a weak negative correlation or no correlation between the control held by school boards and either principals' control or teachers' control.

23. Campbell et al. 1985.

24. See, for example, Chubb and Moe 1990.

25. For an insightful discussion of school boards as instruments of client control, see Tyack 1999.

4. Rules for Teachers

1. For reviews of the variety and range of employee control mechanisms, see, for example, Simpson 1985, Ouchi 1977, Edwards 1979, and Perrow 1986.

2. For a discussion of the objectives of employee control mechanisms, see Dornbusch and Scott 1975, and Edwards 1979.

3. In my field interviews, I asked respondents about school rules and policies for a wide range of issues and activities—parallel to those on decision-making influence described in Chapter 3. Table 4.1 illustrates the range of issues I investigated and indicates for which issues each of the schools had formal rules and policies of one kind or another. As in the previous chapter, I grouped these data into three types of activities: administrative, social, and instructional.

4. See, for example, Coleman and Hoffer 1987; Bryk, Lee, and Holland 1993.

5. In the Research for Better Schools (RBS) School Assessment Survey, for each of fifteen "activities of the professional staff" at their schools, teachers were asked, "whether such a policy exists, and if such a policy exists, how consistently it is enforced." In reference to the existence of a policy, the questionnaire used a four category scale: "yes, written; yes, unwritten; no policy; I don't know." Figure 4.1 shows the percent of teachers who reported that their school did have a policy, either written or unwritten, for each issue. As with the earlier field data on rules, I grouped these data into three types of activity: administrative, social, and instructional.

   The survey collected data from the entire faculty of each school selected, and the average school building response rate was 86 percent. I used the data from secondary schools only. The sample was 6,907 teachers from 158 public secondary schools. RBS developed the survey through four phases over the eleven-year period of its use (from 1979 to 1990). The questionnaire itself underwent slight alterations in each phase. As a result, some of the questions on school rules for teachers were used with only portions of the entire concatenated sample analyzed here. See Firestone and Wilson 1989; and Wilson, Firestone, and Herriott 1985 for details on the survey.

6. For a news report on this set of reform measures, see, for example, Saunders 1995.

7. For discussion of the conservative perspective on character education, see, for example, Bennett 1993; Murray and Herrnstein 1992; Josephson 1992; Crawford 1980; Kellman 1982.

8. See Weber 1946, p. 198.

9. For discussion of the phenomenon of bureaucracy from below, see, for example, Edwards 1979.

10. The data on schools with formal teacher evaluation programs are from the school questionnaire of the 1990–91 SASS. Sample sizes were 3,724 public secondary schools and 465 private secondary schools. The 1987–88 SASS yielded very similar results.

11. For detailed national data on the types, frequency, and criteria of public-school teacher performance evaluation, see Nolin, Rowand, and Farris 1994.

12. There is a voluminous literature on the advantages and disadvantages of the various methods and approaches to teacher assessment and evaluation. For a summary of methods and the debate, see Ingersoll 2002. Among the overviews of research and policy concerned with teacher assessment that I found most useful were Dwyer and Stufflebeam 1996; Haertel 1991; Haney, Madaus, and Kreitzer 1987; and Kennedy 1992. In addition, for a useful collection of articles, see Millman and Darling-Hammond 1990.

13. For discussion of the limitations of classroom performance assessments, see, for example, Shulman 1986; Haertel 1991; Stodolsky 1984; Murnane and Raizen 1988.

14. See Dwyer and Stufflebeam 1996.

15. Data on the usefulness of teacher evaluations are from the fourth

phase of RBS's School Assessment Survey, conducted in the late 1980s. The sample size was 456 teachers in 23 public secondary schools.

16. For discussion on the use of student scores to assess teachers, see, for example, Peterson and Lomeaux 1990, Educational Research Service 1988, Dwyer and Stufflebeam 1996; Kirst 1989.

17. For discussion of criticisms of the use of student scores to assess teachers, see, for example, Millman 1981; Berk 1988; Dwyer and Stufflebeam 1996.

18. Data are from the 1996 Survey of the Status of the American Public School Teacher, conducted by the National Education Association. Sample size was 1,325 K–12 public school teachers. For detailed information on the survey, see National Education Association 1996.

19. Data are from a 1998 survey conducted by Public Agenda, an education-oriented public opinion research group based in New York. Sample size was 700 K–12 public school teachers. For detailed information on the survey, see Farkas et al. 1999.

20. Data on the interference of rules are from the 1987–88 SASS. Sample size was 24,031 secondary school teachers. An identical question in the 1993–94 SASS yielded very similar results.

21. See, for example, Meyer and Scott 1983.

22. See, for example, the report in *Time* magazine, Hull 1994.

23. Examples of these kinds of arguments can be found in the writing of most of those who subscribe to the disorganization perspective. See Lortie 1969, 1975, 1977; Meyer and Scott 1983, pp. 50–51, 57–58, 74–75, 84; and also others, such as Urban League 1999.

24. For a detailed analysis of data on the flow of teachers within and between school districts, see Ingersoll 1995b and 1999.

25. For discussion and analysis of merit pay plans, see Murnane and Cohen 1986.

26. For a classic and insightful discussion of why teachers, even those deemed "good," have often opposed merit pay programs, see Lortie 1969.

The data on merit and incentive plans are from the public district and private school questionnaires of the 1990–91 and 1993–94 SASS. For the public district data, sample sizes were 4,884 districts in 1990–91 and 4,993 districts in 1993–94. For the private school data, sample sizes were 465 secondary schools in 1990–91 and 535 secondary schools in 1993–94.

27. See Weber 1946, pp. 202, 215–216, and also Kohn and Schooler 1983.

28. For a report on problems of accountability in charter schools, see Walsh 2001. For a series of articles in the *New York Times* on the problems of patronage in decentralized schools and districts where many of the normal bureaucratic rules were eliminated, see Berger 1989 (cited in Murnane et al. 1991, p. 94). For a colorful history of the teacher union movement and the motives behind the development of teacher tenure, salary scales, and seniority systems, see Selden 1985. Also see Tyack 1974.

29. See, for example, Crozier 1964; Perrow 1986: Kanter 1977; Pfeffer and Salancik 1978; Thompson 1967; Selznick 1949.

30. For an insightful discussion of the demands on high school teachers' time, see Sizer 1992a.

31. One notable exception to the lack of recognition for the prevalence and importance of out-of-field teaching is Sizer's 1992 study of high school teaching. For data on out-of-field teaching, see Ingersoll 1999. For data on the lack of state regulations on teacher employment and utilization, see Robinson 1985.

32. See, for example, Finley 1984.

33. In the School Assessment Survey, for each of fifteen important activities at their schools, teachers were asked, first, whether a written or unwritten policy exists, and, second, "if such a policy exists, how consistently it is enforced." In reference to the enforcement of a policy, a seven-category scale was used: "never; almost never; occasionally; frequently; almost always; always; I don't know." Figure 4.2 presents teachers' average reports of how consistently policies were enforced.

Again, I grouped these data according to type of activity: administrative, social, and instructional.

34. See, for example, Lukes 1974 or Gaventa 1980.

5. The Teacher in the Middle

1. For reviews of the variety and range of employee control mechanisms, see, for example, Perrow 1986, Simpson 1985, Ouchi 1977, Edwards 1979.

2. For discussion of the methodological difficulties in examining normative control in organizations see, for example, Etzioni 1961; Warren, Rose, and Bergunder 1974; Lukes 1974; Gaventa 1980; Perrow 1986.

3. My discussion pertaining to the unusual technology and clients of teaching and the problem of obtaining regular work from irregular workers is indebted to the seminal work of Bidwell (1965) and Lortie (1975, 1977).

4. For a review of the implications of the technology of occupations for control, see Simpson 1985.

5. See Waller 1932.

6. For detailed discussion of the limits to formal rules and regulations as control mechanisms, see, for example, Perrow 1986, pp. 128–131; Ouchi 1977; Bidwell and Quiroz 1991; Gaventa 1980.

7. For a discussion of the issue of measurability, see Sorensen and Kalleberg 1981.

8. My analysis of structural control is indebted to Perrow's discussion of what he calls bureaucratic control (1986), and Edwards's discussion of what he calls technical control (1979).

9. Discussion of these types of discretion draws from March and Simon 1958, pp. 145–150.

10. The right of professionals to pick and choose their clientele is, of course, a subject of debate—for example, as in the heated controversy in the 1980s over whether doctors were obligated, by professional eth-

ics, to treat patients with AIDS. For an insightful discussion, see Bosk and Frader 1990.

11. The data on teachers' workloads are from the teacher questionnaire of the 1993–94 SASS. Sample size was 26,624 (public and private) secondary school teachers. The 1987–88 and 1990–91 SASS both yielded similar results.

12. For an insightful description of this problem, see Sizer 1992a.

13. For discussion of rate busting, see Roy 1952 and Burawoy 1979.

14. There is a large and varied literature critiquing the social and political interests embedded in "objective" standards and testing. See, for example, Cicourel and Kitsuse 1963, Freire 1973, Cicourel et al. 1974, Labaree 1988, Bowles and Gintis 1976, Bourdieu and Passeron 1977, Giroux 1981.

15. Especially useful for understanding deskilling and its implications for organizational control is the well-known research of Harry Braverman (1974).

16. For classic organizational theory and research on the relationship between employee replaceability and power, see Hickson et al. 1971 and Hinings et al. 1974.

17. For discussion of the complexities of teaching, see, for example, Darling-Hammond 1986, McKeachie 1994, Shulman 1986.

18. For empirical data from cross-occupational research, see, for example, Kohn and Schooler's well-known comparative study of work and occupations. They concluded that secondary teaching involved greater substantive complexity than the work of accountants, salespersons, machinists, and managers in service industries and the retail trade (Kohn and Schooler 1983, p. 68).

19. See Shanker (1985) for an essay condemning out-of-field teaching as education's "dirty little secret."

20. Notable exceptions to this include Conant 1963; Haggstrom, Darling-Hammond, and Grissmer 1988; and Sizer 1992a.

21. For reports of my research on out-of-field teaching, see Ingersoll 1995b, 1999, 2001a.

22. Beginning in the mid-1990s, the SASS data on out-of-field teaching were widely reported in the national media and featured in numerous major education policy reports. Among these: *What Matters Most: Teaching for America's Future* (1996) and *Doing What Matters Most: Investing in Quality Teaching* (1997), both by the National Commission on Teaching and America's Future; *Quality Counts* (1998, 1999, 2000), special annual supplements to *Education Week* magazine; and *Education Watch* (1996, 1998, 2000), by the Education Trust.

23. For a personal account of the problems of teaching high school subjects one does not know, see Sizer 1992a, pp. 187–191.

24. There is an extensive body of empirical research, going back decades, devoted to assessing the effects of teacher qualifications on teacher and student performance. For measures of qualifications, researchers typically examine whether teachers have a particular credential, such as a degree or a teaching certificate, reflecting a variety of types of teacher education and training. Accurately isolating and capturing the effects of teachers' qualifications on their student's achievement is difficult, and not surprisingly, the results from this literature are often contradictory. However, despite these problems and contrary to the claims of skeptics, many studies have indeed found teacher education and training, of one sort or another, to be significantly related to increases in student achievement (see Greenwald, Hedges, and Laine 1996).

25. See, for example, Shulman 1986.

26. This viewpoint is especially common among news columnists. See, for example, the syndicated columns of David Broder, Thomas Sowell, and Maggie Gallagher for the week of September 14–20, 1996.

27. National Association of State Directors of Teacher Education and Certification 1997.

28. For state regulations on teacher assignment and placement, see, for example, Education Week 2000, Robinson 1985.

29. Empirical assessments of occupational orientation are usually based on respondents' reports of the values and aspirations behind their

own career choices. It is reasonable to expect that these subjective data may suffer from bias. However, a strong service ethic among teachers has consistently been found by a number of different researchers, using different data sources, over a period of four decades. See, for example, Rosenberg 1981; Davis 1965; Lortie 1975; Kohn and Schooler 1983; National Education Association 1972, 1982, 1987, 1992, 1996; and Miech and Elder 1996. Moreover, as I will show later in this chapter, these "subjective" indicators of an altruistic ethic are consistent with another, perhaps more "objective," indicator of altruism—the tendency of teachers to spend their own money on their students' needs.

30. These data are from a 2000 survey conducted by Public Agenda, an education-oriented pubic opinion research group. The sample size was 664 K–12 public school teachers and 802 nonteachers. For details on the data and survey, see Farkas, Johnson, and Foleno 2000.

31. For research on teacher community and collegiality in schools, see Talbert and McLaughlin 1994.

32. Sizer 1992a, pp. 180–181.

33. For insightful discussion of the isolation of classrooms and the individualistic culture of teachers, see, for example, Lortie 1975; Freedman, Jackson, and Boles 1983; Sizer 1992a; Johnson 1990.

34. For examples of the social-scientific literature on professions, see, for example, Mills 1951; Hughes 1965; Vollmer and Mills 1966; Hall 1968; Etzioni 1969; Larson 1977; Collins 1975; Starr 1982; Freidson 1984, 1986; Abbott 1988; Hodson and Sullivan 1995.

35. For an insightful discussion of the ideology of professionalism, see Freedman, Jackson, and Boles 1983.

36. These data are from the 2000 survey conducted by Public Agenda (sample size 664 K–12 public school teachers). See Farkas, Johnson, and Foleno 2000.

37. See Waller 1932, p. 10.

38. For an insightful discussion of the difficulties of teachers' maintaining respect, see Grant 1983.

39. The survey was conducted in 1997 by Public Agenda. The sample size was 900 professors. For details on the data and survey see, Farkas, Johnson, and Duffett 1997.

40. For insightful analyses of the role of context in generating student conflict, see Stinchombe 1964; Metz 1978a, 1978b; Grant 1983, 1988.

41. For an example of a newspaper report on a typical teacher union work-to-rule job action and the response of critics, see Horwitz 1992.

42. The sample size for the Carnegie Foundation's 1990 National Survey of Public School Teachers was 21,389 K–12 teachers. For detailed information on the survey, see Carnegie Foundation for the Advancement of Teaching 1990.

43. The sample size for the NEA's 1996 Survey of the Status of the American Public School Teacher was 1,325 K–12 teachers. For detailed information on the survey, see National Education Association 1996.

44. Data on salaries of recent college graduates are from the 1994 and 1997 cycles of NCES's Baccalaureate and Beyond Survey. For detailed information on these data and surveys, see McCormick and Horn 1996 and McCormick et al. 1999. For further discussion of these salary data, see Ingersoll 2000.

45. Data on cross-occupational annual earnings are from the U.S. Department of Education's 1991 National Adult Literacy Survey. For information on this survey, see Smith et al. 1996, pp. 174–175.

46. See, for example, Lortie 1969, Conley 1991.

47. Especially insightful and illuminating for this purpose is the work of Michael Burawoy (1979). Quotes are drawn from his work.

48. For a classic discussion of co-optation, see Selznick 1949, pp. 259–261.

49. See, for example, Bidwell 1970, Kanter 1977, Lipsky 1980, Smith 1990.

50. See Whyte and Gardner 1945.

6. The Effects of Teacher Control

1. Extensive citations for these two perspectives can be found in Chapter 2.

2. For extensive discussion of the concept of school climate, see Hoy and Miskel 1996.

3. See, for example, Elam 1995.

4. See, for example, Ouchi and Wilkins 1985, Kanter 1977, Perrow 1986, Goodman and Pennings 1977.

5. For examples, see Price 1977, 1989; Mobley 1982; Steers and Momday 1981.

6. See, for example, Ingersoll 1995b, 2001b; Bobbitt et al. 1994; Whitener et al. 1997; Theobald 1990.

7. For example, data from the 1987–88 SASS show that about a fifth of secondary schools have high levels of conflict between staff and students, a quarter have high levels of conflict among teachers, and almost a third have high conflict between teachers and principals. Schools with high conflict are those with mean levels on each of the three conflict measures of more than 2 on a scale of 1 to 4. See Appendix for information on these indicators and their use in the analysis to follow. Similar levels of conflict are found in analogous indicators from the other cycles of SASS.

8. See Ingersoll 2001b. The Bureau of National Affairs, a leading research and information service for both business and nonbusiness organizations, has gathered data on employee turnover for more than two decades through quarterly surveys of human resource and employee relations executives. Its 1997 fourth-quarter survey, for example, included 230 respondents representing about 300,000 employees from a wide range of organizations. The organizations vary in size from those employing less than a hundred to those employing thousands, and include manufacturing, nonmanufacturing, finance, and health care establishments. See Bureau of National Affairs 1998. Perhaps the best, albeit now dated, source of comparative data on occupational turnover rates is Price's seminal study on employee turnover; see Price 1977, chap. 4.

9. For insightful work on student conflict, see Grant 1983, 1988; Metz 1978a, 1978b.

10. The data in Figure 6.1 are from the 1987–88 SASS. The analysis was based on a sample of 47,357 teachers from 10,785 schools. See the Ap-

pendix for detailed information on the sample, measures, methods, and results. For a parallel analysis, see Ingersoll 1996.

11. Underlying this widely believed view is a zero-sum model of power—that teacher empowerment will lead to conflict with administrators because the latter's power will, by definition, decline. For an example of this viewpoint see, Lortie 1969.

12. See Ingersoll 1995b, 1999, 2001b.

13. Data in Figure 6.2 are from the 1991–92 TFS. The analysis was based on a sample of 6,733 teachers from 4,864 schools. See the Appendix for detailed information on the sample, measures, methods, and results.

14. See, for example, Tannenbaum et al. 1974, Tannenbaum and Rozgonyi 1986.

15. I found a statistically significant positive correlation between principals' reports of their own control over decisions and both principals reports of teachers' control and teachers' reports of teachers' control over decisions. At the same time, I found either a weak negative correlation or no correlation between the control held by school boards and either principals' control or teachers' control.

16. These background analyses used measures of principal and board control (presented in Chapter 3) based on school principals' reports. My analysis suggests that while principals' reports were useful for comparing the relative influence of the different groups (as in Chapter 3), the reports were less valid and less reliable than those of teachers for predicting the relationship between control and various school climate outcomes, regardless of whether the outcome indicators were based on teachers' or principals' reports. For instance, teachers' reports of teacher control were strongly related to both actual teacher turnover and principals' reports of teacher turnover, while principals' reports of teacher control showed little relationship to the same outcomes. Hence, for this chapter's multivariate analysis I used measures based on teachers' reports of teacher control and did not pursue the use of measures based on principals' reports.

17. See Kanter 1977.

18. See Whyte and Gardner 1945.

19. See, for example, Kanter 1977, Pfeffer 1981, Tannenbaum et al. 1974, Hinings et al. 1974. For a review of much of this research, see Locke and Schweiger 1979.

20. For a classic discussion of co-optation in organizations, see Selznick 1949.

7. Conclusion

1. Waller 1932, pp. 11, 58; also see Mills 1951, p. 129. For a classic discussion of the semi-professional status of the teaching occupation, see Lortie 1969. For an empirical analysis, using SASS, of the degree of professionalization in schools, see Ingersoll 2000.

2. See, for example, Freedman, Jackson, and Boles 1983; Strober and Tyack 1980; Lerner 1979.

3. Extensive citations for these two perspectives can be found in Chapter 2.

4. Extensive citations for these versions can be found in Chapter 2.

5. See Weber 1946, pp. 196–244.

6. For insightful discussions of the discretion of higher management, see, for example, Caplow 1954, p. 66; Kanter 1977, pp. 73, 118; Kohn and Schooler 1983, chap. 2.

7. Extensive citations for these two policy perspectives can be found in Chapter 2.

8. Arthur Wise has labeled this faith in and desire for more rules and regulations the "hyperrationalization thesis." For his insightful study of this tendency, see Wise 1979.

9. For an insightful review of the advantages and disadvantages of organizational centralization, see Aldrich 1978. For a classic critique of top-down reform, see Goodman 1963.

10. For information on the Teacher Followup Survey, see the Appendix. For information on the Public Agenda survey, see Farkus, Johnson,

and Foleno 2000. For a detailed presentation of my analysis of shortages and turnover, see Ingersoll 2001b.

11. For insightful discussions of the problems of top-down school reforms, see, for example, Dombart 1985; Grant 1988, chap. 6.

12. See Fox 1987.

13. For a detailed summary of my analyses of out-of-field teaching, see
Ingersoll 1999, 2001a.

14. See National Education Summit 1999.

15. For discussion of this approach, see, for example, Whyte and Blasi
1982.

16. For discussion of these kinds of education reforms, see, for example, Shedd and Bacharach 1991. For concrete examples, see Glickman
(1993) on the League of Professional Schools in the Southeast and
Sizer (1992b) on the Coalition for Essential Schools in the Northeast.

17. For discussion of the distinction between participation and power, see,
for example, Berg 1978, Kanter 1977.

18. For an insightful analysis of school decentralization in name only, see
Malen and Ogawa 1988a.

19. See, for example, David 1989; Cistone 1989.

20. Personal communication with Representative Charles Hudson of the
Louisiana House of Representatives, March 2000.

Appendix

1. See, for example, Frey 1970, Lukes 1974, Gaventa 1980.

2. Denzin 1970.

3. Haggstrom, Darling-Hammond, and Grissmer 1988; Ingersoll 1995a.

4. See, for example, Kaufman 1991, Kaufman and Huang 1993,
Abramson et al. 1996.

5. See Choy et al. 1992, 1993b; Henke, Choy, and Geis 1996.

6. For research on the effects of the socioeconomic status and race/
ethnicity of student populations, see, for example, Bryk, Lee, and
Smith 1990; Becker 1953; Stinchcombe 1964; Rist 1970; Katz 1972,

1987; Bowles and Gintis 1976; Willis 1977; Everhart 1983; Metz 1978; Connell 1985. For reviews of the literature on school size, see, for example, Bryk, Lee, and Smith 1990; Guthrie 1979; Walberg and Walberg 1994. For research on the effects of school sector, see, for example, Coleman and Hoffer 1987; Bryk, Lee and Holland 1993.

7. See Ingersoll 1996, 1997, and 2001b.

8. For a multivariate analysis of principals' reports of school-level rates of teacher turnover, using the SASS data, see Ingersoll 1995b.

REFERENCES

Abbott, A. 1988. *The System of Professions: An Essay on the Division of Expert Labor.* Chicago: University of Chicago Press.

Abramson, R., et al. 1996. *1993–94 Schools and Staffing Survey Sample Design and Estimation.* Washington, D.C.: National Center for Education Statistics.

Aldrich, Howard. 1978. "Centralization versus Decentralization in the Design of Human Service Delivery Systems: A Response to Gouldner's Lament." In *The Management of Human Services,* ed. Rosemary Sarri and Yeheskel Hasenfeld, pp. 51–79. New York: Columbia University Press.

Anyon, J. 1980. "Social Class and the Hidden Curriculum of Work." *Journal of Education* 162:67–92.

————. 1997. *Ghetto Schooling: A Political Economy of Urban Educational Reform.* New York: Teachers College Press.

Apple, M. W. 1982. *Education and Power.* Boston: Routledge and Kegan Paul.

Bacharach, Samuel, ed. 1981. *Organizational Behavior in Schools and School Districts.* New York: Praeger.

————. 1990. *Education Reform: Making Sense of It All*. Boston: Allyn and Bacon.

Bacharach, Samuel, P. Bamberger, and S. Conley. 1990. "The Dimensionality of Decision Participation in Educational Organizations: The Value of a Multi-Domain Evaluative Approach." *Educational Administration Quarterly* 26:126–167.

Bacharach, Samuel, Scott Bauer, and Joseph Shedd. 1988. "The Learning Workplace: The Conditions and Resources of Teaching." In *Conditions and Resources of Teaching*, pp. 8–40. Washington, D.C.: National Education Association.

Baker, D., M. Han, and C. Keil. 1996. *How Different, How Similar? Comparing Key Organizational Qualities of American Public and Private Secondary Schools*. Washington, D.C.: National Center for Education Statistics.

Barnard, Chester. 1938. *The Functions of the Executive*. Cambridge, Mass.: Harvard University Press.

Barr, R., and R. Dreeben. 1983. *How Schools Work*. Chicago: University of Chicago Press.

Barth, Roland. 1985. "Outside Looking In—Inside Looking In." *Phi Delta Kappan* 66:356–358.

Becker, Howard. 1953. "The Teacher in an Authority System." *Journal of Educational Sociology* 26:128–41.

Bendix, Reinhard. 1956. *Work and Authority in Industry*. New York: Wiley.

Bennefield, R. 1997. "Black America and the Great Debate over School Reform." *The Crisis* October: 27–32.

Bennett, W. 1993. *The Book of Virtues*. New York: Simon and Schuster.

Berg, Ivar. 1978. *Managers and Work Reform: A Limited Engagement*. New York: Free Press.

Berger, J. 1989. "New York Schools and Patronage." *New York Times*, December 11, p. 1.

Berk, R. A. 1988. "Fifty Reasons Why Student Achievement Gain Does Not Mean Teacher Effectiveness." *Journal of Personnel Evaluation in Education* 1:345–363.

Bidwell, Charles. 1965. "The School as a Formal Organization." In *Handbook of Organizations*, ed. J. March, pp. 973–1002. Chicago: Rand McNally.

———. 1970. "Students and Schools: Some Observations on Client Trust in Client-Serving Organizations." *Organizations and Clients: Essays in the Sociology of Service*, ed. William Rosengren and Mark Lefton, pp. 37–71. Columbus, Ohio: Charles Merrill.

Bidwell, C., K. Frank, and P. Quiroz. 1997. "Teacher Types, Workplace Controls and the Organization of Schools." *Sociology of Education* 70:285–307.

Bidwell, C., and N. Friedkin. 1988. "The Sociology of Education." In *The Handbook of Sociology*, ed. N. Smelser, pp. 449–471. Beverly Hills, Calif.: Sage.

Bidwell, C., and P. Quiroz. 1991. "Organizational Control in the High School Workplace: A Theoretical Argument." *Journal of Research on Adolescence* 1:211–229.

Blase, J., and G. Anderson. 1995. *The Micropolitics of Educational Leadership: From Control to Empowerment*. New York: Cassell.

Blau, Peter. 1968. "The Hierarchy of Authority in Organizations." *American Journal of Sociology* 73:453–467.

Block, F., and L. Hirschorn. 1987. "New Productive Forces." In *Revising State Theory: Essays in Politics and Postindustrialism*, ed. F. Block. Philadelphia: Temple University Press.

Bluedorn, A. C. 1982. "A Unified Model of Turnover from Organizations." *Human Relations* 35:135–153.

Bobbitt, S., et al. 1994. *Characteristics of Stayers, Movers, and Leavers: Results from the Teacher Follow-up Survey, 1991–92*. Washington, D.C.: National Center for Education Statistics.

Boocock, Sarane. 1978. "The Social Organization of the Classroom." *Annual Review of Sociology* 4:1–28.

Borman, Kathryn, and Joel Spring. 1984. *Schools in Central Cities*. New York: Longman.

Bosk, C., and J. Frader. 1990. "AIDS and Its Impact on Medical Work: The

Culture and Politics of the Shopfloor." *Milbank Memorial Fund Quarterly* 68(2):257–279.

Bourdieu, Pierre, and Jean-Claude Passeron. 1977. *Reproduction: In Education, Society and Culture.* Beverly Hills, Calif.: Sage.

Bowles, Samuel, and Herb Gintis. 1976. *Schooling in Capitalist America.* New York: Basic Books.

Braverman, Harry. 1974. *Labor and Monopoly Capitalism.* New York: Monthly Review Press.

Brint, Steven. 1998. *Schools and Societies.* Thousand Oaks, California: Pine Forge Press.

Brint, Steven, M. Contreras, and M. Mathews. 2001. "Socialization Messages in Primary Schools: An Organizational Analysis. *Sociology of Education* 74(3):157–180.

Bryk, Anthony, V. Lee, and P. Holland. 1993. *Catholic Schools and the Common Good.* Cambridge, Mass.: Harvard University Press.

Bryk, Anthony, V. Lee, and J. Smith. 1990. "High School Organization and Its Effects on Teachers and Students: An Interpretive Summary of the Research." In *Choice and Control in American Education,* ed. W. H. Clune and J. F. Witte, vol 1, pp. 135–226. New York: Falmer Press.

Bullough, R. V., A. Gitlin, and S. Goldstein. 1984. "Ideology, Teacher Role and Resistance." *Teachers College Record* 86:339–358.

Burawoy, Michael. 1979. *Manufacturing Consent: Changes in the Labor Process under Monopoly Capitalism.* Chicago: University of Chicago Press.

Bureau of National Affairs. 1998. "BNA's Quarterly Report on Job Absence and Turnover." In *Bulletin to Management.* Washington, D.C.: Bureau of National Affairs.

Burns, T., and G. M. Stalker. 1961. *The Management of Innovation.* London: Tavistock.

Callahan, Raymond. 1962. *Education and the Cult of Efficiency.* Chicago: University of Chicago Press.

Cameron, Kim, and David Whetten. 1983. *Organizational Effectiveness: A Comparison of Multiple Models.* New York: Academic.

Campbell, R., L. Cunningham, and R. McPhee. 1985. *The Organization and Control of Schools*. Columbus, Ohio: Charles Merrill.

Caplow, Theodore. 1954. *The Sociology of Work*. Minneapolis: University of Minnesota Press.

Carey, C., and E. Farris. 1994. *Curricular Differentiation in Public High Schools*. Washington, D.C.: National Center for Education Statistics.

Carnegie Forum on Education and the Economy. 1986. *A Nation Prepared: Teachers for the 21st Century*. New York: Carnegie Forum.

Carnegie Foundation for the Advancement of Teaching. 1990. *The Condition of Teaching*. New York: Carnegie Foundation.

Choy, Susan, et al. 1992. *Schools and Staffing in the U.S.: A Statistical Profile, 1987–88*. Washington, D.C.: National Center for Education Statistics.

———. 1993a. *America's Teachers: Profile of a Profession, 1990–91*. Washington, D.C.: National Center for Education Statistics.

———. 1993b. *Schools and Staffing in the U.S.: A Statistical Profile, 1990–91*. Washington, D.C.: National Center for Education Statistics.

Chubb, J. E., and T. Moe. 1990. *Politics, Markets and America's Schools*. Washington, D.C.: Brookings Institute.

Cicourel, Aaron, and John Kitsuse. 1963. *Educational Decision-Makers*. New York: Bobbs-Merrill.

Cicourel, Aaron, et al. 1974. *Language Use and School Performance*. New York: Academic.

Cistone, Peter. 1989. "School Based Management/Shared Decision-Making in Dade County (Miami)." *Education and Urban Society* 21:393–402.

Clark, B. 1987. *The Academic Life: Small Worlds, Different Worlds*. New York:. Carnegie Foundation for the Advancement of Teaching.

Clune, W. H., and J. F. Witte. 1990. *Choice and Control in American Education*, vol 1: *The Theory of Choice and Control in Education*. New York: Falmer Press.

Cohen, M., J. March, and J. Olsen. 1972. "A Garbage Can Theory of Organizational Decision Making." *Administrative Science Quarterly* 17:1–25.

Coleman, James. 1987. "Families and Schools." *Educational Researcher* 16 (7):32–38.

Coleman, James, and T. Hoffer. 1987. *Public and Private Schools: The Impact of Communities.* New York: Basic Books.

Collins, R. 1975. *Conflict Sociology.* New York: Academic Press.

Conant, J. 1963. *The Education of American Teachers.* New York: McGraw-Hill.

Conley, Sharon. 1991. "Review of Research on Teacher Participation in School Decision Making." *Review of Research in Education,* vol. 17, ed. G. Grant, pp. 225–266. Washington, D.C.: American Educational Research Association.

Conley, S., and B. Cooper. 1991. *The School as a Work Environment: Implications for Reform.* Boston: Allyn and Bacon.

Connell, Robert W. 1985. *Teacher's Work.* Boston: George Allen.

Corbett, H. T., J. L. Dawson, and William Firestone. 1984. *School Context and School Change.* New York: Teachers College Press.

Corcoran, Thomas, Lisa Walker, and J. Lynne White. 1988. *Working in Urban Schools.* Washington, D.C.: Institute for Educational Leadership.

Cornbleth, Catherine. 1989. "Cries of Crisis, Calls for Reform and Challenges of Change." *Crisis in Teaching,* ed. L. Weis et al., pp. 9–32. Albany: State University of New York Press.

Corwin, Ronald. 1981. "Patterns of Organizational Control and Teacher Militancy: Theoretical Continuity in the Idea of 'Loose Coupling.'" *Research in the Sociology of Education and Socialization* 2:261–291.

Crawford, Alan. 1980. *Thunder on the Right.* New York: Pantheon.

Cremin, L. 1964. *The Transformation of the School.* New York: Vintage.

Crozier, Michel. 1964. *The Bureaucratic Phenomena.* Chicago: University of Chicago Press.

Cuban, L. 1982. "Persistent Instruction: The High School Classroom 1900–1980." *Phi Delta Kappan* 64:113–118.

Cyert, Richard, and J. March. 1963. *A Behavioral Theory of the Firm.* Englewood Cliffs, N.J.: Prentice Hall.

Dahl, Robert. 1984. *Modern Political Analysis,* 4th ed. Englewood Cliffs, N.J.: Prentice Hall.

Dahrendorf, Ralf. 1958. "Toward a Theory of Social Conflict." *Journal of Conflict Resolution* 7:170–183.

Darling-Hammond, Linda. 1986. "A Proposal for Evaluation in the Teaching Profession." *Elementary School Journal* 86:531–551.

———. 1987. "Teacher Quality and Equality." In *Access to Knowledge,* ed. P. Keating and J. I. Goodlad. New York: College Entrance Examination Board.

———. 1994. "National Standards and Assessments: Will They Improve Education?" *American Journal of Education* 102:479–510.

Darling-Hammond, L., and B. Berry. 1988. *The Evolution of Teacher Policy.* Santa Monica, Calif.: Rand Corporation.

Darling-Hammond, Linda, and Arthur Wise. 1985. "Beyond Standardization: State Standards and School Improvement." *Elementary School Journal* 85:315–335.

David, Jane. 1989. "Synthesis of Research on School-Based Management." *Educational Leadership,* 46(8):45–52.

Davis, J. A. 1965. *Undergraduate Career Decisions.* Chicago: Aldine.

Deal, Terrence, and L. D. Celotti. 1980. "How Much Influence Can and Do Educational Administrators Have on Classrooms?" *Phi Delta Kappan* 61:471–473.

Denzin, Norman. 1970. *The Research Act.* Chicago: Aldine.

Dewey, John. 1974 (1902). *The Child and the Curriculum.* Chicago: University of Chicago Press.

———. 1934. *A Common Faith.* New Haven, Conn.: Yale University Press.

Dombart, P. 1985. "The Vision of an Insider: The Practitioner's View." *Educational Leadership* 43(November):71–73.

Dornbusch, Sanford, and W. R. Scott. 1975. *Evaluation and the Exercise of Authority.* San Francisco: Jossey-Bass.

Dreeben, Robert. 1968. *On What Is Learned in School.* Reading, Mass.: Addison-Wesley.

———. 1973. "The School as a Workplace." In *Second Handbook of Research in Teaching,* ed. R. Travers, pp. 450–473. Chicago: University of Chicago Press.

———. 1976. "The Organizational Structure of Schools and School Systems." In *Explorations in General Theory in Social Science,* ed. J. J. Loubser et al., vol. 2, pp. 857–873. New York: Free Press.

———. 1994. "The Sociology of Education." *Research in the Sociology of Education and Socialization* 10:7–52.

Durkheim, Emile. 1961 (1925). *Moral Education: A Study in the Theory and Application of the Sociology of Education,* trans. E. K. Wilson and H. Schnurer. New York: Free Press.

———. 1956 (1911). *Education and Sociology.* New York: Free Press.

Dwyer, Carol, and Daniel Stufflebeam. 1996. "Teacher Evaluation." In *Handbook of Educational Psychology,* ed. D. Berliner and R. Calfee, pp. 765–786. New York: Prentice-Hall.

Educational Research Service. 1988. *Teacher Evaluation: Practices and Procedures.* Arlington, Va.: ERS.

Education Trust. 1996, 1998, 2000. *Education Watch.* Washington, D.C.: American Association for Higher Education.

Education Week. 1998, 1999, 2000. *Quality Counts: A Report Card on the Condition of Public Education in the 50 States.* Washington, D.C.: Education Week.

Edwards, Richard. 1979. *Contested Terrain.* New York: Basic Books.

Elam, Stanley. 1995. *How America Views Its Schools: The PDK/Gallup Polls, 1969–1994.* Bloomington, Ind.: Phi Delta Kappa Press Educational Foundation.

Elmore, R. 2000. *Building a New Structure for School Leadership.* New York: Albert Shanker Institute.

Etzioni, Amitai. 1961. *A Comparative Analysis of Complex Organizations.* New York: Free Press.

———. 1996. *The New Golden Rule.* New York: Basic Books.

———, ed. 1969. *The Semi-Professions and Their Organizations: Teachers, Nurses and Social Workers.* New York: Free Press.

Everhart, Robert. 1983. "Class Management, Student Opposition and the Labor Process." In *Ideology and Practice in Schooling,* ed. M. Apple and L. Weiss, pp. 169–192. Philadelphia: Temple University Press.

Fantini, Mario, Marilyn Gittell, and Richard Magat. 1979. *Community Control and the Urban School.* New York: Praeger.

Farkas, S., and J. Johnson. 1996. *Given the Circumstances: Teachers Talk about Public Education Today.* New York: Public Agenda.

Farkas, S., J. Johnson, and A. Duffett. 1997. *Different Drummers: How Teachers of Teachers View Public Education.* New York: Public Agenda.

Farkas, S., J. Johnson, and T. Foleno. 2000. *A Sense of Calling: Who Teaches and Why.* New York: Public Agenda.

Farkas, S., et al. 1999. *Reality Check.* New York: Public Agenda.

Filby, N. N., et al. 1980. *What Happens in Smaller Classes.* San Francisco: Far West Laboratory.

Finley, M. 1984. "Teachers and Tracking in a Comprehensive High School." *Sociology of Education* 57:233–243.

Finn, C., M. Kanstoroom, and M. Petrilli. 1999. *The Quest for Better Teachers: Grading the States.* Washington, D.C.: Thomas B. Fordham Foundation.

Firestone, William. 1985. "The Study of Loose Coupling: Problems, Progress, and Prospects." *Research in the Sociology of Education and Socialization* 5:3–30.

Firestone, William, and B. Bader. 1991. "Professionalism or Bureaucracy? Redesigning Teaching." *Educational Evaluation and Policy Analysis* 13(1):67–87.

Firestone, W., and B. Wilson. 1989. "Administrative Behavior, School SES, and Student Achievement: A Preliminary Report." Paper presented at the annual meeting of the American Educational Research Association.

Floden, R., et al. 1988. "Instructional Leadership at the District Level: A Closer Look at Autonomy and Control." *Educational Administration Quarterly* 24:96–124.

Fox, T. 1987. "Rampage: Values Are Not in the Curriculum." *Philadelphia Inquirer.* April 26, p. 7E.

Freedman, S., J. Jackson, and K. Boles. 1983. "The Other End of the Corridor: The Effect of Teaching on Teachers." *Radical Teacher* 23:2–23.

Freidson, Eliot. 1970. "Dominant Professions, Bureaucracy, and Client Services." In *Organizations and Clients: Essays in the Sociology of Service,* ed. William Rosengren and Mark Lefton, pp. 71–92. Columbus, Ohio: Charles Merrill.

———. 1973. *The Professions and Their Prospects.* Beverly Hills, Calif.: Sage.

———. 1984. "The Changing Nature of Professional Control." *Annual Review of Sociology* 10:1–20.

———. 1986. *Professional Powers: A Study in the Institutionalization of Formal Knowledge.* Chicago: University of Chicago Press.

Freire, Paulo. 1973. *Education for Critical Consciousness.* New York: Continuum.

Frey, Frederick. 1970. "The Determination and Location of Elites: A Critical Analysis." Paper presented at the 66th annual meeting of the American Political Science Association, Los Angeles, California.

———. 1971. "On Issues and Non-Issues in the Study of Power." *American Political Science Review* 65:1091–1104.

———. 1978. "The Analysis of Social Structure." Paper presented at the World Congress of Sociology, Uppsala, Sweden.

———. 1985. "The Problem of Actor Designation in Political Analysis." *Comparative Politics* 2:127–152.

Fuhrman, S., W. Clune, and R. Elmore. 1988. "Research on Educational Reform: Lessons on the Implementation of Policy." *Teachers College Record* 90:237–257.

Fuhrman, S., and R. Elmore. 1990. "Understanding Local Control in the Wake of State Education Reform." *Educational Evaluation and Policy Analysis* 12(1):82–96.

Futrell, M. 1988. "Teachers in Reform: The Opportunity for Schools." *Educational Administration Quarterly* 24:374–380.

Gaventa, John. 1980. *Power and Powerlessness*. Chicago: University of Illinois Press.

Giroux, H. 1981. *Ideology, Culture and the Process of Schooling*. Philadelphia: Temple University Press.

Gitlin, Andrew. 1983. "School Structure and Teachers' Work." In *Ideology and Practice in Schooling*, ed. M. Apple and L. Weiss, pp. 193–212. Philadelphia: Temple University Press.

Glickman, C. 1993. *Renewing America's Schools*. San Francisco: Jossey-Bass.

Goffman, Erving. 1959. *The Presentation of Self in Everyday Life*. New York: Doubleday.

Goodlad, John. 1984. *A Place Called School*. New York: McGraw-Hill.

———. 1985. "Structure, Process and an Agenda." In *The Ecology of School Renewal*, ed. J. Goodlad. Chicago: University of Chicago Press.

Goodman, Joan. 2001. *The Moral Stake in Education*. New York: Longman.

Goodman, Paul. 1963. *People or Personnel*. New York: Vintage.

Goodman, P., and J. Pennings. 1977. *New Perspectives on Organizational Effectiveness*. San Francisco: Jossey-Bass.

Granovetter, Mark. 1985. "Economic Action and Social Structure: The Problem of Embeddedness." *American Journal of Sociology* 91:481–510.

Grant, Gerald. 1981. "The Character of Education and the Education of Character." *Daedalus* 110:135–150.

———. 1983. "The Teachers' Predicament." *Teachers College Record* 84(3):593–609.

———. 1988. *The World We Created at Hamilton High*. Cambridge, Mass.: Harvard University Press.

Grant, Gerald, and Christine Murray. 1999. *Teaching in America: the Slow Revolution*. Cambridge, Mass.: Harvard University Press.

Greenwald, R., L. Hedges, and R. Laine. 1996. "The Effect of School Resources on Student Achievement." *Review of Educational Research* 66:361–396.

Guthrie, J. 1979. "Organizational Scale and School Success." *Educational Evaluation and Policy Analysis* 1:17–27.

Hackman, Richard, and Gregg Oldham. 1980. *Work Redesign*. Reading, Mass.: Addison-Wesley.

Haertel, Edward. 1991. "New Forms of Teacher Assessment." In *Review of Research in Education*, vol. 17, ed. G. Grant, pp. 3–29. Washington, D.C.: American Educational Research Association.

Hage, Jerald. 1980. *Theories of Organization: Form, Process and Transformation*. New York: Wiley.

Haggstrom, G. W., L. Darling-Hammond, and D. Grissmer. 1988. *Assessing Teacher Supply and Demand*. Santa Monica, Calif.: Rand Corporation.

Hall, R. 1968. "Professionalization and Bureaucratization." *American Sociological Review* 33:92–104.

Haney, Walter, G. Madaus, and A. Kreitzer. 1987. "Charms Talismanic: Testing Teachers for the Improvement of American Education." In *Review of Research in Education*, vol. 14, pp. 169–238. Washington, D.C.: American Educational Research Association.

Hannaway, J. 1993. "Political Pressure and Decentralization in Institutional Organizations: The Case of School Districts." *Sociology of Education* 66:147–163.

Hannaway, J., and M. Carnoy. 1993. *Decentralization and School Improvement*. San Francisco: Jossey-Bass.

Hannaway, J., and J. Talbert. 1993. "Bringing Context into Effective Schools Research: Urban-Suburban Differences." *Educational Administration Quarterly* 29(2):164–186.

Hanson, E. Mark. 1981. "Organizational Control in Educational Systems: A Case Study of Governance in Schools." In *Organizational Behavior in Schools and School Districts*, ed. Samuel Bacharach, pp. 245–276. New York: Praeger.

Harris, Louis, and Associates. 1986. *Metropolitan Life Survey of the American Teacher*. New York: Metropolitan Life Insurance Co.

Haycock, K. 1998. "Good Teaching Matters." *Thinking K–16* 3(2):1–14. Washington, D.C.: Education Trust.

Henke, R., S. Choy, and S. Geis. 1996. *Schools and Staffing in the U.S.: A Sta-*

tistical Profile, 1993–94. Washington, D.C.: National Center for Education Statistics.

Henke, R., et al. 1997. *America's Teachers: Profile of a Profession, 1993–94.* Washington, D.C.: National Center for Education Statistics.

Henry, Jules. 1965. *Culture against Man.* New York: Vintage.

Herndon, James. 1968. *The Way It Spozed to Be.* New York: Bantam.

————. 1971. *How to Survive in Your Native Land.* New York: Bantam.

Hess, F. 1999. *Spinning Wheels: The Politics of Urban School Reform.* Washington, D.C.: Brookings Institute.

Hickson, David, J. 1966. "A Convergence in Organizational Theory." *Administrative Science Quarterly* 11:225–237.

Hickson, David, et al. 1971. "A Strategic Contingencies Theory of Intraorganizational Power." *Administrative Science Quarterly* 2:216–229.

Hinings, C. R., et al. 1974. "Structural Conditions of Intraorganizational Power." *Administrative Science Quarterly* 19:22–44.

Hirsch, E. D. 1987. *Cultural Literacy: What Every American Needs to Know.* Boston: Houghton Mifflin.

Hodson, R., and T. Sullivan. 1995. "Professions and Professionals." In *The Social Organization of Work,* pp. 287–314. Belmont, Calif.: Wadsworth.

Holmes Group. 1986. *Tomorrow's Teachers.* East Lansing, Mich.: Holmes Group.

Horwitz, S. 1992. "D.C. Teachers Threaten to Trim Work Schedules." *Washington Post,* February 3, pp. A-1, A-12

Howsam, R., et al. 1985. *Educating a Profession.* Washington, D.C.: American Association for Colleges of Teacher Education.

Hoy, W., and C. Miskel. 1996. *Educational Administration.* New York: McGraw-Hill.

Hughes, E. 1965. "Professions." In *The Professions in America,* ed. K. Lynn and the editors of *Daedalus,* pp. 1–14. Boston: Houghton Mifflin.

Hull, J. 1994. "Do Teachers Punish According to Race?" *Time Magazine* 151(April 4):30–31.

Ingersoll, R. 1993. "Loosely Coupled Organizations Revisited." *Research in the Sociology of Organizations* 11:81–112.

———. 1994. "Organizational Control in Secondary Schools." *Harvard Educational Review* 64:150–172.

———. 1995a. *An Agenda for Research on Teachers and Schools: Revisiting NCES' Schools and Staffing Survey.* Washington, D.C.: National Center for Education Statistics.

———. 1995b. *Teacher Supply, Teacher Quality and Teacher Turnover.* Washington, D.C.: National Center for Education Statistics.

———. 1996. "Teachers' Decision-Making Power and School Conflict." *Sociology of Education* 69:159–176.

———. 1997. *Teacher Professionalization and Teacher Commitment: A Multilevel Analysis.* Washington, D.C.: National Center for Education Statistics.

———. 1999. "The Problem of Underqualified Teachers in American Secondary Schools." *Educational Researcher* 28(2):26–37.

———. 2000 "The Status of Teaching as a Profession." In *Schools and Society: A Sociological Perspective,* ed. Jeanne Ballantine and Joan Spade, pp. 115–129. Belmont, Calif.: Wadsworth.

———. 2001a. "Misunderstanding the Problem of Out-of-Field Teaching." *Educational Researcher* 30(1):21–22.

———. 2001b. "Teacher Turnover, Teacher Shortages: An Organizational Analysis." *American Educational Research Journal* 38(3):499–534.

———. 2002. "Teacher Assessment and Evaluation" In *Education and Sociology: An Encyclopedia,* ed. D. Levinson, P. Cookson, and A. Sadovnik, pp. 651–657. New York: RoutledgeFalmer.

Institute for Educational Leadership. 2001. *Leadership for Student Learning: Redefining the Teacher as Leader.* Washington, D.C.: Institute for Educational Leadership.

Jackson, Philip. 1968. *Life in Classrooms.* New York: Holt, Rinehart and Winston.

Johnson, Susan Moore. 1984. *Teacher Unions in Schools.* Philadelphia: Temple University Press.

———. 1990. *Teachers at Work: Achieving Success in Our Schools*. New York: Basic Books.

Josephson, M. 1992. *Ethical Values, Attitudes, and Behaviors in American Schools: A Report*. Marina del Rey, Calif.: Joseph and Edna Josephson Institute of Ethics.

Kamens, David. 1977. "Legitimating Myths and Educational Organizations: The Relationship between Organizational Ideology and Formal Structure." *American Sociological Review* 42:208–219.

Kanter, Rosabeth. 1977. *Men and Women of the Corporation*. New York: Basic Books.

———. 1981. "Organization Performance: Recent Developments in Measurement." *Annual Review of Sociology* 7:321–349.

Katz, Michael. 1972. *Class, Bureaucracy and Schools*. New York: Vintage.

———. 1987. *Reconstructing American Education*. Cambridge, Mass: Harvard University Press.

Kaufman, Steven. 1991. *1987–88 Schools and Staffing Survey Sample Design and Estimation*. Washington, D.C.: National Center for Education Statistics.

Kaufman, Steven, and H. Huang. 1993. *1990–91 Schools and Staffing Survey Sample Design and Estimation*. Washington, D.C.: National Center for Education Statistics.

Kellman, Shelly. 1982. "What in God's Name Is Going on in Schools." *New Age*, October, pp. 30–53.

Kennedy, M. 1992. "The Problem of Improving Teacher Quality While Balancing Supply and Demand." In *Teacher Supply, Demand and Quality*, ed. E. Boe and D. Gilford, pp. 63–126. Washington, D.C.: National Academy Press.

Kirst, M. 1984. *Who Controls Our Schools?: American Values in Conflict*. New York: W. H. Freeman and Co.

———. 1989. "Who Should Control the Schools?" In *Schooling for Tomorrow*, ed. T. J. Sergiovanni and J. Moore. Boston: Allyn and Bacon.

Kliebard, Herbert. 1987. *The Struggle for the American Curriculum*. New York: Routledge and Kegan Paul.

Kochan, T., H. Katz, and R. McKersie. 1986. *The Transformation of American Industrial Relations*. New York: Basic Books.

Kohn, M., and C. Schooler. 1983. *Work and Personality*. Norwood, N.J.: Ablex.

Kozol, Jonathan. 1967. *Death at an Early Age*. Boston: Houghton Mifflin.

———. 1991. *Savage Inequalities*. New York: HarperCollins.

Krause, E. 1971. *The Sociology of Occupations*. Boston: Little, Brown and Co.

Kuhn, Thomas. 1962. *The Structure of Scientific Revolutions*. Chicago: University of Chicago Press.

Labaree, David. 1988. *The Making of an American High School: The Credentials Market and the Central High School of Philadelphia*. New Haven, Conn.: Yale University Press.

Larson, M. 1977. *The Rise of Professionalism: A Sociological Analysis*. Berkeley: University of California Press.

Lawler, Edward, and Samuel Bacharach. 1983. "Political Action and Allignments in Organizations." *Research in the Sociology of Organizations* 1:83–107.

Le Compte, Margaret. 1978. "Establishing a Workplace: Teacher Control in the Classroom." *Education and Urban Society* 11:87–105.

Lerner, G. 1979. "The Lady and the Millgirl." In *A Heritage of Her Own: Toward a New Social History of American Women*, ed. Nancy F. Cott and Elizabeth H. Pleck, pp. 188–189. New York: Simon and Schuster.

Levin, H. 1998. "Education Performance Standards and the Economy." *Educational Researcher* 27(4):4–10.

Lightfoot, S. 1986. "On Goodness in Schools: Themes of Empowerment." *Peabody Journal of Education* 63(3):9–28.

Likert, Rensis. 1967. *The Human Organization*. New York: McGraw-Hill.

Linn, Robert, E. Baker, and S. Dunbar. 1991. "Complex, Performance-Based Assessment Expectations and Validation Criteria." *Educational Researcher* 20(8):15–21.

Lipset, S. M., M. Trow, and J. Coleman. 1956. *Union Democracy.* Glencoe, Ill.: Free Press.

Lipsky, Michael. 1980. *Street Level Bureaucracy.* New York: Basic Books.

Locke, E., and D. Schweiger. 1979. "Participation in Decision Making: One More Look." *Research in Organizational Behavior* 1:265–339.

Lortie, Dan. 1969. "The Balance of Control and Autonomy in Elementary School Teaching." In *The Semi-Professions and Their Organizations: Teachers, Nurses and Social Workers,* ed. A. Etzioni, pp. 1–53. New York: Free Press.

———. 1973. "Observations on Teaching as Work." In *Second Handbook of Research in Teaching,* ed. R. Travers, pp. 474–497. Chicago: University of Chicago Press.

———. 1975. *School Teacher.* Chicago: University of Chicago Press.

———. 1977. "Two Anomalies and Three Perspectives: Some Observations on School Organization." In *Perspectives on Organizations,* ed. R. Corwin and Roy Edelfelt, pp. 20–38. Washington, D.C.: American Association of Colleges for Teacher Education.

Lukes, Steven. 1974. *Power: A Radical View.* London: Macmillan.

Malen, B., and R. Ogawa. 1988a. "Professional-Patron Influence on Site-Based Governance Councils: A Confounding Case Study." *Educational Evaluation and Policy Analysis* 10:251–270.

———. 1988b. "School-Based Management: Disconcerting Policy Issues, Critical Policy and Choices." In *Restructuring the Schools: Problems and Prospects,* ed. J. Lane and E. Epps. Berkeley, Calif.: McCutchan.

Malen, B., R. Ogawa, and J. Kranz. 1990. "What Do We Know about School-Based Management? A Case Study of the Literature—A Call for Research." In *Choice and Control in American Education,* vol. 2: *The Practice of Choice, Decentralization and School Restructuring,* ed. W. H. Clune and J. F. Witte. pp. 289–342. New York: Falmer Press.

March, James, and J. Olsen. 1976. *Ambiguity and Choice in Organizations.* Bergen, Norway: Universitesforlaget.

March, James, and H. Simon. 1958. *Organizations.* New York: Wiley.

Marks, H., and K. Louis. 1997. "Does Teacher Empowerment Affect the Classroom? The Implications of Teacher Empowerment for Instructional Practice and Student Academic Achievement." *Educational Evaluation and Policy Analysis* 19:245–275.

McCormick, A., and L. Horn. 1996. *A Descriptive Summary of 1992–93 Bachelor's Degree Recipients One Year Later.* Washington, D.C.: National Center for Education Statistics.

McCormick, A., et al. 1999. *Life after College: A Descriptive Summary of 1992–93 Bachelor's Degree Recipients in 1997.* Washington, D.C.: National Center for Education Statistics.

McDonnell, L. 1989. *The Dilemma of Teacher Policy.* Washington, D.C.: Rand Corporation.

McKeachie, Wilbert. 1994. *Teaching Tips.* Lexington, Mass.: D.C. Heath and Co.

McLaughlin, M., J. Talbert, and N. Bascia. 1990. *The Contexts of Teaching in Secondary Schools: Teachers' Realities.* New York: Teachers College Press.

McNeil, Linda. 1988. *Contradictions of Control.* New York: Routledge.

McPherson, Gertrude. 1972. *Small Town Teacher.* Cambridge, Mass.: Harvard University Press.

Mehan, Hugh. 1978. "Structuring School Structure." *Harvard Educational Review* 48:32–65.

Metz, Mary. 1978a. "Clashes in the Classroom: The Importance of Norms for Authority." *Education and Urban Society* 11:13–47.

———. 1978b. *Classrooms and Corridors: The Crisis of Authority in Desegregated Secondary Schools.* Berkeley: University of California Press.

Meyer, John. 1984. "Organizations as Ideological Systems." In *Leadership and Organizational Culture: New Perspectives in Administrative Theory and Practice,* ed. T. J. Sergiovanni and J. E. Corbally, pp. 186–205. Urbana: University of Illinois Press.

Meyer, John, and Brian Rowan. 1977. "Institutionalized Organizations: Formal Structure as Myth and Ceremony." *American Journal of Sociology* 83:340–363.

————. 1978. "The Structure of Educational Organizations." In *Environments and Organizations*, ed. M. Meyer, pp. 78–110. San Francisco: Jossey-Bass.

Meyer, John, and W. R. Scott. 1983. *Organizational Environments: Ritual and Rationality*. Beverly Hills, Calif.: Sage.

Meyer, John, et al. 1978. "Instructional Dissensus and Institutional Consensus." In *Environments and Organizations*, ed. M. Meyer, pp. 233–263. San Francisco: Jossey-Bass.

Meyer, Marshall. 1968. "The Two Authority Structures of Bureaucratic Organization." *Administrative Science Quarterly*, 13:211–238.

Michels, Robert. 1959 (1915). *Political Parties*. New York: Macmillan.

Midgley, C., and S. Wood. 1993. "Beyond Site-Based Management: Empowering Teachers to Reform Schools." *Phi Delta Kappan* 75:245–252.

Miech, R., and G. Elder. 1996. "The Service Ethic and Teaching." *Sociology of Education* 69:237–253.

Millman, J. 1981. *Handbook of Teacher Evaluation*. Beverly Hills, Calif.: Sage.

Millman, J., and L. Darling-Hammond. 1990. *The New Handbook of Teacher Evaluation*. Newbury Park, Calif.: Sage.

Mills, C. W. 1951. *White Collar*. New York: Oxford.

Mobley, W. 1982. *Employee Turnover: Causes, Consequences and Control*. Reading, Mass.: Addison-Wesley.

Morgan, Gareth. 1980. "Paradigms, Metaphors and Puzzle Solving in Organization Theory." *Administrative Science Quarterly*, 25:605–622.

Morris, M. 1982. *The Public School as a Workplace*. Dayton, Ohio.: Institute for Development of Educational Activities.

Murnane, R., and D. Cohen. 1986. "Merit Pay and the Evaluation Problem." *Harvard Educational Review* 56:1–17.

Murnane, R., and S. Raizen, eds. 1988. *Improving Indicators of the Quality of Science and Mathematics Education in Grades K–12*. Washington, D.C.: National Academy Press.

Murnane, R., et al. 1991. *Who Will Teach? Policies That Matter*. Cambridge, Mass.: Harvard University Press.

Murray, C., and R. Herrnstein. 1992. "What's Really behind the SAT-Score Decline?" *The Public Interest* 106:32–56.

National Association of State Directors of Teacher Education and Certification. 1997. *Manual on Certification and Preparation of Educational Personnel in the United States and Canada.* Washington, D.C.: NASDTEC.

National Commission on Excellence in Education. 1983. *A Nation at Risk: The Imperative for Educational Reform.* Washington, D.C.: U.S. Government Printing Office.

National Commission on Teaching and America's Future. 1996. *What Matters Most: Teaching for America's Future.* New York: National Commission on Teaching and America's Future.

———. 1997. *Doing What Matters Most: Investing in Quality Teaching.* New York: National Commission on Teaching and America's Future.

National Education Association. 1972, 1982, 1987, 1992, 1996. *Status of the American Public School Teacher.* Washington, D.C.: National Education Association.

National Education Goals Panel. 1997. *National Education Goals Report.* Washington, D.C.: U.S. Government Printing Office.

National Education Summit. 1999. *National Education Summit.* Washington, D.C.: Achieve Inc.

National Governor's Association. 1987. *Results in Education.* Washington, D.C.: National Governor's Association.

Neill, A. S. 1960. *Summerhill: A Radical Approach to Child Rearing.* New York: Hart Publishing Co.

Newmann, F., and R. Rutter. 1989. "Organizational Factors That Affect School Sense of Efficacy, Community and Expectations." *Sociology of Education* 62:221–238.

Nolin, M., C. Rowand, and E. Farris. 1994. *Public Elementary Teachers' Views on Teacher Performance Evaluations.* Washington, D.C.: National Center for Education Statistics.

Nord, Walter. 1983. "A Political-Economic Perspective on Organizational

Effectiveness." In *Organizational Effectiveness: A Comparison of Multiple Models,* ed. K. Cameron and D. Whetten, pp. 95–130. New York: Academic.

Oakes, J. 1985. *Keeping Track: How Schools Structure Inequality.* New Haven, Conn.: Yale University Press.

———. 1990. *Multiplying Inequalities: The Effects of Race, Social Class, and Tracking on Opportunities to Learn Mathematics and Science.* Santa Monica, Calif.: Rand Corporation.

Oakley, A. 1974. *Women's Work: The Housewife, Past and Present.* New York: Vintage.

Organization for Economic Co-operation and Cultural Development (OECD). 1995. *Decision-making in 14 OECD Education Systems.* Paris: OECD.

———. 1998. *Education at a Glance: OECD Indicators.* Paris: OECD.

Ouchi, William. 1977. "The Relationship between Organizational Structure and Organizational Control." *Administrative Science Quarterly* 22:95–113.

Ouchi, William, and A. Wilkins. 1985. "Organizational Culture." *Annual Review of Sociology* 11:457–483.

Parsons, Talcott. 1959. "The School Class as a Social System: Some of Its Functions in American Society." *Harvard Educational Review* 29:297–318.

———. 1960. *Structure and Process in Modern Societies.* Glencoe, Ill.: Free Press.

Perrow, Charles. 1986. *Complex Organizations: A Critical Essay.* New York: Random.

Peterson, P., and M. Comeaux. 1990. "Evaluating the Systems: Teachers' Perspectives on Teacher Evaluation." *Educational Evaluation and Policy Analysis* 12:3–24.

Pfeffer, Jeffrey. 1981. *Power in Organizations.* Marshfield, Mass.: Pitman.

———. 1982. *Organizations and Organization Theory.* Marshfield, Mass.: Pitman.

Pfeffer, J., and J. Baron. 1988. "Taking the Workers Back Out: Recent Trends in the Structuring of Employment." *Research in Organizational Behavior* 10:257–303.

Pfeffer, J., and G. Salancik. 1978. *The External Control of Organizations: A Resource Dependence Perspective.* New York: Harper and Row.

Polanyi, Karl. 1944. *The Great Transformation.* Boston: Beacon.

Porter, L. W., E. E. Lawler, and J. R. Hackman. 1975. *Behavior in Organizations.* New York: McGraw-Hill.

Price, J. 1977. *The Study of Turnover.* Ames: Iowa State University Press.

———. 1989. "The Impact of Turnover on the Organization." *Work and Occupations* 16:461–473.

Ravitch, Diane. 1974. *The Great School Wars.* New York: Harper.

Rice, M., and G. Schneider. 1994. "A Decade of Teacher Empowerment: An Empirical Analysis of Teacher Involvement in Decisionmaking." *Journal of Educational Administration* 32:43–58.

Rinehart, J., et al. 1998. "Teacher Empowerment and Principal Leadership: Understanding the Influence Process." *Educational Administration Quarterly* 34:608–630.

Rist, Ray. 1970. "Student Social Class and Teacher Expectations: The Self-Fulfilling Prophecy in Ghetto Education." *Harvard Educational Review* 40:411–451.

Robinson, V. 1985. *Making Do in the Classroom: A Report on the Misassignment of Teachers.* Washington, D.C.: Council for Basic Education and American Federation of Teachers.

Rogers, David. 1968. *110 Livingston Street.* New York: Vintage.

Rosenberg, M. 1981. *Occupations and Values.* New York: Arno Press.

Rosenholtz, Susan. 1985. "Political Myths about Educational Reform: Lessons from Research on Teaching." *Phi Delta Kappan* 66:349–355.

———. 1989. *Teacher's Workplace: The Social Organization of Schools.* New York: Longman.

Rowan, Brian. 1990. "Commitment and Control: Alternative Strategies for the Organizational Design of Schools." In *Review of Research in*

Education, vol. 16, ed. C. Cazden, pp. 353–389. Washington, D.C.: American Educational Research Association.

Roy, D. 1952. "Quota Restriction and Goldbricking in a Machine Shop." *American Journal of Sociology* 57:427–442.

Sadker, Myra, and David Sadker. 1994. *Failing at Fairness.* New York: Scribner.

Salaman, Graham. 1978. "Towards a Sociology of Organizational Structure." *The Sociological Review* 26:519–554.

Salancik, Gerald, and Jeffrey Pfeffer. 1974. "The Bases and Use of Power in Organizational Decision Making: The Case of a University." *Administrative Science Quarterly* 19:453–473.

Sarason, S. 1971. *The Culture of School and the Problem of Change.* Boston: Allyn and Bacon.

————. 1996. *Revisiting the Culture of School and the Problem of Change.* New York: Teachers College Press.

Saunders, D. 1995. "The Loyalty Oath, circa 1995." *San Francisco Chronicle,* June 21, p. A21.

Schlechty, P., and V. Vance. 1981. "Do Academically Able Teachers Leave Education?" *Phi Delta Kappan* 63:106–112.

Schneider, B., and Stevenson, D. 1999. *The Ambitious Generation: America's Teenagers, Motivated but Directionless.* New Haven, Conn.: Yale University Press.

Scott, W. Richard. 1987. *Organizations: Rational, Natural and Open Systems.* Englewood Cliffs, N.J.: Prentice Hall.

————. 1988. "The Adolescence of Institutional Theory." *Administrative Science Quarterly* 32:493–511.

Selden, D. 1985. *The Teacher Rebellion.* Washington, D.C.: Howard University Press.

Selznick, Philip. 1948. "Foundations of a Theory of Organizations." *American Sociological Review* 13:25–35.

————. 1949. *TVA and the Grass Roots.* Berkeley: University of California Press.

———. 1957. *Leadership in Administration.* New York: Harper and Row.

Sergiovanni, T. J., and J. Moore. 1989. *Schooling for Tomorrow.* Boston: Allyn and Bacon.

Shanker, Albert. 1985. "Education's Dirty Little Secret." *New York Times,* October 27, p. E9.

———. 1989. "Reform and the Teaching Profession." In *Crisis in Teaching,* ed. Lois Weis et al., pp. 99–110. Albany: State University of New York Press.

Shedd, Joseph, and Samuel Bacharach. 1991. *Tangled Hierarchies.* San Francisco: Jossey-Bass.

Shepard, P. 2000. "Zero Tolerance Hits Black Students Hardest." *Associated Press.* Reprinted in *Athens Daily News/Banner-Herald,* February 19, p. 5B.

Short, P., and Greer, J. 1997. *Leadership in Empowered Schools: Themes from Innovative Efforts.* Columbus, Ohio: Prentice Hall.

Short, P., and J. Rinehart. 1993. "Teacher Empowerment and School Climate." *Education* 113:592–597.

Shulman, L. 1986. "Those Who Understand: Knowledge Growth in Teaching." *Educational Researcher* 15:4–14.

Simon, Herbert. 1957. *Administrative Behavior.* New York: Macmillan.

Simpson, Richard. 1985. "Social Control of Occupations and Work." *Annual Review of Sociology* 11:415–436.

Silberman, Charles. 1970. *Crisis in the Classroom.* New York: Vintage.

Sizer, T. 1992a. *Horace's Compromise: The Dilemma of the American High School.* Boston: Houghton Mifflin.

———. 1992b. *Horace's School: Redesigning the American High School.* Boston: Houghton Mifflin.

Smith, T., et al. 1996. *The Condition of Education.* Washington, D.C.: National Center for Education Statistics.

Smith, Victoria. 1990. "Restructuring Management and Managing Restructuring." *Research in Politics and Society* 3:221–239.

Smylie, M. 1994. "Redesigning Teachers' Work: Connections to the Classroom." In *Review of Research in Education,* vol. 20, ed. L. Darling-

Hammond, pp. 129–177. Washington, D.C.: American Educational Research Association.

Snyder, T., C. Hoffman, and C. Geddes. 1997. *The Digest of Education*. Washington, D.C.: National Center for Education Statistics.

Sorensen, Aage, and Arne Kalleberg. 1981. "An Outline of a Theory of the Matching of Persons to Jobs." In *Sociological Perspectives on Labor Markets*, ed. Ivar Berg, pp. 49–74. New York: Academic.

Sorokin, P. 1928. *Contemporary Sociology Theories*. New York: Harper and Row.

Starr, Paul. 1982. *The Social Transformation of American Medicine*. New York: Basic Books.

Steers, R. M., and R. T. Momday. 1981. "Employee Turnover and the Post-Decision Accommodation Process." In *Research in Organizational Behavior*, vol. 3, ed. B. M. Shaw and L. L. Cummings. Greenwich, Conn: JAI Press.

Stevens, F. 1993. "Applying an Opportunity-to-Learn Conceptual Framework to the Investigation of the Effects of Teaching Practices." *Journal of Negro Education* 62(3):232–259.

Stevenson, D., and D. Baker. 1991. "State Control of the Curriculum and Classroom Instruction." *Sociology of Education* 64:1–10.

Stinchombe, Arthur. 1964. *Rebellion in a High School*. Chicago: Quadrangle Books.

Stodolsky, S. 1984. "Teacher Evaluation: The Limits of Looking." *Educational Researcher* 13:11–18.

Strober, M., and D. Tyack. 1980. "Why Do Women Teach and Men Manage?" *Signs* 5:499–500.

Swedberg, Richard. 1987. "Economic Sociology: Past and Present." *Current Sociology* 35:1–221.

Swidler, Ann. 1979. *Organization without Authority*. Cambridge, Mass.: Harvard University Press.

Talbert, J. 1993. "Understanding Context Effects on Secondary School Teaching." *Teachers College Record* 95(1):45–68.

Talbert, J., and M. McLaughlin. 1994. "Teacher Professionalism in Local School Contexts." *American Journal of Education* 102:123–153.

Tannenbaum, Arnold, and Tamas Rozgonyi. 1986. *Authority and Reward in Organizations.* Ann Arbor, Mich.: Institute for Social Research.

Tannenbaum, Arnold, et al. 1974. *Hierarchy in Organizations.* San Francisco: Jossey-Bass.

Theobald, N. 1990. "An Examination of the Influence of Personal, Professional and School District Characteristics on Public School Teacher Retention." *Economics of Education Review* 9:241–250.

Theobald, N., and B. Malen, eds. 2000. *Balancing Local Control and State Responsibility for K–12 Education: 2000 Yearbook of the American Education Finance Association.* Larchmont, N.Y.: Eye on Education.

Thompson, J. 1967. *Organizations in Action.* New York: McGraw-Hill.

Turner, A. N., and P. R. Lawrence. 1964. *Industrial Jobs and the Worker.* Cambridge, Mass.: Harvard University Press.

Tyack, David. 1974. *The One Best System.* Cambridge, Mass.: Harvard University Press.

———. 1999. "Choice Options: School Choice, Yes–But What Kind?" *American Prospect* 42:61–66.

Tyler, William. 1985. "Organizational Structure of the School." *Annual Review of Sociology* 11:49–73.

———. 1988. *School Organization.* New York: Croom Helm.

Urban League. 1999. *The State of Black America.* New York: Urban League

U.S. Bureau of the Census. 1998. *Statistical Abstract,* 117th ed. Washington, D.C.: U.S. Department of Commerce.

Vollmer, H., and D. Mills. 1966. *Professionalization.* Englewood Cliffs, N.J.: Prentice Hall.

Walberg, H., and H. Walberg. 1994. "Losing Local Control." *Educational Researcher* 23(5):19–26.

Waller, Willard. 1932. *The Sociology of Teaching.* New York: Wiley.

Walsh, J. 2001. "Who's Minding the Schools?" *Minneapolis Star Tribune,* October 14, p. 01B

Walton, R. E. 1980. "Establishing and Maintaining High Commitment

Work Systems." In *The Organization Life Cycle*, ed. J. Kimberly and R. Miles. San Francisco: Jossey-Bass.

Warren, Roland, S. Rose, and A. Bergunder. 1974. *The Structure of Urban Reform*. Lexington, Mass.: Lexington Books.

Weber, Max. 1946. *From Max Weber: Essays in Sociology*, ed. H. Gerth and C. W. Mills. New York: Oxford University Press.

———. 1947. *The Theory of Economic and Social Organization*, ed. T. Parsons. New York: Oxford University Press.

Weick, Karl. 1976. "Educational Organizations as Loosely Coupled Systems." *Administrative Science Quarterly* 21:1–19.

———. 1979. *The Social Psychology of Organizing*. Reading, Mass.: Addison-Wesley.

———. 1984. "Management of Organizational Change among Loosely Coupled Elements." In *Change in Organizations*, ed. P. Goodman, pp. 375–409. San Francisco: Jossey-Bass.

Weis, Lois, et al. 1989. *Crisis in Teaching*. Albany: State University of New York Press.

Whitener, S. K., et al. 1997. *Characteristics of Stayers, Movers, and Leavers: Results from the Teacher Follow-up Survey, 1994–95*. Washington, D.C.: National Center for Education Statistics.

Whyte, W. F., and J. Blasi. 1982. "Worker Ownership, Participation and Control: Toward a Theoretical Model." *Policy Sciences* 14:137–163.

Whyte, William F., and B. Gardner. 1945. "The Man in the Middle." *Applied Anthropology* 4:1–28.

Willis, Paul. 1977. *Learning to Labor*. New York: Columbia University Press.

Wilson, Bruce, W. Firestone, and R. Herriott. 1985. *School Assessment Survey: A Technical Manual*. Philadelphia: Research for Better Schools.

Wilson, Bruce, Robert Herriott, and William Firestone. 1990. "Explaining Differences between Elementary and Secondary Schools: Individual, Organizational and Institutional Perspectives." In *Advances in Educational Administration*, vol. 2, ed. P. Thurston and P. Zodiates. Greenwich, Conn.: JAI Press.

Wirt, F., and M. Kirst. 1989. *Schools in Conflict.* Berkeley, Calif.: McCutchan.

Wise, Arthur. 1979. *Legislated Learning: The Bureaucratization of the American Classroom.* Berkeley: University of California Press.

Wise, Arthur, et al. 1985. "Teacher Evaluation: A Study of Effective Practices." *Elementary School Journal* 86:61–121.

Woodward, Joan. 1965. *Industrial Organization.* London: Oxford University Press.

Wrong, Dennis. 1961. "The Oversocialized Conception of Man in Modern Sociology." *American Sociological Review* 26:183–193.

Zeigler, Harmon, and Wayne Peak. 1970. "Political Functions of Educational Systems." *Sociology of Education* 42:115–141.

Zey-Ferrell, Mary, and Michael Aiken, eds. 1981. *Complex Organizations: Critical Perspectives.* Glenview, Ill.: Scott, Foresman and Co.

Zucker, Lynne. 1977. "The Role of Institutionalization in Cultural Persistence." *American Sociological Review* 42:726–743.

———. 1987. "Institutional Theories of Organization." *Annual Review of Sociology* 13:443–464.

———. 1988. *Institutional Patterns and Organizations.* Cambridge, Mass.: Ballinger.

INDEX

Academic achievement, 192–193
Academic freedom, 44, 102
Academic instruction: as the work of teachers, 49–52, 226–227; teacher control and, 75–76, 78–79, 199–207; standardized curricula and, 103–104; division of labor in schools and, 148–154; organizational climate and performance of schools and, 192–193; teacher turnover and, 204–208; teacher control over, 223

Accountability: centralized control and, 5–6; debate over the control of teachers' work and, 8; implications for research, 13; problem of control and consent and, 30; disorganization viewpoint, 43; teacher disempowerment view, 43; school reforms and, 45; evaluation of control in schools, 57; performance evaluations, 61–62; standardized curricula and, 103–104; rules for teachers and, 108; evaluation programs and, 112; student achievement and teacher, 113–115; record-keeping and teacher,

118–119; enforcement of rules for teachers and, 120; merit pay and, 122; ethos of schools and teacher, 170–182; effects of teacher control and, 191; teacher control and, 221–223; implications for policy and reform, 234–242; power and teacher, 244

Administrator(s): conflict with teachers and implications for research, 13–14; conflict with teachers at Suburban High, 25–26; bureaucracy and, 64; organizational control of schools and, 64; power comparisons with teachers, 83; board/district administrator comparisons, 84–86; school-to-school differences, 87–95; enforcement of rules for teachers by, 120–135; control of resources in enforcement of teacher rules by, 126–127; out-of-field teaching and, 128–130, 164–167; student discipline and control by, 131–132; support of teachers by, 174–175; teacher control and conflict between teachers and, 196–215; teacher control and conflict

Administrator(s) *(continued)*
with, 201–203; control over teachers
work by, 221–222; evaluating control in
schools and, 229–230; measuring control in schools and, 231–234; empowerment reform and, 242–243, 245;
teacher control and conflict with, 245–
246
Administrator-Teacher Supplement of the
High School and Beyond Survey, 257
American Association for Higher Education, 70
American Association of University
Women, 38–39, 70
American Civil Liberties Union, 70
American Council for Education, 70
American Federation of Teachers (AFT),
24–26, 44; service assignments and,
103; bureaucratic rules in Urban High
and, 109–110
American Historical Association, 70
Association of Catholic Teachers, 23
Authority: defined, 18
Autonomy: defined, 18; academic freedom and teacher, 44; control and consent and, 45–46; disorganization viewpoint and, 48; evaluation of control in
schools and, 57; control of schools and,
73–74; teacher control and, 81; curriculum control in Friends School and, 105;
curriculum control in Suburban High
and, 105; academic instruction and
teacher, 149–154; measuring control in
school and teacher, 232, 234

Back-to-basics, 36
Bendix, Reinhard, 16–17
Bidwell, Charles, 33–35
Braverman, Harry, 16–17
Burawoy, Michael, 16–17
Bureau of National Affairs, 197

Bureaucracy: school disorganization perspective and, 5–10; loosely coupled perspective and, 6–7; decentralization and,
7; as a machine model of organization,
12; defined, 17–18; rationality and, 17–
18; organizational coordination and
control, 30; Max Weber and, 30–31;
"iron cage," 31; organizational theory
of schools and, 31–32; anomaly of educational organizations and, 33; power
and control in organizations and, 63–
65; rules for teachers and, 97–135; standardized curricula and, 103–104; administrator control and, 124; school accountability and, 141–143; division of
labor in schools and, 143–154; class size
and, 151; curricula standardization and,
158; control and consent and, 177; implications for theory and research, 226;
measuring control in schools and, 230–
233
Bureaucratic model: of organizational administration, 30–31; mass character of
education and, 34; limits of, 34–35;
evaluation of control in schools and,
57–58

Carnegie Forum on Education and the
Economy, 44
Carnegie Foundation, 70
Carnegie Foundation for the Advance-
ment of Teaching, 179, 256
Catholic education, 23, 93
Catholic High: Association of Catholic
Teachers and, 23–24; teacher control
and, 98; rules for teachers of, 101–102;
evaluation programs and, 113; enforce-
ment of rules by teachers in, 146; cur-
ricula standardization at, 149; class size
at, 150
Centralization: teacher disempowerment

efficient and ineffective bureaucracy, 5–9; implications for research, 12–13; teachers' work and, 40–41; community control and, 42–43; zone view and, 48–49; evaluation of control in schools and, 56; school variations in control, 95; enforcement of rules for teachers and, 120; enforcement of rules for teachers and, 124–126; effects of teacher control and, 191; empowerment reform and, 243

School size: and school control, 88–92, and school conflict, 198, 199, 202, 204

Schools and Staffing Survey (SASS): data and methods for research, 21–22; decision-making by teachers and, 75; teacher decision-making and, 79–83; school-to-school differences and, 87–95; policies for teachers and, 105–107; evaluation programs and, 112; teacher record-keeping and, 117; enforcement of school policies and, 132–134; out-of-field teaching and, 159, 162, 187–188, 241–242; teacher control and school climate and, 195–216; field research and, 252, 253; as primary source data, 254–258; measurement and methodological issues, 264

Scott, W. Richard, 33, 61

Secular humanism, 55

Seniority: enforcement of rules and teacher, 121; administrative control and teacher, 129; measuring control in schools and teacher, 231; empowerment reform and teacher, 243

Site-based management, 44, 242, 244, 245

Social capital, 50, 51

Socialization: role of schools in student, 11–13; defining the role of teachers in student, 49–54; teacher control of student, 77–79; rules for teachers and student, 106–108; administrator control of

teachers and student, 131–132; role of teachers in student, 139–140; organizational climate and performance of schools and student, 192; teacher control and student, 199–207, 212–216, 221, 223, 227; teacher turnover and student, 204–205; defining the work of teachers and student, 226–227; accountability reform and student, 234; educational reforms and student, 247; multiple regression analysis and student, 257, 269

Special interest groups, 70, 86–87

Standardized tests, 113–115. See also Testing

Stratification, 50–51, 53

Student(s): testing, 8; grades, 147, 153–154; conflict between school staff and, 196–203; teacher conflicts with, 211–212. See also Socialization

Student discipline: debate over the control of teachers' work and, 5; teacher decision-making and, 13; teacher disempowerment view and, 43; socialization and, 53–55; teacher control of, 78–79, 198–201; power perceived by administrators and, 83; rules for teachers and, 102–103; record-keeping by teachers and, 117–119; race and, 118–119; administrator control of teachers and, 131–132; division of labor in schools and, 144–148; ethos in the school and, 171–176; teacher in the middle and, 187; teacher control over social issues and, 213–216; measuring control in schools and, 233; accountability reforms and, 238–241; educational reforms and, 247–249

Suburban High: description of, 25–26, 98; evaluation programs and, 113; enforcement of rules by teachers in, 145–146, 148; class size at, 150–151; student